Cash and

Cash and Carry

The Spectacular Rise and Hard Fall of C.C. Pyle, America's First Sports Agent

JIM REISLER

McFarland & Company, Inc., Publishers
Jefferson, North Carolina, and London

LIBRARY OF CONGRESS CATALOGUING-IN-PUBLICATION DATA

Reisler, Jim, 1958–
    Cash and carry : the spectacular rise and hard fall of C.C. Pyle,
America's first sports agent / Jim Reisler.
        p.   cm.
    Includes bibliographical references and index.

    ISBN 978-0-7864-3846-4
    softcover : 50# alkaline paper ∞

    1. Pyle, Charles C., 1882–1939.   2. Sports agents — United
States — Biography.   I. Title.
GV734.5.R45   2009
338.4′77960973 — dc22   2008043935
[B]

British Library cataloguing data are available

On the cover: C.C. Pyle aboard the S.S. *Leviathan* (Library of Congress); brick wall ©2008 Shutterstock; background: Red Grange
carries the football against Michigan, 1924 (Library of Congress).

Manufactured in the United States of America

McFarland & Company, Inc., Publishers
    Box 611, Jefferson, North Carolina 28640
    www.mcfarlandpub.com

For Tobie and Julia

Table of Contents

Preface   1

Introduction   5

1. "How Would You Like to Make $100,000?"   11
2. "Three or Four Men and a Horse Rolled into One"   34
3. "One of the Finest Men I Have Ever Known"   64
4. "Football for All and All for Football"   88
5. "People Will Pay to See Anyone They Hate"   106
6. "The Most Stupendous Athletic Accomplishment in
      All History!"   138
7. "It Is a New Racket Altogether"   156
8. "Everyone Will Be Satisfied"   176
9. "More Ideas Than Most Men Came Up With in a Lifetime"   191

Epilogue: "Everything He Touched Turned to Gold"   199

Chapter Notes   203

Bibliography   213

Index   217

Charles C. Pyle is a character out of a book. He is today the most interesting man in sports. A news person could keep his notebook, and for that matter his entire paper, pretty well filled up merely by assigning himself to follow Charles about the country, and observe the birth, the incubation and the hatching of the various schemes that enable him to make page one of the Metropolitan dailies, free for nothing, most any time he cares to do so.

— Paul Gallico, *New York Daily News*, May 29, 1928

Preface

I learned about C.C. Pyle in an unlikely way. As a member of the Kenyon College cross country team in the fall of 1977, I was at practice one afternoon when a man stopped by to ask if any of us were interested in trying out for a new play to be staged in early 1978 on campus called "C.C. Pyle and the Bunion Derby."

A play about a man staging a 1928 trans–America footrace? "Well, why not?" several of us figured. Directing Tony award winning playwright Michael Cristofer's script was Paul Newman, a 1949 Kenyon graduate. So we gave it a shot, read some lines — and to a man, were positively dreadful. "Stick to running boys," I remember the man in casting advised us, "and we'll get some actors instead."

In early 1978, I attended the play, which was great, after which I forgot all about C.C. Pyle. But a few years later, a funny thing happened: After I started writing sports books, I'd find myself poring through microfilm in search of some tidbit about Babe Ruth or Walter Johnson or Damon Runyon, and bam, there would be an item about Pyle. I learned that in the mid-to-late 1920s, C.C. Pyle was promoting not just distance running, but football, tennis and even hockey as well, and usually at the same time. Slowly, a portrait of one of the era's most energetic, influential — and forgotten — sports figures emerged.

I started a file on C.C. Pyle. The file grew, but most of the articles and citations were distressingly brief, generally no more than a few paragraphs. For all the headlines C.C. Pyle captured in his day, a sense of Pyle, the man, was proving elusive. Sure, Pyle was quotable, verbose and always a bit shifty, but who exactly was he? Pyle was said to be a gambler — but that wasn't quite right. He gambled — not in the traditional sense, but by losing vast quantities of other people's investments in schemes that rarely worked. Pyle was said to have inherited his golden-tongued ability to talk anyone into any-

1

thing from his father, who had been a famous preacher from Ohio. Oh, so that was it. No, it wasn't; Pyle's father was indeed an Ohio preacher, but he was hardly famous and died young.

There were other reasons why Pyle was hard to fathom, starting with C.C. himself. Though Pyle talked all the time about his latest and greatest schemes, he seldom revealed much about himself. When he did, his tales of an itinerant early adulthood in the Pacific Northwest seemed a little too fantastic to be completely true. But Pyle didn't care. His primary goal seemed to be making a lot of money in sports, being a big shot, and sticking it to the establishment. Doing so required he take on several sports bureaucracies, much to the intense dislike of football and tennis officials. Tim Mara, founder of football's New York Giants, loathed Pyle, and seldom failed to say nasty things about him. Tennis star Bill Tilden didn't like C.C. either, and the dismissive comments of those men and others meant that Pyle seldom received the credit he deserved.

Adding a particular challenge to any understanding of C.C. Pyle was the brevity of his overall sports career. Starting in 1925, Pyle's star "rose like a rocket," as Theodore Roosevelt once said of himself, and burst almost as quickly, sunk by 1930 by overwhelming financial troubles, poor health and the Depression. Pyle's sports career lasted only five years — about the length of an average tenure of a big-league football or baseball player. Less than a decade later, he was dead.

Only now is an accurate portrait of C.C. Pyle starting to emerge. In recent years, accomplished sports historians like John M. Carroll, Robert Peterson, Larry Engelmann, Molly Levite Griffis and Geoff Williams have put together important books that cover Pyle's exploits. Carroll and Peterson wrote about football in the 1920s, Engelmann about the dawn of women's professional tennis, and Griffis and Williams on the bunion derby, all of which provide major contributions to our growing appreciation of Pyle's legacy, warts and all. Consider this study then an attempt to add context and a bit of cohesion to the mounting scholarship.

I am grateful to several people whose help was integral to producing this work. Gina Laitinen, C.C. Pyle's great-granddaughter, was gracious in her time and knowledge of her family background. Historians at the Wheaton College Archives & Special Collections in Wheaton, Illinois, and the Library of Congress in Washington, D.C., were patient with my questions on photo usage and copyrights. Debbie Elmenhorst of Carnegie Library in El Reno, Oklahoma, helped track down some vintage photos of bunion derby, and Dub Hornberger of Haynes Photo and Framing in El Reno produced the prints. At mygenealogist.com, Elizabeth Kahn and Christopher Johnson unearthed more about Pyle's background that I ever thought possible. And most of all, my wife Tobie and daughter Julia were more than understanding of all the hours I spent in the microfilm room. Sincere thanks — and a C.C. Pyle–engineered "Red Grange" meat-loaf recipe — to all.

C.C. Pyle got it right sometimes, and a lot of times, he failed. With luck, this biography gets it right most of the time.

Introduction

If C.C. Pyle was nervous, he didn't let on. "The human foot is going to come into its own," he started, speaking rapidly. "I have made such a study of the ailments of the human walking mechanism as has never been equaled, and I claim to know more about toe trouble, heel trouble, instep trouble and ankle trouble than any man living. I can tell you exactly what to do for anything that goes from the knee down."

The pack of reporters who had gathered in Pyle's spacious suite at the Vanderbilt Hotel in New York City in search of genuine news were taken aback. On this otherwise lazy Sunday morning of Memorial Day weekend in 1928, a slow day in the news business, was the promise of a bona fide story — whether Pyle, the flamboyant midwestern sports promoter, had actually come up with the money to pay participants in his just-completed 3,470-mile transcontinental footrace, among the most flamboyant sporting events of a flamboyant era. But here was Pyle talking about ... foot injuries.

C.C. was just starting to cook, delivering his words in spitfire form and making it hard to interrupt. "I am going to write a treatise on chiropody in English, who he who runs may read, and I am going to give away one copy with every purchase of C.C. Pyle's Patent Foot Box, which will contain remedies for every one of the 3,000 maladies of the human foot. I will make vast sums out of this because this country is going marathon. We are just entering the golden age of the foot."[1]

Reporters dutifully recorded Pyle's words. But "the golden age of the foot?" They hadn't given up their Sunday morning to hear about that, and they wanted to focus on a true tabloid headline as only New York could produce. Pyle had promised for days that he would have no problem in securing the $48,500 in prize money for the top 15 finishers. Then again, each and every one of the 78 bedraggled runners who had snaked all the way from Los Angeles through deserts, mountains, heat, wind and rain to the concrete

5

canyons of New York deserved more, far more than just a pat on the back and train fare home. So did he have it?[2]

How grand, Pyle had thought all those months ago, the race would be: heroic marathoners passing through the small towns of America, where town fathers and citizens alike would welcome them — and Pyle's traveling carnival — with admiration, affection and, most importantly, open pocketbooks. That this magical mystery tour hadn't quite worked out that way hardly seemed to faze Pyle who, rumor had it, was broke. But no worries, C.C. assured everyone present. Though the runners had arrived in New York to shouts of sympathy and anger about their emaciated condition, it was really not a problem. No, not in the least bit, Pyle said, because in six days, they would finish up their grand journey at a grueling 26-hour finale at Madison Square Garden. There, the stands would be packed, the coffers filled and the runners getting the tremendous send-off they deserved. Everyone would go home happy, C.C. said. Just wait; you'll see.[3]

So where *was* the prize money? "There are going to be more marathons, more 26-hour footraces, more six-day footraces and more transcontinental footraces than anybody would have dreamed to be possible," Pyle was saying now, longing to get back to his latest fixation about sore feet. "All along our route, children who could hardly walk were out there trying to keep up with my transcontinental runners. We are going to have hundreds of thousands of distance runners in this country, and every one of them will naturally buy C.C. Pyle's Patent Foot Box. All that I hope is that the present rage for traveling great distances on foot do not too far. Some of my best friends are in the automobile business."

But the prize money? "I will not have to wait for profits to accrue from the miraculous foot fixer in order to pay my athletes their prizes," Pyle said. "They will get them immediately after the 26-hour foot race. My contract does not stipulate that I pay them at any particular time."[4]

So reporters had their answer, sort of. How typical of Pyle, who could talk rings around anyone and sound convincing in the process. Powerfully built from having been an athlete himself— a boxer and bicycle racer despite a heart condition — the 46-year-old promoter radiated both importance and confidence. The 6'3" Pyle had sandy, gray hair, a pencil-thin mustache, and looked like a heftier version of the actor William Powell. C.C. dressed well, always wearing in a pin-striped suit and usually a hat, which he used to his advantage — dominating most rooms he entered and commanding attention. And Pyle talked and kept talking in a kind of rat-a-tat that mixed bold dreams, bravado and the promise of a big payoff just ahead. So it went in the 1920s when wonderful excess was in, illegal booze flowed, the stock market boomed — and C.C. Pyle road the stage, albeit briefly, as one of the era's most flamboyant figures. Pyle excelled in talking anyone, anywhere to join him — sometimes making it big, dazzlingly big, but of late, coming up short, really short.[5]

He fit the times. It was an era of excess, of ballyhoo. Babe Ruth could be just as magnificent striking out, his body theatrically coiled up as he swung and missed, as he could hitting one of his moon-shot home runs. The same could be said of C.C. Pyle, who, when faced with the rumored likelihood that this transcontinental run, dubbed by columnist Westbook Pegler as the "Bunion Derby," had bankrupted him, still commanded a crowd at the Vanderbilt Hotel's penthouse suite. That was Pyle, who even as he was losing everything, always wound up sounding convincing — and somehow, staying at the best hotels. That was Pyle who during the course of the Derby had resided in the luxury of a $25,000 custom-built "land yacht," the Hummer of its time, while his runners slept in tents, barns and under stadium bleachers. Anything was possible to Pyle's way of thinking and nothing was impossible — qualities he displayed again and again to the delight of reporters who took to his colorful quotes and ready stock of Prohibition liquor.[6]

Few other sports promoters of the time attracted more attention than C.C. Pyle, who Pegler had taken to calling "Cash and Carry," based on his insistence on never taking a check and getting cash upfront. What a fast ride it had been! Pyle's name blazed across the American sports pages for the first time in the fall of 1925 for rocking the sports world by inducing Harold "Red" Grange to leave the leafy confines of the University of Illinois for pro football. The academics had howled in protest — and lectured Pyle on how he was soiling the college game and keeping a bright, young student from earning his degree and making his way in the world. But C.C. thumbed his nose at such indignities. He and Grange made a mint, perhaps $100,000 — the equivalent of about $2 million today — and showed the world that pro football had a shot to make it big.[7]

Then Pyle had made another killing and stuck it to the establishment — again — by signing French tennis star Suzanne Lenglen, the six-time Wimbledon champion and her sport's reining ice goddess. In a day when many woman still wore ground-length dresses to play tennis, Lenglen was a rebel — wearing her dress just above the calf, and shaking up the staid amateur tennis establishment by sipping brandy between sets, pouting and often weeping when a call went against her. Popular at home but exceedingly disliked abroad, Lenglen didn't stand a prayer of making it big in the U.S., the critics charged. Why on earth would C.C. want to convince her to turn pro when, as one said, "People hate her." But that was just the point, Pyle figured. "People will pay to see anybody they hate," he counseled. So they did, and C.C. and Lenglen earned a fortune.[8]

Back at the Vanderbilt, Pyle rattled on, like the swift rat-a-tat of a Tommy gun, in working to ease the concerns of reporters over the previous few days' barrage of unwelcome headlines on the condition of his runners, many of whom were gaunt, even cadaver-like, from the long grind. "I believe in tapering off," C.C. said. "When you've been through torture like this, it is a dangerous thing to stop agony all at once. When all the misery's gone, you feel kind of lonesome and lost. A lot of the boys are feeling terrible and don't know what is the matter with them. I'll tell you what's the matter with them. The thing they are suffering from is lack of pain."

Oh, so that was it. And not only that, but apparently the most common ailment suffered by the runners was shin splints, prompting Pyle to devote a special chapter in his foot study to this particular problem, which was caused, he said, by running rapidly down a hill. So Pyle was really using his runners as both a promotion *and* as a science experiment regarding the best ways to cure foot problems.

"Those fellows are men; they're not crying," C.C. said in response to those who dared question the haggard appearance of his athletes. "Of course, they've been through a lot. A transcontinental race is no kissing bee. It's done 'em a world of good. All those boys are in marvelous health — from the ankles up."[9]

And with that, Pyle stood up and left the room, still needing to deal with the task of finding the elusive $48,500 in prize money. The press conference had been a whirlwind, as were most things involving C.C. Pyle. So it went for an American original, this combination preacher meets Amway salesman, or as writer Larry Engelmann put it, a man "as close as the decade of the 1920s would ever come to combining the talents of P.T. Barnum, Don King, Col. Tom Parker and Oral Roberts."[10]

C.C. Pyle *was* one of a kind, a man with an answer for everything, some of it true and much of it malarkey — usually comprised on the fly, especially when he was broke, which was often. Pyle was a dreamer and a schemer, occasionally practical but often completely illogical. He was a businessman — though not a good one — and an incurable spendthrift. You could say that the Golden Age of Sport got a good dose of its color, its chutzpah and a sizable chunk of rascally charm from C.C. Pyle. To some, he was visionary. Others called him a villain, a phony and a fraud. Either way, sports as we

C.C. Pyle aboard the S.S. Leviathan *in New York, 1926. From* New York World-Telegram *and the* Sun *Newspaper Photograph Collection (Library of Congress, Prints and Photographs Division, NYWT&S Division).*

know it today owes a giant debt of gratitude to C.C. Pyle, a promoter who burst on the scene, and seemed to vanish just as quickly, swept into the dust-bin of history and relegated to a few paragraphs found here and there via Google and an occasional mention in a documentary. But the tale of C.C. Pyle was quite a ride while it lasted. Here is how it happened.

1

"How Would You Like to Make $100,000?"

New York's premier baseball palace, the Polo Grounds, had seen the crush of big crowds in its day: three of the previous five World Series had been contested at the massive, horseshoe-shaped ballpark built between a jagged cliff called Coogan's Bluff and the Harlem River in the northern reaches of Manhattan. But on this damp, overcast Sunday in early December 1925, the stadium was given over to something just starting to dawn on the conscience of American sports fans — professional football.

With excitement high, many were still hoping to score one of the last few tickets available for the 2:00 P.M. game between the Chicago Bears and the New York Giants. Gates were set to open at 11:00 A.M., but the crowds had ignored temperatures in the mid-30s and started forming hours before, snaking from the gate, out the plaza, and down the block.[1]

The scene was reminiscent of the swarms of people who often poured from the Eighth Avenue elevated train for big World Series and college football games, filling the streets and watering holes around the big ballpark for hours before and after game time. While the fortunes of the baseball Giants consumed the Polo Grounds for up to seven months a year, fall at the Polo Grounds had in more recent years become the scene of big-time college football clashes, like the annual clash between local power West Point and its great rival, Notre Dame. It was at the Army–Notre Dame game on October 18, 1924, when Grantland Rice, the famous syndicated columnist, had memorably renamed the Notre Dame backfield as the "Four Horsemen," creating a legend with a few deft key strokes.[2]

"Outlined against a blue-gray October sky, the Four Horsemen rode again," Rice wrote in his *New York Herald Tribune* lead, among the most quoted of all-time. "In dramatic lore, they are known as famine, pestilence, destruction and death. These are only aliases. Their real names are (Harry) Stuhldreher, (Don) Miller, (Jim) Crowley and (Elmer) Layden."[3]

Rice and the nation's other top sportswriters — men like Damon Runyon, Paul Gallico, Westbrook Pegler and more than 100 other reporters — along with 65,000 spectators were back on this day as well. The cause of this latest fuss was the first appearance in New York of a Bears rookie running back named Red Grange. A member of the team for all of two weeks, Grange had just closed a storied career at the University of Illinois by turning pro — and giving this struggling pro game and the six-year-old professional National Football League (NFL) a shot at reaching the big time.[4]

Signed by C.C. Pyle, Grange had closed out his college career on November 20 against Ohio State, and joined the Bears in time for their traditional Thanksgiving bash against the cross-town Cardinals, drawing a crush of 40,000 to Cubs Park. From there, he and the Bears had worked steadily eastward, attracting another 28,000 to Cubs Park a week before, 8,000 Wednesday in St. Louis, and 35,000 to Shibe Park in Philadelphia. While the 111,000 spectators to date could be attributed to Grange, the grueling schedule and mania for this camera-shy football hero was all Pyle's doing.[5]

In the space of two weeks, Grange had been transformed from a college football player to a folkloric, even mythological figure. He was no longer merely the "Wheaton Iceman," a reference to his former summer job delivering ice for Luke Thompson's company in his hometown of Wheaton, outside Chicago, or the "Galloping

After Red Grange joined the Chicago Bears in 1925, there weren't many places he went without C.C. Pyle (at right), even on the football field (Red Grange Collection [SC-20], Special Collections, Buswell Memorial Library, Wheaton College).

Ghost," as Rice called him, but simply "the dream of every boy come true," as Paul Gallico of the *New York Daily News* labeled him. While the college administrators yowled that the lure of playing for cash would cause the more popular college game irreparable harm, it hadn't seemed to have happened. The college game seemed quite healthy without the former University of Illinois star. Meantime, Grange's every move and every utterance of what the *New York Times* later called his "meteoric football career" made headlines. All of 23, he was one of the famous public figures in America.[6]

Grange rarely smiled in the photos that cropped up almost daily in the newspapers. With a leather football helmet usually enveloping his head — faceguards were still several decades away — Grange stared soberly and uncomfortably at the camera, looking like a man visiting the dentist. But his smoldering good looks and weekly exploits had captured national attention, a status confirmed October 5 when Grange, wearing a necktie and not a helmet this time, made the cover of *Time* as only the third athlete after heavyweight champ Jack Dempsey and golfer Bobby Jones to grace the front of the 2½-year-old weekly news magazine. "Eel-hipped runagade, no man could hold him; he writhed through seas of grasping moleskin-flints with a twiddle of his buttocks and a flirt of his shin-bone," wrote the magazine, demonstrating that sports writing was not exactly its strength. "His knee-bolt pumped like an engine piston; his straight arm fell like a Big-Wood tree.... Even juvenile imaginations must strain if they are to exaggerate the prowess of Grange. Only 23, legend has already begun to barnacle his babyhood."[7]

No wonder that Red Grange on this raw, early–December afternoon in New York was the darling of the tabloids, the man of the moment. Suddenly more popular an athlete than Babe Ruth, he was ever richer by the day — earning a remarkable $82,000 in his first 11 days as a professional, an average of $16,000 a game — all of it at a time when the average American's annual salary was perhaps $2,000. By his side, even on the sideline bench, was Pyle, the Chicago-based sports promoter whose own rise could be termed "meteoric," a man who seemed to have a knack for getting his client — and himself — into the limelight, and making it look effortless.[8]

Anticipating a rush for tickets, Polo Grounds officials had for most of the previous week extended the hours at the Giant ticket office on West Forty-second Street to meet the demand for tickets, which ranged from $2.50 at midfield to 50 cents in the bleachers. On Sunday, game day, the newspapers had published detailed accounts on what gate ticket-holders should enter. Wisely, Giant officials had the gates opened extra early, at 11:00

A.M., three hours prior to game-time, so the throng could enter the big ball-park and find their seats in comfort.[9]

At noon, an enterprising entrepreneur in a yellow ice wagon drove up Eighth Avenue to the Polo Grounds, disappeared into the ballpark and wasn't spotted again for hours. By then, the box office supply of tickets was long gone, and the crowds were steadily streaming from the Eighth Avenue elevated train and into the stadium. Policemen did their best to keep the crowd moving.

Ten minutes to kickoff, all but a handful of all the park's 65,000 seats were filled, a stunning sight for a league straining to move beyond its sand-lot roots. Hundreds of spectators stood in back of the stadium, up and down the aisles, and on its rafters. Others occupied long benches placed on the sidelines and running almost the length of the field. On top of Coogan's Bluff, the rocky crevice that abutted the Polo Grounds, another crowd had gath-ered, peering downward for a look at a sliver of the field. No precise crowd figure was ever tallied; organizers said it was 70,000 inside the stadium with another 5,000 or so on Coogan's Bluff, and that seemed accurate enough.[10]

Scanning the enormity of the crowd, and not quite believing his sud-den luck, was the 38-year-old bookmaker Tim Mara, who had been per-suaded the previous August to spend $500 for ownership of New York's NFL franchise. Born on the Lower East Side of Manhattan, Mara had risen from poverty and become a self-made man in the then-legal profession of book-making, most notably in the enclosure at Belmont Park. Well entrenched in the political world of Tammany Hall, Mara had tentatively entered the foot-ball business at the insistence of his friend, boxing manager Billy Gibson.[11]

The two men had met when Mara asked Gibson for a piece of one of his fighters, Gene Tunney. Not just any boxer, Tunney was the light-heavy-weight champion who would eventually move up a division and become heavyweight champ, defeating Jack Dempsey. But Gibson decided to keep Tunney for himself while he deftly changed the subject to football. Joining their meeting were two others: Joe Carr, an Ohio sportswriter-turned-NFL commissioner, and a retired army surgeon named Harry March.

Carr and March had already been in Gibson's office most of the morn-ing, anxious to secure an NFL franchise for New York while trying to con-vince their boxing friend to buy a team. Gibson wasn't biting, and claimed he had already lost $15,000 trying to finance a football team. So he turned to Mara, thinking he might be interested.

"It's a better deal than Tunney over the long haul," March told Mara. "You might lose some money at first but you would have exclusivity in New York and down the road that could mean big money."

"How much for a franchise?" Mara asked.

"Five hundred dollars," Carr said.

"Deal," Mara said, sticking out his hand. "I figured," he would say years later, "that even an empty store with two chairs in it would be worth $500."

Hoping to capitalize on a recognizable name, Mara named his new team the Giants, which was the same as the city's National League baseball franchise, which had made the Polo Grounds famous. For a man who had never attended a pro football game, buying a team was an impulsive, gutsy decision. And though Giants had performed well to date during the 1925 season, crowds had been sporadic, giving Mara plenty of sleepless nights. By early December, he had already absorbed $40,000 in losses.[12]

But with Red Grange on the premises and a huge crowd anxious to see him, Mara had quite suddenly forgotten his plight. While Red Grange and C.C. Pyle didn't create pro football on that chilly Sunday at the Polo Grounds, as some historians would insist, they had given it a major shot in the arm and demonstrated to skittish owners like Mara that the game had a promising future indeed. That wasn't a half-bad proposition for a team that had played its first home game less than two months before — a 14–0 loss on October 18 to the Frankford Yellow Jackets before a crowd generously estimated at a "few thousand." At least the home opener hadn't been a total bust, thanks to Mara's nine-year-old son, Wellington. Arriving home with a cold, which Tim attributed to watching the game from the shadows of the Polo Grounds, young Wellington was ordered to watch future games in the sun. And with that, his mother delivered an edict, placing the Giant home bench forever after on the sunny side of the field, where it remains to this day.

Making the days leading up to the Giants-Bears game particularly challenging was a steady downpour. For much of Friday and Saturday, it rained hard, leaving the field muddy and treacherous and fraying the nerves of promoters, nervous that the uncomfortable conditions would keep ticket-holders at home. Fortunately, at 3:00 A.M. prior to the game, a friend of Mara's woke him up with a phone call. "Look out the window!," he yelled. "The moon is out!"

By game-time, the rain had held off and the atmosphere was electric. New Yorkers were pumped. "When I saw that crowd and knew that half the cash in the house was mine," Mara said, "I said to myself, 'Timothy, how long has this gravy train been running?'"[14]

Most of the afternoon actually. Trotting onto the field a few minutes before kickoff, Grange was surrounded by photographers, like a visiting statesman. "I'll have to sue that bum," joshed Babe Ruth, sitting in the pricy $2.50 seats near the 50-yard line and watching the commotion that surrounded America's newest sports icon. "They're *my* photographers."[15]

Then Grange shredded the overmatched Giants, piling up 128 total yards, including 53 from running, 13 on kickoff returns, 23 from catching a pass, and 35 from returning an interception for a touchdown. Considering this was his fifth game in two weeks, it was an doubly impressive day, all of it accomplished on a muddy, treacherous field and against a hard-hitting Giant defense. The Bears won, 19–7, but the real story of the day was that Grange had performed magnificently on pro football's biggest stage ever. At the end of the day, Grange played only one whole quarter and parts of two others, but from all accounts, had been the key to the game, even throwing the key block that allowed quarterback Joey Sternaman to score one of his two touchdowns. "Although we had won, it was one of the most bruising battles I had ever been in," Grange said, citing one play when Giants center Joe Alexander wrenched his head. "It was clear we were all beginning to show the wear and tear of our crowded schedule."[16]

Grange had weathered some other jarring hits against the Giants. In the second quarter while playing defensive back, Grange knocked down a New York pass just as Joe Williams slammed him on the back of his head. In the fourth quarter, Red was kicked on the forearm. Grange had also picked up a head cold, in part because the Bears had worn the same soggy, muddy-splattered uniforms they had donned for the previous day's game in the rain and wind at Philadelphia. "This tour will make you so wealthy," Pyle told Bears owner George Halas, "that next year you'll be able to afford two sets of uniforms."[17]

The professional game was more physically challenging than in college, and C.C. Pyle was making sure things were a whole lot busier as well. At the University of Illinois, Grange could run rampant on the football field and disappear to his fraternity house, with the reporters content to write about his heroics without even talking to him. But with Pyle now running the show, Grange was center-stage, from interviews to charity commitment and public appearances — all geared to building his visibility and making as much money as possible. The Bears' next game was Tuesday night in Washington, and the team wasn't leaving New York until late Monday, giving every Chicago player but one — Grange — the chance to enjoy New York. Red was in Pyle's hands, and there was a lot to do.[18]

Back at the Hotel Astor, Pyle had Grange grab some dinner and tend to his nagging cold, but not for long. By 10:20 P.M., they were in the studios of WEAF Radio, which also fed a half-dozen other stations, from Washington, D.C., to St. Paul, Minnesota. Grange made a brief address in support of famine relief and war orphans in the Near East before launching into his most expansive public comments on topics ranging from football to training habits.

Red's plea on behalf of famine was brief. "The reason that I am here, in front of a microphone, is that the Near-East Relief asked me to do this as a part of their program for the observance of Golden Rule Sunday," he said. "They told me that it would be a real help to their cause and I am strong for doing anything that I can to help them."

Saying he had caught a cold that afternoon, Red apologized for not being "quite as clear as you would like." His flat, midwestern delivery underscored his genuine sincerity, and he came off as a humble hero who assured his listeners that he played football not for the money, but because it was in his blood. "Football, I am convinced, is the best game that was ever invented," Grange said. "It demands more than any other game from the players. Its rewards are spiritual rather than material, but they are certain. I am sure I am a better man for having played. The monetary reward is secondary."

Adding that he received a lot of letters from boys asking for advice about how to become a football star, Grange offered some practical, plain-spoken tips. "Get lots of sleep and live a normal, regular, healthy life," he advised. "Keep away from the bright lights and eat plain food... Don't eat too much meat... Don't smoke. Don't drink liquor. Don't be a loafer on the street. Think, dream and believe that you will come to the top, and you'll get there."

So what had worked for him? "Several things," Grange said. "I have never smoked in my life. My father always saw to it that I kept good hours until I got my growth. After starting athletics during boyhood days, I never stopped training."[19]

The next morning at the Astor, Pyle, who was sharing a suite with the young football star, was up early as he prepared for the onslaught of presentations from people anxious to have Grange endorse their products. Here was C.C.'s day of reckoning — the moment when he would discover the true value of his new and unique partnership with the toast of New York — and a day that would change sports history. Headed on the train two days before from Philadelphia to New York, C.C. had been shaving when he pointed his straight-edge razor at Grange and uttered what became his mantra: "Son, this is the blade that knows no brother. We are going to take a deep cut at the dough on old Broadway, let the gyps fall where they may."

Pyle had it all worked out. He alone would pour over the mountain of endorsement offers, turning the day into a kind of old-fashioned auction, with Red banished to the room next-door, to be made available as needed for a quick "hello" and a handshake. "The only thing I needed to do was just meet the people," Grange recalled later. "I never had any part in the discussions or anything." Pyle took care of it, his commanding voice carrying to all corners of the drawing room of his large suite. "Don't be impatient gentlemen," he told the lineup of sales-people. "Everybody will be heard in due course."[20]

Indeed, they were — and those who didn't offer enough were unceremoniously and quickly dispatched. When one man offered $100 to Grange for an endorsement, Pyle grasped the salesman by the elbow and firmly edged him toward the exit, a sign that the offer was nowhere near acceptable. "Just take that elevator," Pyle told the salesman. "Press the button and when the car stops, tell the man you want to go to the bargain basement."

By the end of the day, C.C. had signed the young football star to an astounding list of contracts that dwarfed the $30,000 he had reportedly earned from Sunday's game. There was a $300,000 movie contract, and another $40,000 for various and sundry endorsements, including $13,000 from a sweater manufacturer, $10,000 from a doll maker, $5,000 each for shoes and ginger ale, and $2,500 from a cap manufacturer. The smallest deal: $500 for lending his name to a "Red Grange" toy savings bank in the shape of a football. There was even a deal for a fountain pen, and another for a meat-loaf recipe. But Pyle drew the line at hawking cigarettes, sort of, agreeing for $10,000 to a modest endorsement in which Grange would actually be quoted as saying, "I don't smoke but my best friends smoke."[21]

Pyle was at the top of his game, wheeling and dealing as if had been doing this his whole life. "He was frisking like a barn-fed old wagon horse knee deep in bluegrass," Grange told Westbrook Pegler. "Charlie was in the big money and, while I suppose he did turn down a few thousand dollars of easy increment for the sheer voluptuous joy of rejecting these trifles, it was worth the loss to see him expand."[22]

The day was a windfall, amounting to about $125,000 in endorsements since the movie contract was more like $50,000 and a lot less than originally thought, and after it was finished, C.C. wrote a check to Grange for $50,000. The reported $300,000 film deal that newspaper scribes had at first breathlessly reported was way out of line, and a bit of vintage blarney from Pyle, who, to heighten the stakes, had written out a check for that amount and flashed it around. Strictly a "friendly promotion" was how Grange later remembered the deal, signed with an outfit called the Arrow Production Company for a film to be shot in March after the football tour. Grange was up for it, but adamantly refused "to be a sheik," a reference to the famous role and film of that name played by Rudolph Valentino. Taking note were Grange's teammates, who immediately pegged him "Rudy" for the rest of the tour.[23]

Grange admired Pyle's boldness. "Where the average fellow would ask for $5,000, Charley would ask for $25,000," Grange told sportswriter Myron Cope in 1974. "Mostly, he got cash. Cash or a check. He didn't fool around very much." No, he didn't, and that Monday, Pyle made sure that Grange worked just as hard as he did on a football field and earned every penny, always with an eye to the next big deal. Big business in the world of professional sports had arrived.[24]

Amidst all the deals that Monday, Pyle paused long enough to arrange a quick meeting and photo op with a special guest, the one and only Babe Ruth. Before a gaggle of flashbulb-popping photographers in Grange's room, the Babe dispensed some advice. "Kid," said the Babe, who couldn't remember names if his life depended on it, "don't pay any attention to what they write about you, and don't pick up too many checks." That got Grange thinking about Ruth, famous for tipping $100 for a $10 meal. "That's just what the Babe was always doing — picking up too many checks," Red said.[25]

On Monday night, the Bears took a train to Washington, with Grange still nursing a cold and slightly banged up. On Tuesday, the team went to the White House to meet President Calvin Coolidge. Never one for words — when challenged by a dinner companion to say at least three words, the president responded, "You lose" — Coolidge seemed a bit distracted and baffled by the backgrounds of the men visiting him. Meeting Pyle, Grange and Chicago Bears head coach George Halas, the president was cordial, saying, "How are you, young gentlemen? I have always admired animal acts." The president's comments were a jarring reminder that pro football still faced a long road.[26]

Even so, Pyle and Grange had already made quite a mark. The endorsements would continue to mount, with the pair adding another dozen or so deals over the next year. And that December game when Red Grange ran though the mud at the Polo Grounds had sealed the pro game's credibility and its future. "(Pro football) had been slowly gathering momentum," wrote Damon Runyon in the *New York American*. "It invaded new territory, including New York City, and it commenced getting valuable word-of-mouth advertising as a thing worth seeing. But it needed a Jumbo ... one big name

In December 1925 in the mist of his first pro tour, Red Grange (second from right) and Pyle (far right) sign a reported $300,000 movie contract. The actual figure was never revealed but it was nowhere near the reported amount, though Grange did shoot his first film four months later. Representing the Arrow Production Company at the Hotel Astor in New York are W.E. Schallenberger (left), the company president, and Harry Kosh (second from left), Schallenberger's attorney (Library of Congress, Prints and Photographs Division).

of known drawing power.... Professional football needed a Jumbo, and it got its Jumbo when it landed Red Harold Grange, of the University of Illinois."[27] Concurring was Allison Danzig in the *New York Times*.

> To call these 70,000 spectators football followers needs correction. There were thousands in that tremendous assemblage who probably never saw a game before, who did not have the slightest idea of what the proceedings were all about. They knew only that Grange was out there on the field among the 22 young warriors clad in moleskins and they watched to see what were the things he did and how he did them.

It is a point of pride with the men most concerned about the future of college football that it is the fame of the colleges and for the colleges. It is

President Calvin Coolidge was probably more at ease communing in a wheat field than making policy at the White House. From the Bain Collection (Library of Congress, Prints and Photographs Division).

the great college game, so they say. It was a game of America yesterday, calling to those who never saw a college campus as well as to those who have. And it was Red Grange who made it so.[28]

How appropriate that the film destined to change the face of professional football was *The Freshman*, which detailed the efforts of funnyman Harold Lloyd to make his college football team. It was October 1925, and Grange was taking a break from his studies at the University of Illinois at the start of his senior year to go the movies at the stately Virginia Theatre in Champaign, near campus. While there, an usher handed him a card. It was a free pass from the manager that was also good for the Park Theatre.[29]

You would think that Grange, as the greatest, most lionized college football star in America, would be blasé about receiving a free movie pass. Hardly. "I was very pleased with the offering not only because I liked going to the movies, but since this was the first time I had ever received anything free while I was at Illinois," Grange said. So much for the preferential treatment of big-time college athletes in the Golden Age of Sports.

Several days later, Grange used his pass to attend another movie at the Virginia, where this time, the manager of both movie houses, one C.C. Pyle, was in the lobby to greet him. Inviting Grange to his office, Pyle got right to business.

"Grange, how would you like to make $100,000, or maybe even $1 million?" Pyle asked.

Suspecting a bribe, Grange, who was standing, took a step back and stated he didn't do those things. "You'll have to get someone else," said Red.[30]

No, that wasn't the idea at all, Pyle countered. This would be a legitimate exercise — a plan in which Grange would become a professional and tour the country to packed stadiums from coast to coast. The math was simple, Pyle explained. Fans would pay top dollar for tickets to see the man sportswriters called "The Galloping Ghost" for his unrivaled ability to elude tacklers, making Grange and Pyle rich beyond their dreams.

Grange was taken aback, uncertain about what he was hearing. "I thought he was crazy," he said. But the football star responded as most would, especially somebody who hadn't grown up with much. "Naturally, (I'd like to make that kind of money)" he said. "Anyone does."

That was the only opening Pyle needed. "Sit down," he said finally, shifting into details of how the arrangement would work. "I'll get back to you inside of a few weeks."[31]

Grange went back to watch the rest of the movie, promising at Pyle's insistence that he would not utter a word of their conversation to anyone —

yet. That's the story anyway, which was true, except for the fact that the famous meeting that night at the Virginia Theatre wasn't the first time Grange and Pyle had met. Though no one can say for sure when the two men first met, it had probably been months earlier, perhaps in May 1925 when Pyle accompanied Grange to Milwaukee to negotiate a film contract. Pyle and fellow theater manager H.E. McNevin, as the *Milwaukee Journal* reported, "seem to have convinced producers that the famous football star is a second Wallace Reid."

Red's friends said that indeed the two men had met the previous spring after Grange had been upset that an automobile company was using his name without permission. Supporting the claim was a man named E.P. Albertsen of Kokomo, Indiana, who swore in an affidavit that C.C. had hired him to serve as Grange's press agent. That Pyle had pursued America's shyest sports superstar is in little doubt, though C.C. spun a different tale, saying that it had been Grange, who in 1924 had approached *him* for counsel after another promoter had offered the football star $60,000 to turn professional.[32]

"Wait," Pyle insisted he had told Grange in 1924, figuring the Illinois running back would only get better and be able later to attract a bigger paycheck. "The inevitable came, of course," Pyle told *NEA News Service* in 1926. "Red waited and while he waited, he kept getting better all the time.... After the Penn game (in 1925), our fortune was made. Then it was time to begin talking turkey. So we talked." The reserved Grange as the pursuer? The story is almost certainly hokum.[33]

The day after their meeting at the movie theater, Pyle left for Chicago to put the first step of his plan into action, which was convincing George Halas and Ed "Dutch" Sternaman, co-owners of the NFL's Chicago Bears, to sign Grange after his last college game of the season, on November 21 against Ohio State. Agreeing to meet in three weeks at the Morrison Hotel in Chicago, Halas prepared accordingly. Making inquiries about Pyle through a mutual acquaintance, a Chicago film distributor named Frank Zambrino, Halas learned that C.C. owned two theaters in Champaign and a third in Kokomo, Indiana, but had virtually no background in professional sports.[34]

C.C. has beaten Halas and Sternaman to the punch. He knew the Bear owners were desperate to sign Grange and had already written him several times. Winners of the NFL championship in 1921, the Bears had signed several top ex-collegians in the years since, men like Ed Healey of Dartmouth, Notre Dame's Hunk Anderson, Duke Hanny of Indiana and Oscar Knop of Illinois. Though they helped the Bears to finish in second place three years in a row, the team was still in need of one special player to put them on top again and draw crowds. "We had seen the 'Galloping Ghost' in the flesh," said Halas. "As an owner, manager, coach and player, I was determined to have Red on the Bears.... He was a true rarity, a perfectly coordinated athlete."[35]

Halas and Sternaman didn't know Pyle, but they were about to meet him in all his glorious bluster. Striding into the Bear offices, C.C. Pyle firmly shook hands with each man and looked them in the eye, stating in no uncertain terms that if they wanted Grange, they had better deal with him. Taller than both of his hosts and elegantly tailored in a gray flannel suit and gray spats with fashionable pearl buttons, Pyle cut an imposing figure. "I noted how carefully he dressed and how well tended was his mustache," Halas recalled in his autobiography. "His shoes were brilliant. He spoke well. He was suave. I felt I was in the presence of a born promoter."[36]

Halas was an NFL pioneer and a football innovator, and a leading coach and executive who even at the relatively young age of 30 was a veteran in negotiating contracts. An accomplished two-sport athlete at the University of Illinois, Halas had even had a brief stint as an outfielder with the New York Yankees and knew just about anyone who was anyone in the sports world. But seated before him was a man who owned downstate movie theaters for goodness sakes, and someone who represented an entirely new concept as the manager *of a player* of all things. It was as if C.C. had burst in from the ether.

"Although neither Sternaman nor I ever had heard of C.C. Pyle, we had nothing to lose. Frankly, Dutch and I figured that a middle-aged, small-town theater owner who wore spats might not prove too tough a negotiator for a couple of bright young football executives from Chicago."

At the same time, the Bear co-owners recognized that they had better deal with Pyle. He was their ticket to Red Grange, the man who could prop up the rickety financial legs of the NFL and move professional football into the big time. Besides, Halas had heard the rumors that rival NFL teams were also after Grange, and realized that Pyle was offering him the inside track. Just after the Ohio State game, those rumors were confirmed when the Associated Press reported that the New York Giants, in their first NFL season, had offered the Illinois running back a whopping $40,000 for the team's last three games of the schedule.[37]

Rumors of the imminent signing had already set off a firestorm of protest. The prospect of a top collegian turning pro before he had graduated fired up the academics, most of all college presidents who said the concept of a young man leaving school before earning his degree was abhorrent.

Their real concern, however, was the bona fide threat Grange's departure meant for the future of college football and its new status as a surefire moneymaker. Major John L. Griffith, head of the Big Ten Athletic Conference, of which Illinois was a member, went further, saying that the professional game just didn't measure up to the quality of the collegians. "Grange needs perfect, well-timed interference to enable him to get away on his thrilling runs, and he will not get this in the professional game," Griffith said. "They will simply hand him the ball and say to Grange, 'There it is; now see what you do can do.' The college spirit in lacking in professional football."[38]

George Halas, C.C. Pyle's first great football ally, was more than a pro football pioneer. He was a football and baseball star at the University of Illinois, MVP of the 1919 Rose Bowl, and in 1919, an outfielder with the New York Yankees for 12 games. In 1920, the Yankees would add a new outfielder: Babe Ruth. From the Bain Collection (Library of Congress, Prints and Photographs Division).

Grange remained torn about what he should do. University of Michigan coach Fielding "Hurry-Up" Yost felt Red should try something other than pro football. University of Illinois head coach Bob Zuppke agreed, but less vehemently, saying his star running back should do what was best for him. Arguing that Grange should turn professional without a second thought was syndicated columnist Westbrook Pegler. "Grange may bring into a butcher shop many books of clippings," Pegler wrote. "But after he has exhibited them all, the butcher will say, 'The chops are still 68 cents.'" It was Pegler's way of urging Pyle and the Illinois football star to go for the money.[39]

Back at the Morrison Hotel, Halas opened the financial discussions with the prospect of sharing their earnings. How would a two-to-one split sound?

Without a word, Pyle agreed, which just about floored Halas. "I anticipated at least some discussion," he said. "My astonishment may have stirred my generosity, because I then volunteered that the Bears would pay costs."

"Of course," Pyle said coyly.

Halas added that he hoped Grange would find the arrangements acceptable.

"He will," Pyle said.

The negotiations were proceeding smoothly, too smoothly, thought Halas. "A sense of unease came over me," he said, so much so that he started over.

"All right," he said to Pyle, "it is agreed the Bears will get two-thirds, and...."

Pyle cut him off. "Oh, no, George," he said, "Grange and I will get two-thirds. The Bears will get one-third."[40]

Halas was stunned. He told Pyle that the arrangement was unacceptable. He and Sternaman had to pay the players. They needed to foot the bill for the tremendous costs of such a tour. Then, if luck prevailed, they might break even, Halas said.

But Pyle was just getting started, revealing his skill at steely eyed bargaining, which had suddenly been drained of its optimism and lightness. Through the night and into the following afternoon the men haggled and bartered. In the end — *26 hours later* — Pyle and the Bears had agreed to a 50–50 split of the profits, with the Bears set to pay the tour costs. So Red Grange would become a pro after all, thanks mostly to Pyle, who had proven anything but a pushover. "It was a fair arrangement," Halas said. "Pyle would provide Red (and) Red would provide the crowds."[41]

In the end, Pyle had earned Halas' grudging respect. "I would never have dared think of such a sweeping enterprise," he said years later of the Grange tour. "But Pyle had unlimited vision.... I would not have known where to begin. Pyle had been around. I was just a country boy."[42]

In Champaign, Red Grange was doing his part to ensure that the upcoming tour, now a secret to everyone but himself, Pyle and the Bear owners, would be a big success. He did so by focusing on accumulating vast yardage on the football field. And in the process, he built his legend.

That legend had grown since Grange's first collegiate game when, as a sophomore in 1923, he scored three touchdowns and ran for 202 yards against Nebraska. At 5', 11" and 175 pounds, the swivel-hipped halfback was born for football, a player whose speed, hesitation and instincts were attributes passed down from the gods. Had there been a Heisman Trophy for the nation's top player in those days, Grange would have already won it once, probably twice and possibly three times by 1925. He was college football's most electrifying player since Jim Thorpe.

Grange described himself as a "green country punk." Born in the isolated eastern Pennsylvania hamlet of Forksville, about halfway between Wilkes-Barre and Williamsport, he took the physical attributes of his father, Lyle. As a foreman at three nearby logging camps, the 6' 1" Lyle weighed 200 pounds, and was powerfully built and quick with his fists. Red worshipped his father, calling him the reason "why I could never get a swelled head." Lyle had 300 men under him, Red said, "and he had to be able to lick" any one of them. "One day," Red added, "(Lyle) had a fight that lasted four hours."[43]

But the Granges weren't long for Pennsylvania. Red's mother died when he was five, prompting Lyle to move his family, which included Red's two older sisters and a younger brother, Garland, back to his hometown, Wheaton, Illinois, some 30 miles west of Chicago.

With a population of 4,000, Wheaton was a thriving farming and manufacturing community that fronted the railroad. It was a promising place to find work, in part because Lyle Grange could lean on a big network of siblings to help raise his children. So Lyle joined his brother's moving business, and economized as best he could by sending Red's sisters back to Pennsylvania to live with relatives. Times were still hard; in Wheaton, Red and his brothers moved frequently, usually a step ahead of creditors. For a time, Red lived with an uncle, a lawyer, and another who farmed.[44]

Grange seldom complained, but he loathed the year he spent at age 15 on his Uncle Ernest's farm outside Wheaton. Rising each day at 5:00 A.M., Red did two hours of chores and then drove a milk wagon to town and back before hopping on his bicycle for the two-mile ride to school. At night, he did another round of chores and only then end his day. "I earned my keep — and then some," Red said of life at the farm. Concerned that Red was overworked, Lyle took him back to live at the family's apartment in town.

Gradually, the Grange family's fortunes improved. Lyle Grange earned a steady paycheck as an assistant to the police chief and then city marshal. Meantime, Red became the town's humble football star, his character quite possibly shaped by the loss of his mother at an early age as it was by his no-nonsense father. "A man for a kid to brag about," Red recalled of Lyle, who remained his role model forever.[45]

Red took easily to sports in Wheaton, where he was a star from the get-go. "I don't remember ever losing a footrace as a kid," he said. "I'd go to these church picnics and I'd win a baseball, and then my father would give me a quarter every time I won."[46]

As a member of the 1918 Wheaton High School football team, Grange was a seldom-used end, but gave a glimpse of what was ahead by returning a punt 70 yards for a touchdown. Shifting to halfback in 1919, he became a star, blending deft moves and an effective stiff arm to score 15 touchdowns in seven games. He even kicked nine extra points, and Wheaton High won five of seven games.

In the summer of 1919, Grange took a job delivering ice for Luke Thompson's Company. Using oversized tongs to haul 75-pound blocks of ice was the 1920 equivalent of hitting the weight room. The job added muscle to Grange's arms, shoulders and legs, and became the basis of his future moniker, "The Wheaton Iceman." Stronger, miles ahead of others in conditioning and motivated by Lyle's payment of a quarter for every touchdown he scored, Grange piled up the yardage on the football field in 1920.

That year, Wheaton High School hired Charles "Dink" Weldon as football coach and athletic director. A member of the first Wheaton High team back in 1910 and a U.S. Marine in World War I, Weldon recognized Grange's greatness. He also did Grange a favor by leaving him at running back while working behind the scenes to toughen the team's competition. Playing against bigger schools closer to Chicago, Grange continued to excel, gaining an unworldly 504 yards in one game and continuing to roll up the touchdowns — 36 in 1920 alone.

In four varsity seasons at Wheaton High, Grange scored 75 touchdowns and booted 82 extra points for 532 total points, nearly 15 a game. For Lyle, the scoring got expensive. At a quarter for each touchdown, he forked over $2 after Red tallied *eight* touchdowns against Batavia High. "I was a pro that early, and I must admit that the money incentive was almost as strong as high school loyalty about then," Red joked. Along the way, he earned 16 letters in four sports, playing basketball, baseball and running track. In the spring, Red split his time between baseball and track, and at the state championships won the 220-yard dash and long jump in 1921 and the 100 in 1922. In baseball, Red was good enough for the Boston Braves to offer him a tryout.[47]

At the 1922 state track championships at Champaign, University of Illinois football coach Bob Zuppke approached Grange with the idea of enrolling at Illinois to play football. Head coach since 1913, Zuppke had already earned a well-deserved reputation as a successful innovator. A German immigrant from Milwaukee, Zuppke had orchestrated a real turnaround at Illinois by winning his first Big Ten title after two years; it was first of four titles he would earn in the next decade. In doing so, Zuppke had created the spiral pass from center, the screen pass, the huddle and the hidden on-side kick, earning him, along with Fielding Yost of Michigan, Knute Rockne of Notre Dame, Amos Alonzo Stagg of the University of Chicago and Glenn "Pop" Warner of the Carlisle Indian School, a reputation as one of the era's top coaches.[48]

In light of Grange's extraordinary gifts, it is remarkable Zuppke was the only big-name coach to recruit him. Grange said he wanted to play basketball and run track at Illinois — *and not football* — but once at Illinois, members of his fraternity, Zeta Psi, convinced him to reconsider. "They figured that since I also had a pretty good record in football at Wheaton High, it would be much more desirable, prestige-wise for the fraternity, if I were to concentrate on football."[49]

So he did, drawing his famous number 77 jersey on his first day of practice. The reason? The guy in front of me got 76; the guy in back got 78," Grange explained. Peering at his bigger, beefier teammates, Grange figured he didn't stand a chance of even making the team. Among his fellow freshmen teammates were future All-Americans Ralph "Moon" Baker from Rockford at quarterback (by then playing for Northwestern) and Frank Wickhorst of Aurora at tackle (for Navy), along with fullback Earl Britton of Elgin, a future Bears teammate. But after a week of practice, it was clear that Grange had superior speed and better ball-handling skills than anyone else on the field. Any remaining doubt was removed in a pre-season intra-squad game in which Grange, the freshman team's starting halfback, threaded the varsity all day, scoring two touchdowns, including a 60-yard punt return. Zuppke took note, calling the game the first of many times that Grange would capture his attention.[50]

In addition to speed, Grange had a combination of gifts, from remarkable lateral mobility to a change of pace, an innate ability in finding an opening, and a devastating straight-arm to stifle tacklers. It was as if carrying a football was part of Grange's DNA, something he was destined to do. Grange "seemed to glide, rather than run, and he was a master at using his blockers," W.C. Heinz wrote. "What made him great, however, was his instinctive ability to size up a field and plot a run the way a great general can map not only a battle but a whole campaign." Grange chose just to run and not give it too much analysis. "The sportswriters wrote that I had peripheral vision," he said. "I didn't even know what the word meant. I had to look it up."[51]

Grange's next three years would become a litany of big moments, recorded by gushing reporters and performed before big and increasingly enthusiastic crowds. With Illinois struggling through a dismal 2-5 varsity record in 1922 — it would be several more decades before freshmen could play varsity football — there was Grange starting at halfback in the first game of 1923 against the powerful Nebraska Cornhuskers, which had dismantled Rockne's Notre Dame the year before. With the benefit of another summer delivering ice supplemented by Zuppke's intense nine-week training regimen, Grange ran rings around Nebraska to help Illinois coast, 24–7. There were more heroics to come — many more — and by season's end, Grange was a consensus All-American with 1,260 yards and 12 touchdowns to power Illinois to an 8-0 record and the co-championship with Michigan in the Big Ten.[52]

By 1924, Grange had taken to piling up one epic performance after another. On November 3 against the University of Chicago, more than 60,000 braved a steady rain to watch Grange peel off runs of 60, 42, 30 and 23 yards in Illinois' hard-fought 7–0 victory, capped by his five-yard scoring plunge. It was the largest crowd ever assembled in central Illinois, and underscored how Grange had helped make Illinois football a happening. With many of the Illinois spectators now owning cars, the Chicago and St. Louis newspapers published detailed pre-game roadmaps to Champaign, with the entire Illinois state trooper force dispatched to major roads to keep the traffic flowing. Even the *New York Times*, beginning to wake up to this extraordinary happening in the Midwest, reported that some fans reached Champaign by airplane, while "some youthful enthusiasts, lacking carfare ... walked all night."[53]

But it was a warm-up next to the epic Michigan game of October 18, 1924, the inaugural game at the university's massive new $1.7 million, 67,000-seat Memorial Stadium, and the first Illinois game to be broadcast by radio. In all the thousands upon thousands of football games ever played, Grange's performance against Michigan, the Illini's major rival, may have been the most spectacular and closest to perfect 60 minutes of football ever played, a game in which the Illinois running back scooted up and down the field seemingly at will, not so much un-tackled as untouched.

Undefeated Michigan was a heavy favorite against the Illini, which had dropped its opener to Nebraska, and lost a significant number of starters from 1923 to graduation. Michigan had prepared for Grange, or so they thought, by sending the opening kickoff to him by design — a challenge to see if this Grange was as good as advertised. "Mr. Grange will be a carefully watched man every time he takes the ball," Michigan coach Fielding Yost had said of his team's strategy for handing the Illinois running back. "There will be just about 11 clean, hard Michigan tacklers headed for him at the same time. I know he is a great runner, but great runners usually have the hardest time gaining ground when met by special preparation."[54]

Grange would later say the opening kickoff was headed to Wally McIlwain when he dropped back, gathered the ball and headed upfield, waiting a spilt second for the linemen to form in front of him. Twisting, slithering, darting here and there, changing speeds and instinctively using his blockers as a shield, Grange passed 10 Michigan defenders. Still needing to beat one more man, safety Tod Rockwell, Grange turned on the speed and scored. Touchdown, 95 yards.

Getting the ball four minutes later with a 7–0 lead, Zuppke called for Grange, at tailback, to take a short pass and swing around right end. Catching the ball, Grange headed 67 yards for another touchdown. Then on Illinois' next set of downs, he took off for 56 yards for his third touchdown. Touchdown number 4 came a few minutes later, a 44-yard sprint running right and cutting back, down the middle, and across the goal line. With 12 minutes gone in the first quarter, Grange had gained 262 yards and scored all four of the game's touchdowns. Illinois led 27–0. "You knew something was happening that was out of the ordinary," said Illinois end Dwight Follett. "When it came off, it seemed like he did the impossible."[55]

Leaning against the Michigan goal post during a water break after his fourth touchdown, Grange admitted he was whipped. "I'm so dog-tired I can hardly stand up," he told Illinois trainer Matt Bullock. "Better get me outta here."[56]

The break finished, Bullock delivered the message to the bench. Zuppke obliged for a time, but put his star player back in the lineup a few minutes later. "You should have had five touchdowns," the coach told Grange when the offense left the field. "You didn't cut right on that one play." Red scored the fifth a few minutes later — and then a sixth. When the game ended, Red had gained an astounding 402 yards on 21 carries. Final score: Grange 38, Michigan 14.[57]

In all of a single quarter, Grange had demolished a powerful team, all the while transforming himself from a regional star to a national sensation. "The most spectacular single-handed performance ever made in a major game," Amos Alonzo Stagg said of Grange's epic performance. From the *Detroit Free Press*, "Grange must be given his place with those old heroes, Richard the Lion-hearted, Frederick Barbarossa, and Eric the Red." It didn't

The great Red Grange carries the football in his epic performance against Michigan in 1924. The next fall, Grange, represented by C.C. Pyle, turned pro (Library of Congress, Prints and Photographs Division).

hurt that the Grange phenomenon was taking root just as tabloid journalism was enjoying an explosion of its own in the Golden Age of Sports. Nor did it hurt that in 1924 the other sports icons of the day, heavyweight boxing champion Jack Dempsey and Babe Ruth, were having their troubles. Dempsey was an engaging champ but had faced a barrage of negative publicity that he was a draft dodger (not true) and had married a prostitute (true), which sullied his reputation.[58]

Ruth, meantime, had just polished off a sub-par season — for him anyway — in which he had hit *only* 46 home runs, which led the major leagues, but paled in comparison to his performances in earlier seasons when he had twice walloped more than 50. Nor was it enough to keep his Yankees from beating out the Washington Senators for the American League pennant. Behind their ace right-hander Walter Johnson, the Senators went on to win an exciting seven-game World Series, the team's only championship.[59]

But considering what 1925 had in store, Grange's performance was all a prologue.

2

"Three or Four Men and a Horse Rolled into One"

Just after Thanksgiving of 1924, Red Grange returned home to Wheaton, where 250 townspeople and old friends held a testimonial in his honor. The town newspaper described him as sitting "rather bored and fatigued" through the speeches and testimonials.[1]

But Grange would need his energy in the new year because the Michigan game — those 12 minutes of glory — had transformed him into a national celebrity. "A streak of fire, a breath of flame ... eluding all who reach and clutch," Grantland Rice wrote of the Illinois running back after the Michigan game. "(He is) a gray ghost ... that rivals hands may rarely touch." As part of year-end review of 1924, the *Boston Globe* featured Grange and a description of his heroics against Michigan alongside other comparable news, including the deaths of former President Woodrow Wilson and labor leader Samuel Gompers and the visit of the Prince of Wales to America.[2]

As 1925 opened, coverage of Grange had become what his biographer, John M. Carroll, called "a media frenzy." A *Chicago Journal* poll named Grange one of the world's best athletes, behind Jack Dempsey, Olympic swimmer Johnny Weissmuller and Jim Thorpe, but well ahead of Babe Ruth and fellow baseball stars Walter Johnson and Ty Cobb. That spring, Red met Pyle for the first time, traveling to Milwaukee for the screen test with Universal Studios.

Despite coming down with a case of mumps that spring, Grange closed out his junior year at Illinois and went home for the summer. Resuming his job delivering ice for $30 a week, Grange was often trailed by reporters and was periodically stopped for conversation and posing for photos with customers. In a sense, the media interest in Grange was preordained. By the mid–1920s, a technological explosion of newsprint and a generation of talented, new writers were conspiring with an American culture intent on enjoying itself.[3]

Symbolizing this new frivolity on the sports pages was the arrival of the one and only "Babe," the era's most electrifying athlete. The Babe reached stardom as a left-handed pitcher in the teens with the Red Sox, and probably would have remained there for the rest of his career had it not been his unusual propensity to hit home runs, an astounding skill for a pitcher and especially in the days when power simply wasn't an integral part of the game. By mid–1918, Red Sox manager Ed Barrow faced a dilemma: Should he let Ruth pitch and bat every fourth day and occasionally pinch hit? Or was it better to put him in the outfield and see what he could do while batting every day? Barrow made him an outfielder — and the results revolutionized baseball. In 1919, Ruth set the major league single-season home run mark by belting 29, and a year later, as a member of the Yankees, hit an unfathomable 54, breaking his own record *in mid–July*. The confluence of heroics on the field and doing it in America's biggest city made Ruth a superstar, leading reporters to follow him everywhere.[4]

Readers craved news of this flamboyant new hero. In the newspapers, Ruth was "Big Bertha," "the Son of Swat," the man "who made sick ball games well," and for Damon Runyon, simply "Mr. Ruth." Everything about him projected excitement, and he was attracting bigger crowds than the Yankees had ever seen, including, in 1920, baseball's first home "million" gate. "Ruth looks good when he makes a home run," said one Polo Grounds fan to another. "True," cracked the friend, but "Ruth looks good even when he strikes out." Even the staid *New York Times* couldn't contain itself from gushing purple prose about this new prodigy. "Ruth has become the most alarming menace big league pitchers have ever bucked against," its reporter wrote. "An extra outfielder stationed in the upper grand stand may be necessary to curb the clouter. But that wouldn't stop Ruth, for they would also have to plant another outfielder out in Manhattan Field, and maybe before the season is over another would have to be scouting flies out in Eighth Avenue."[5]

It didn't hurt that the Babe was charismatic, belting all those home runs and carousing all night, but doing it with a glint in his eye. He was quotable without trying to be, and carried on a genuine love affair with children, always finding time to visit them in hospitals and orphanages similar to the one where he was raised in Baltimore. Purposely omitted by writers were the naughty bits, like Ruth's coarse language, much of it related to sex and body parts. "I can knock the c__k off any ball that ever was pitched," Ruth enjoyed boasting to anyone within earshot. Baseball historian Fred Lieb recalls sitting on the train and playing cards with other writers on a barnstorming trip when Ruth suddenly burst down the aisle, pursued by an irate, raven-haired woman carrying a knife pointed at the Babe's back. Ruth got away, and the woman, the wife of a Louisiana state senator, calmed down, but the writers chose to keep on playing cards and ignore the incident. "I still wonder why we newspapermen acted as we did," Lieb pondered years later. "There were 11 of us sitting there and no one said a word. We just went on typing, reading magazines, and playing cards."[6]

The most likely explanation? It was the writers' code in those days, where anything on the field was fair game for the sports page, with extracurricular exploits and the bad language not fit for print. And why hurt the Babe? He oozed charm and was incurably newsworthy. By the mid–1920s, he had become not only the best baseball player in the land, but the most publicized athlete in U.S. history, a man known far and wide. Ushered in the Yankee locker room in St. Louis to meet their hero, three cowboys told Ruth they had ridden three days on horseback to catch a train in Wyoming. "Baby Ruth," one of them said to the Babe, "I'd have ridden all the way to St. Louis to see you hit them home runs."[7]

By 1920, Manhattan alone had 11 major dailies, all of which saw in Ruth a big "feel good" story, particularly in a country just two years removed from the more than 54,000 American soldiers killed in World War I, and a year or so after an extraordinarily devastating flu epidemic that started in the soldier camps and by the time it had laid waste to wide parts of the country, had claimed more than 600,000 lives. Feeding a public weary of both war and illness with a steady dose of copy on sports, gossip, the social scene, fashion, crime and movie stars was a vast improvement on the dreadful drumbeat of death on the front pages. Fueling the trend was an explosion of newsprint, aided by the birth of tabloids featuring oversized photos, eye-catching headlines and short, snappy copy, perfect for immigrants just learning the language. Setting the standard was the birth in 1919 of William Randolph Hearst's *Illustrated Daily News*, soon renamed the *Daily News*, where snappy headlines like "Baby Sleeps As Parents Are Robbed" and "Waitress Battles Alleged Thief Until Police Arrive" became staples. Circulation soared, reaching 750,000 within five years.

Feeding the public clamor for more sports news was a talented breed of young journalists like Runyon, Rice, Pegler and Ring Lardner, who used humor, a healthy dose of irreverence, and often poetry in turning the sports page — "a train wreck," in Jimmy Breslin's opinion — to an essential stop for any reader. They were the young bucks of the trade willing to overlook tradition and change the way sports was covered — a perfect anecdote to a public weary of bad news. They became celebrities in their own right, playing golf with presidents and enjoying the ride.[8]

No one was immune from their humor. Turning to President Harding between tee shots, Lardner pronounced he wanted to be named ambassador to Greece.

"Greece?" said the president, puzzled. "Why Greece?"

"My wife doesn't like Great Neck," said Lardner.[9]

Pegler, then a young sportswriter, branded the 1920s as "The Era of Wonderful Nonsense," and the description was accurate. "Totally surrounded by billionaires, Mr. Babe Ruth felt more at home here this afternoon than at any time since he joined the Yankees," Runyon of the *New York American* wrote from Yankee spring training camp about a game played at a Palm Beach country club. "It was an atmosphere to which his price tag has accustomed him. He realized that he cost almost as much as a white chip at Bradley's or one of the Pomeranians in the arms of a lady fan."[10]

Talented writers like Runyon could get away with material like that. Hard drinkers and hard partiers, they were more interested in turning a phrase and trying to outwit one another than always reporting what exactly had happened. Who cared that they rarely quoted anyone or ventured to the locker room? Or that that they failed to report a crucial injury? Lardner and Runyon could fall back on humor and didn't need to try terribly hard to track down news. It amounted to a style and an attitude different than today, with the gulf between wealthy ballplayers and middle-class baseball reporters wider than Lake Michigan. Not so then. Instead of stories on salary arbitration, agate with every kind of conceivable statistic or game summaries full of analysis from players, coaches and managers, coverage in the 1920s was more like public relations — collegial, chatty, seldom challenging, and rarely unpleasant.[11]

Top byliners pulled in $35,000 a year if they had a syndicated column. Top journalists had additional opportunities to contribute to a growing legion of young sassy magazines like the *Saturday Evening Post, Vanity Fair, Cosmopolitan*, and starting in 1925, *The New Yorker*, all of which recognized that writing on sports sold copies.[11]

Grange was no match for Babe Ruth's personality. The shy star from Wheaton, Illinois downplayed his exploits, adding little insight into his remarkable gifts. "If you have the football and 11 guys are after you, you'll run," he said. "It was no big deal." Of the legendary 1924 game against Michigan, he said matter of factly that "I cut back for the first time in my career, and it was the greatest single factor in my being able to break away consistently for long runs." But his modesty didn't matter because sportswriters were more than willing to create the hype, writing that Red was not just a running back, but a heartland product who had grown strong by hauling ice. To them, Red was a humble hero who answered kids' letters, went to class and took his success in stride, all of which was basically true.[12]

Short of scoring six touchdowns a game, what could Grange possibly do in 1925 to top his already legendary 1924 season? Considering the Illini had lost its entire offensive line to graduation, the odds were against him. Making things more challenging was the condition of quarterback Harry Hall, who had not fully recovered from an injury suffered in the previous season's Minnesota game. "It's going to be some job to fill the places of the experienced players," Zuppke admitted. Even Grange's younger brother, Garland, who had been a standout on the 1924 freshman team and slotted as a varsity starter, was injured in preseason and withdrew from school.

Adding to the gloom was a fall on the flat plains of Illinois where it rained just about every Saturday, making it hard for Grange, or any running back for that matter, to compile much yardage. With its lineup, taped together with inexperienced sophomores and juniors, Illinois lost its opener, a rain-soaked 14–0 thrashing by Nebraska in the mud in which Grange gained only 49 yards and no first downs.[13]

The Illini then lost two of its three games before Grange began finding his stride. Against Butler, Grange gained 185 yards, and then 208 yards at Iowa. Although the team would recover from its poor start and finish 6–4 with Grange gaining more yardage (in one more game) than in 1924, some football historians took Grange to what they perceived was a lackluster year. One historian, James Mark Purcell, argued that yardage were merely "the good sound stats one expects of a great offensive star on a mediocre team," adding that Johnny Mack Brown of Alabama and Eddie Tryon of Colgate had better seasons and deserved first-team All-American status.[14]

But just when the largely eastern press corps was ready to write Grange off, he delivered another epic performance. On October 31 in the driving rain and muck of Franklin Field against the powerful University of Pennsylvania, Grange saved his best for his first eastern trip by gaining 363 yards and scoring three touchdowns in Illinois' 24–2 thrashing of the highly favored Quakers. Grange had come East for the first time and triumphed, sending Runyon, Rice and their colleagues into new fits of prose. It was the exclamation mark of a great collegiate career, a defining moment of what would become his third consecutive All-American season.

"This man Red Grange, of Illinois, is three or four men and a horse rolled into one for football purposes," Runyon extolled. "He is Jack Dempsey, Babe Ruth, Al Jolson, Paavo Nurmi and Man o' War. Put them all together, they spell Grange. At 2:05 this afternoon by the watch, this man Red Grange broke out against the University of Pennsylvania football eleven, and at 4:30 he had 65,000 men, women and little children sitting positively dumbfounded by his performance."[15]

Grange's convincing performance removed any doubt about his ability to run in mud or measure up against what many considered the more powerful eastern college football teams. "In case you wonder why so much fuss is made about Red Grange, it is because he is the kind of football player every one whoever thought anything about the game would like to be," wrote Paul Gallico of the *Daily News*. "In my boyhood dreams, I would see myself thundering down the Yale Bowl with 80,000 yelling encouragement to me. I had in my imagination a peculiar loping gait that Harvard found it impossible to solve.... Well, Red Grange is the dream of every boy come true."[16]

Writers compared Grange to the legendary Jim Thorpe, the former Carlisle Indian School football star who did a few other things as well, such as winning good medals in the decathlon and pentathlon at the 1912 Olympic Games, playing six years of major league baseball, and joining the NFL in its charter season of 1920. The hype took care of the fact that Grange was virtually unavailable for comment — seldom interviewed and barely consulted. In the little that he did say, he credited others for his performance, namely Coach Zuppke and "his brilliant strategy," according to his memoirs, "that called for our using weak side plays against the Quakers" as well as his "psychological build-up" that had the team at its "absolute peak," as they had been in 1924 against Michigan.[17]

Stepping off the train Sunday in Champaign after the trip home from the Penn game, Grange got a taste of what it meant to be a star. More than 20,000 stormed the railroad station, and Grange tried leaving the car by ducking off the rear platform, only to be caught by the festive crowd, hoisted to its shoulders and carried two miles to his fraternity house. "I was embarrassed," Grange recalled years later of the adulation. "You wish people would understand that it takes 11 men to make a football team." Only after he made two curtain calls at the window and gave some remarks did people disperse. On Monday, university athletic officials announced that Grange's uniform number 77 would be retired after the season.[18]

With only three games left in his senior year, rumors that Grange was

headed for the pros were rampant. At Pyle's insistence, Red had to repeat-
edly deny the stories that he had already signed for big money. So reporters
headed to Wheaton for Lyle Grange's view on whether his son should join
the NFL. The elder Grange urged him to make the plunge, arguing that "he's
entitled to 'cash-in' on the long runs his gridiron fame has brought him."

"It has been expensive for me to send Harold and his brother Garland
through the University," Lyle Grange added. "We are not rolling in wealth,
and I think the public would approve of anything Harold does."

Most everyone. Hearing the talk, University of Illinois president David
Kinley became worried that his famous student had already become a professional and might have to leave the college game immediately. But after a
chat with Grange, he was convinced that "he was not tied up with anybody."
Agreeing was Big Ten commissioner John Griffith, who said he had investi-
gated the reports and found that Grange had broken no rules.[19]

Grange was finding it difficult to focus on his studies. Newsreel men
camped outside his fraternity house to record his coming and going. The
shy star described it as "all confusion" and "no privacy." Meantime, the
Chicago Tribune reported that Grange had been "besieged with offers of every
description," so many that Grange went home to Wheaton for two days to
sort through the offers with his father. About the same time, Tim Mara took
off for Illinois on a unnamed mission, though it was an open secret that he
intended to offer Grange $40,000 to play the season's last three games with
the Giants.[20]

Back on campus, Grange ducked from class to practice, avoiding as
many interviews as possible and telling his fraternity mates to answer neither questions from reporters nor the telephone. He even threw off Zuppke,
promising his coach he would tell him "anything he wanted to know" after
the final game against Ohio State. But if Grange was feeling besieged, he
never let on, despite gaining only 51 yards November 7 on another soggy,
muddy field at home against the University of Chicago, and barely playing
the following week, an easy 21–0 win over Wabash College. But just when
he seemed spent, the great Red Grange finished off his collegiate career with
a solid performance, chewing up 113 yards in a hard-fought 14–9 victory
against Ohio State before a record college football crowd of 85,500 at Ohio
Stadium, the Big Horseshoe, in Columbus.[21]

After the game came reckoning time. Facing a mob of reporters crowded
around his locker in the cramped locker room, Grange finally spoke. It was
a bombshell announcement that confirmed the rumors that he would drop
out of college to play professional football. Grange said he would soon be

leaving for Wheaton to organize his own pro team. His words were slightly disingenuous, designed at Pyle's insistence to throw reporters off track. This way, C.C. would be able to make his own splash by announcing that Grange would soon join the Bears, with his first game set for Thanksgiving Day at Cubs Park against the Cardinals. (*In 1926, Cubs Park was renamed Wrigley Field.*)[22]

Zuppke was floored. After Grange had showered and dressed, he invited the halfback to share a cab back to the hotel, hoping to change the mind of the young star he had recruited and mentored. The ride lasted more than an hour — Zuppke ordered the hack to keep driving — during which the coach tried hard to change Grange's mind. "Keep away from professionalism and you'll be another Walter Camp," Zuppke urged, his reference to the great Yale coach who was a paragon of amateurism, honor and clean play. "Football isn't a game to play for money."

But Grange's mind was set. After a childhood marked by constant moving and keeping one step ahead of the creditors, he craved security and a steady paycheck. Didn't Zuppke make a living teaching and coaching football? Grange's coach didn't find it paradoxical. "So what's the difference if I make a living playing football?" Red asked his former coach.

Back at the hotel, the two shook hands. Grange headed through a side door to avoid the crowd in the lobby, and went up to his room. He then packed his luggage, left by a fire escape, and caught the next train to Chicago. Checking into the Belmont Hotel under an assumed name, he met the following day with Pyle, made him his manager, and signed a contract with the Bears. Just like that, Red Grange was a professional, having turned C.C. Pyle into the world's first sports agent in the modern sense. But minefields were just ahead.[23]

C.C. Pyle had fooled them all, managing to stay out of sight most of November in Florida as he negotiated what was going to be part of Red Grange's triumphant tour of America and the real birth of pro football.

True to his word, Pyle had orchestrated everything. Immediately after signing the contract, he and Grange attended that afternoon's Bears game against Green Bay at Cubs Park. Emerging from the baseball dugout and onto the sideline, Pyle insisted Grange wear a lavish, oversized raccoon coat to attract maximum attention. Sitting on the Bears bench, Red looked out of place next to his new uniform-clad teammates, though no one seemed to mind. Spying Grange, many in the crowd of 3,000 rose and let out a tremendous roar, the kind that the *Milwaukee Sentinel* reported, "Babe Ruth or Jack Dempsey, in their palmiest days, were never accorded."[24]

Zuppke remained unimpressed, his mood growing increasingly bitter at what he saw as his star's disloyalty. When Grange went back to Champaign some days later to attend the team's post-season banquet, the coach berated him in front of his teammates. Grange just stood up and walked out, and it was several months before the two men patched up their differences. With Grange's decision final, other college officials stepped up their profound displeasure, quickly passing rules to dismiss any college player signing as a professional. "The professional game is not only taking students away from school before they complete their courses, but it is wrecking what might otherwise be successful careers as coaches and athletic directors because no conference will hire anyone who has had anything to do with it," bellowed University of Missouri professor W.G. Manley, the university's faculty representative on the Missouri Valley Conference board. "While we feel the professional game is on the decline and will die a natural death, we wish to be instrumental in hastening its demise."[25]

The collegiate crowd spun Grange's decision as an affront on the sanctity of college athletes. In reality, the college game was far from pure, riddled as it was with "ringers," a common term for players hired by big-name schools for a game or two. Another practice was for college players to hire themselves out for semi-pro teams, a steady form of income that the great Notre Dame coach Knute Rockne did years before. Left unsaid was concern by many college professors and administrators that professionals posed a genuine threat to the college football that filled university stadiums and coffers.[26]

So who was Charles C. Pyle the man responsible for all the commotion? Bursting from obscurity, he had invented a profession all by himself, becoming America's first full-scale sports agent, a man who represented an athlete in micro-managing each and every deal, from contracts to what to wear, what to say to the newspapermen, and where and when to play. That's common practice today, but in Pyle's day, it was a revolutionary concept. Other athletes had managers, commonly in boxing, where larger-than-life characters like Madison Square Garden owner Tex Rickard worked more as promoters hyping a particular fight or securing a venue. Also, most boxers had managers like Doc Kearns, who worked with Jack Dempsey, but their role was focused on getting their fighters in shape for the ring. Nowhere in the sports world had there been anyone like Pyle, who actually did a player's bidding at contract time, told him what to say to the press and which charity ball to attend.[27]

Athletes from team sports had been slow to catch on to the use of managers or agents. Just imagine the uncertainty of a poorly educated ballplayer heading into contract negotiations with an owner like the Yankees Jacob Ruppert or the White Sox Charles Comiskey, who typically intimidated — and underpaid — his players. The closest anyone had come to having an agent had been Babe Ruth, who as a Red Sox pitcher had hired Boston restaurant and drugstore owner John Igoe to answer his mail and set up appearances. The two men had met through Ruth's first wife, Helen, who was a waitress at Igoe's coffee shop. In 1921, Ruth hired sportswriter-turned-manager Christy Walsh, who contacted the Babe by entering his apartment at the Ansonia Hotel in New York by posing as an ice man. Walsh ghost-wrote and negotiated contracts for Ruth's articles in newspapers. In later years, he conspired with Ruth's second wife, Claire, in investing the Babe's considerable earnings and keeping him on a strict budget so he wouldn't revert to former habits like tipping waitresses $100. The strategy worked; Walsh's shrewd money management made Ruth a wealthy man in retirement. But Walsh wasn't an agent in the modern sense, never negotiating a contract with Ruppert and seldom advising Ruth where to go or what to wear.[28]

Pyle had seemingly burst from nowhere to become one of the most talked about sportsmen in America. But in a sense, this was a role for which he had prepared his entire life. At 43, C.C. was the huckster's huckster — a slick, fast-thinking talker with a fertile mind, boundless optimism, chutzpah and an itch for affluence and playing the big shot. Equal parts circus barker, showman and snake-oil salesman, Pyle enjoyed sticking it to tradition and making a lot of money his way, preferably in cash, which earned him the enduring nickname "Cash and Carry," a play on "C.C." Most accounts of Pyle attribute his gift of gab to being a son of a famous Methodist minister from Delaware, Ohio, near Columbus. But that depiction is a half-truth, most likely due to Pyle's tendency to make his background appear more fanciful than reality, a tendency driven home in an adoring and probably exaggerated 1928 profile of him in The *New Yorker*.[29]

The most notable aspect of Pyle's small-town upbringing may have been how ordinary it was. Pyle's family — originally spelled "Pile" — were farmers from Ohio and Pennsylvania. According to 1860 census figures, his paternal grandfather, Noah, was born in Pennsylvania and moved at some point to Mercer County, in the western part of Ohio near Indiana. He became a successful farmer, with a property and an estate valued at $3,600, fairly prosperous for the times. By 1870, William, by then 16, was working as a laborer on his parents' farm. Likewise, Pyle's mother, Sidney McMillan, was from a farming family, who according to 1860 census figures, was born in 1856 in Van Wert County, just north of Mercer County. With a last name of Scottish origin, genealogical research suggests that some of C.C. Pyle's ancestors were part of the large Scots-Irish immigration to the U.S. in the seventeenth century.

William and Sidney married in 1876 and moved to Van Wert County, Ohio, where they started a family. Their daughter, Anna, was born in 1878; son, Ira, in 1880, and Charles, on March 25, 1882. In the same spirit that C.C. would in later years spin tall tales about his background, there is uncertainty about his real middle name, the second "C," which was sometimes "Cassius" in documents and other times "Clifton."[30]

William was a farmer by trade but was unable to work by the mid-1880s, disabled by a chronic heart condition, which as it turns out he had passed on to his sons. Around the same time, Pyle changed the family from "Pile" for unrecorded reasons, though it may have been to escape a minor embarrassment triggered by the name. "Pile" was a common late-nineteenth-century term for hemorrhoids.[31]

William Pyle had a gift for gab, a skill he did pass on to his youngest son, Charles. And he was indeed a minister, though far from famous in his second career as an itinerant preacher. No longer able to farm, William moved to his family to Delaware, a Methodist community 25 miles north of Columbus in central Ohio, which was a good place for a man of the cloth seeking work. Founded in 1808, the thriving town of Delaware was a popular health resort in mid-century and home to the prestigious liberal arts college Ohio Wesleyan University, founded in 1842 by Methodists. In 1851, the Cleveland, Columbus & Cincinnati Rail Road established a stop in Delaware, which gave the community access to major cities and markets throughout the country by the time the Pyles lived there. At the turn of the century, the Delaware County population had grown to a shade above 26,000, and Delaware, the town and county seat, had its own electric street railway system.

Most residents of Delaware were staunch Republicans — the 19th president of the United States, Rutherford B. Hayes, a Republican, had been born there. Yet, Delaware, Ohio, was a progressive, even liberal town by nineteenth-century midwestern standards. Before the Civil War, the Underground Railway had gone through the area to which its Africa Road owes its name. During the war, Camp Delaware was one of the few grounds safe enough to send African-American soldiers for training.[32]

As an itinerant or a "local" preacher, William substituted for ordained

Methodist clergy, most of whom had more than one church and traveled between them. But sadly, Pyle's pastoral career was brief. In the Delaware-based Archives of Ohio Methodism, William is listed as a local pastor for precisely one year, 1889, which has no other documentation about him. In 1890, when C.C. turned eight, William Pyle died of tuberculosis, plunging his widow and three children into the workforce.[33]

In Delaware, the Pyles lived in a house on North Washington Street, between Winter Street and Central Avenue, two blocks north of the Ohio Wesleyan campus. There, the widowed Mrs. Pyle worked as a dressmaker, with the children taking a variety of jobs to make ends meet. In their early teens, C.C. and Ira worked as train butchers, strolling through trains and selling cigarettes, fruit and candy to people headed to one of their father's old churches. According to the census figures from 1900, the family was still hard-working, with Sidney making dresses, 17-year-old C.C. clerking at a grocery on weekends and after school, 20-year-old Ira managing the local Western Union Telegraph Company, and 22-year-old Anna serving as operator at Citizens Telephone Company.[34]

Sports captivated C.C. from the get-go. In 1890, Ohio Wesleyan fielded a football team for the first time and dropped its inaugural game to Ohio State. But in all of one season, the team became a powerhouse and completed the 1891 season undefeated. By 1897, Ohio Wesleyan was a bona fide football power, thanks largely to its coach, the 26-year-old "Hurry-Up" Yost, under whom the Red and Black rolled up a 7–1–1 record and the state championship. Along the way, Ohio Wesleyan shut out six opponents, including Ohio State and Michigan. So impressed were Michigan officials by Yost's scoreless tie against the much-bigger Wolverines that they hired him a few years later. A West Virginia native, Yost would leave Ohio Wesleyan for a year each at Nebraska, Kansas and Stanford before joining Michigan in 1901 and coaching a quarter-century there, including the epic game in 1924 against Illinois.[35]

Yost was Pyle's first hero. Years later, he talked reverently of Hurry-Up's skill in motivating his players, and how he willed them to victory when defeat seemed imminent. Along the way, Pyle became a decent athlete himself— at basketball, boxing and bicycle riding — though pleurisy and a genetically weak heart ended any chance he would have to make a college or professional career of it.[36]

C.C. once noted that as a boy it struck him as unfair that a baseball player could be paid for his services, whereas it was a lot harder to make a living as a boxer or a cyclist. Acknowledging her son's gifts of persuasion,

C.C. Pyle's earliest sports triumph was promoting champion driver Barney Oldfield, usually found smoking a cigar. The two men retained a lifelong friendship. From the Bain Collection (Library of Congress, Prints and Photographs Division).

C.C.'s mother wanted him to attend Ohio Wesleyan, a breeding ground for ministers, and become one himself. Enthralled by sports, young Pyle had other ideas, and at 16, he became a promoter. Seeing that a professional bicycle racer named Barney Oldfield was due in Delaware, Pyle set up a race between Oldfield and a local youngster named Holden. On the surface, it seemed to be a certain rout, but seeking to build interest, Pyle made it a winner-take-all event. As expected, Oldfield won the race and pocketed the $25 prize, plus expenses, with the unfortunate Holden shut out for his efforts. Meantime, Pyle had a good payday himself; the event netted him $7 and ignited his passion for the business.

So there was money to be made in the sports business after all. And if it were done the right way, good money. These athletes were personalities, people the public would pay to watch, provided there was someone behind them. Only two years older than Pyle, Oldfield served as C.C. Pyle's test case, his lab rat for the mountaintop that C.C. hoped one day to scale. Oldfield was a good place to start; he was a character himself, a poor kid with an itch for speed and a desire to make bicycling and auto racing his living at a time when "speed sports" were dominated by the rich. Oldfield had left school at 12 or 13 to become a cyclist, leading his Racycle Team in competitions throughout the Midwest. He would find his true calling by racing motorcycles and then automobiles, winning in 1902 his first auto race in Henry Ford's "999," which featured a stripped-down engine and frame with exposed crankshafts.[37]

To win the auto race, Oldfield beat Alexander Winston, the American champion. In doing so, Barney beat a rich man at his own game, a satisfying feat for the speedy young man and a watershed sign in early American car racing that the sport was democratizing. "Up to that point, American auto racing had largely been the cozy preserve of wealthy sportsmen like Winton and William K. Vanderbilt, for whom racing was an avocation," wrote Geoffrey Ward in his biography of heavyweight boxing champion Jack Johnson. Later, Oldfield raced against Johnson, with whom he shared more than a love of sports. The two lived life on the edge, drinking too much, going broke, fighting, and marrying often. Oldfield married four times; Johnson three. "I'd rather be dead than dead broke," Barney said.[38]

Back in Delaware, Ohio, a restless C.C. Pyle contemplated his future. The young grocery clerk could attend Ohio Wesleyan, his mother's fondest wish, but college would have bored him. Fueled by his former job as a train butcher, which took him to towns beyond Delaware, and fortified perhaps by the constant threat of poverty that hung over the family, C.C. longed to make a lot of money and flash it around. And he yearned to see the big cities, ride the fast trains and be a big shot. Then came the opening that would change his life: a diagnosis by his doctor that the weak respiratory condition that he had inherited from his father would be eased somewhat by the fresh air and arid climate of the West.

So, like the young man who Horace Greeley urged to "go west," C.C. did, joining the nineteenth-century exodus of restless entrepreneurs headed to the Pacific Coast, a tradition spearheaded a half-century before by hearty settlers chasing gold in the California mountains. In later years, Pyle would put a different spin on the real reasons for his venturing westward, telling the *New Yorker* that he had developed pleurisy from an injury picked up during a basketball game when he was 16. But that sounds like a bit of Pyle blarney, considering pleurisy is often a hereditary ailment and not something picked up by playing basketball.[39]

Taking a job selling Western Union time-service clocks for a commission of $2 each, Pyle used Western Union passes to travel about on railroads throughout the West. But people weren't buying a lot of clocks, which got

C.C.'s agile mind to thinking. He knew the clocks weren't so popular, but the Western Union passes he used to move about might be if sold for a substantial discount. Bingo! The scheme with the passes worked, and Pyle made a living, in part by using his steadily accumulating knowledge of the West to set up a one-man travel bureau and advise tourists where to go and stay.[40]

But then C.C. blew his earnings on a card game. Stuck deep in the wilds of the Sierra Mountains in Northern California and penniless, Pyle's scheming mind again began working. Wandering into a boxing match, a popular recreation in the mining camps, he spied an aging sore-thumbed 118-pounder in need of an opponent. Aching for a few bucks, C.C. jumped at the chance. What an opportunity! Pyle had boxed a little back in Ohio and outweighed his opponent by a good 40 pounds, so what was there to lose? Plenty, it turns out, because C.C. was no match for the old pug, who as it turns out was a former journeyman professional. To his credit, Pyle hung in there, but without the skills to land many blows on his stooped-over opponent, he took an old-fashioned whipping. It ended as a draw, with C.C. somehow still standing. A crowd of 210 miners paid 50 cents each to watch the mismatch, leaving Pyle with earnings of $52.50, while his opponent picked up a little more than $100. With a few dollars in his pocket, C.C. believed everyone could have enjoyed an even better payday had the fight been properly promoted, like the bicycle race with Barney Oldfield back in Ohio. Finishing school in the wily ways of big-time sports promoting was about to begin in earnest for C.C. Pyle.[41]

It seemed inevitable that C.C. would catch the acting bug. Wandering the highways and byways of the Pacific Northwest, Pyle picked up enough theatrical contacts to organize his own company. To cut expenses, he became his own leading man, and starred in plays like *The Golden Giant Mine* and *The Tennessee Partner*. It's impossible to report whether Pyle had any stage talent, but the reviews were sensational, though C.C. never would say exactly how many reviews he had written on his own behalf. In later years, Pyle recalled with pride that he had been egged in only one town, Brownsville, Oregon.

Pyle wended his way north to the Oregon town of Silverton, just south of Portland, where his rapidly expanding knowledge in the ways of entrepreneurship and talking his way out of scraps took another fortuitous turn. Checking into the hotel in Silverton, he stumbled into a theatrical troupe of a dozen or so, one of whom was a 17-year-old woman named Dorothy Fischer who would soon change his life.

Dorothy, or "Dot," was the daughter of the troupe's manager, John

Fischer, who also owned the hotel. There is no record of when Pyle arrived in Silverton, or when or how he and Dorothy first met. The only thing for certain is that the two soon became a couple, and in September 1905, when Pyle was 23 and Dorothy 21, got married in the coastal Washington town of Aberdeen. By then, Pyle had joined the troupe at a salary of $10 a week, working as an advance man by traveling ahead of the actors and wheeling and dealing with theater and opera house owners. The position required C.C. to become a jack-of-all-trades by posting the handbills, drumming up publicity, and making stagecoach and hotel reservations.[42]

On the surface, Pyle and his new bride had a lot in common. Like C.C., Dot and her younger sister, the 15-year-old Margarita, were entertainers, having been actresses since childhood. By most accounts, Dot was talented, but not on the level as Margarita, who was a revelation. Under the name "Babe Fischer," Margarita had already been playing the troupe's lead role in adult comedies, drama and vaudeville for several years. And she had become so well known in the small northwest towns that John Fischer had renamed the troupe, giving it a moniker designed to draw attention — the Margarita Fischer Company.[43]

Working a day or two ahead of the troupe suited Pyle. His job required mobility, agility, and a knack for doing just about anything that had to be done to achieve maximum attention. At the actual performances, C.C. painted and repaired the stage, shifted scenery, took tickets, and even blew a plugged tuba in the stage band. He was developing an odd assortment of gifts: guts, the soul of a gambler, a love of wanderlust and joy in haggling. Much like "the King and the Duke," Mark Twain's memorable charlatans in *Huckleberry Finn*, Pyle had become part of a slightly shifty but longstanding American backwoods tradition of extracting dollars from people he had just met.

Finding his stride, C.C. became an expert at flattering people to get his way and convincing them that securing the services of the Margarita Fischer Company would guarantee the grandest, most magnificent event to ever hit their small town. A mastery of detail and where precisely to cut corners was critical, as in the time C.C. convinced an Albany, Oregon, hotel manager to provide the entire company with a cut room-rate that included a breakfast consisting of a slab of ham and a single egg each. For the most part, business went well, aided considerably by all those favorable reviews — supplied by one C.C. Pyle.

Back in Ohio, C.C.'s mother fretted, and held out hope that her errant son would see the light to get on with his life's intended work as a minister.

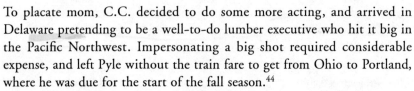

To placate mom, C.C. decided to do some more acting, and arrived in Delaware pretending to be a well-to-do lumber executive who hit it big in the Pacific Northwest. Impersonating a big shot required considerable expense, and left Pyle without the train fare to get from Ohio to Portland, where he was due for the start of the fall season.[44]

C.C. traveled as far as his funds would take him — to Great Falls, Montana, 1,000 miles or so short of Portland. Getting into Great Falls at 4:00 A.M. with 20 cents in his pocket, he turned again to what was becoming his fail-safe: promoting something on the fly. Pyle's predicament and the vast open spaces from Great Falls to western outposts like Seattle, San Francisco, Los Angeles and Denver got him thinking just how many miles it was to get to those places. For that matter, how far was it the other way, from Great Falls to Chicago and New York? And to London, Paris, Tokyo and Shanghai? C.C. figured merchants and townspeople in Great Falls would want to know, and might even be wiling to pay for the information. Working out the distances and striding into a printing office, Pyle designed a poster with "Great Falls" in large type and the distances to the many cities, while adding, for good measure, the Montana game laws. Then, he folded a piece of cardboard into a small four-page leaflet on which he intended to print the information and sell it to merchants.

Bursting from store to store, Pyle pitched merchants to buy ads in his geographical and game-law pamphlet. He guaranteed front-page coverage to at least a dozen merchants, each of whom bought 1,000 copies. But how could a dozen ads fit on the first of a four-page brochure? C.C. determined that depended on how the pages were folded, that is, a four-page brochure could be designed so that every page can conceivably be regarded as page one. So every store owner was happy, noting that their particular establishment had secured a front-page ad. Pyle had come through again, and fortified with $60 in his pocket, caught the train to Portland.[45]

Fate intervened in the spring of 1906 when, with the troupe encamped in Eureka, California, John Fischer died. The event seems to have galvanized Pyle into a realization that it was time for he and Dot to give up the rambling theatrical life and settle down, sort of. In partnership with a Eureka entrepreneur named F.W. Parker, C.C. purchased or rented a theater in the northern California town and grandly renamed it the Theatre Margarita, hoping to trade on his sister-in-law's growing fame. Looking to capitalize on the new sensation of moving pictures, he and Parker decided to permit customers to see the movies first and actually pay later, a kind of forerunner to the concept of a credit card. As Bunion Derby historian Geoff Williams wrote, Pyle's strategy didn't work out, but he was well ahead of his time, decades ahead in fact, as MasterCard and Visa would eventually prove.

The Pyles didn't stay long in Eureka, but their time there taught C.C. the ropes of managing a theater. In 1907, the couple moved south to Oakland, California, where C.C. took a position as business manager for two theaters, one in Oakland and other across the bay in San Francisco. That was only part of a very busy year for the Pyle family. That August, Dot gave birth to a daughter, born Mary Margaret but forever known as Kathy. Around the same time, C.C.'s ability to talk to anyone about anything, including the benefits of California sunshine, convinced the rest of his immediate family to try their luck on the West Coast, as Pyle's mother, Sidney, and his brother, Ira, moved to Santa Rosa, north of San Francisco. Ira was the rock of the Pyle family; a lifelong bachelor, he would house and look after Sidney for the remainder of her life. In Santa Rosa, he managed the town's Western Union office and led an exemplary life as a civic leader and a businessman. Ira became the exalted leader of Santa Rosa's Elks' lodge, and during World War I, chaired the town's Red Cross chapter. As a prominent real estate developer, he specialized in property along the Russian River.

Ira and Sidney moved into a home on Sonoma Avenue in Santa Rosa. Anna would join them in time, with her husband, Verner Ronk, taking a position with Ira as a realtor. Anna would preside over Santa Rosa's Saturday Afternoon Club and the Sonoma County Federation of Women's Clubs.[46]

Meanwhile in Oakland, C.C. was getting edgy, finding that he missed the roaming life, and wanted to flee a marriage that had turned sour. The exact reasons for the Pyles' marital troubles are lost to history, though court records indicate that C.C. was jailed some six months after Katherine's birth for nonsupport. Pyle responded to the allegation by spinning a fantastic tale of woe to the judge, telling him his wife had become an invalid living at a local hospital and was completely unwilling to answer his pleas to move home. In later years, Margarita would agree that Dot had been ill at the time — with what isn't recorded — and say that she had been the one to provide for her sister and niece.

Chances are that C.C. Pyle was destitute. Author Geoff Williams uncovered a revealing morsel from a May 1908 edition of the *Oakland Tribune,* a notice for an auction sale of the contents of the Pyles' home. By listing some of the items for sale — quality furniture made of bird's-eye maple, mahogany and oak, as well as lace curtains and carpets — the ad is a glimpse into what appeared to be, for a while anyway, the family's solid, middle-class life. That it all was for sale suggests a family in financial distress.[47]

Itching to leave, Pyle found a reason: He simply had to travel to take advantage of the booming silent-movie industry, where C.C. was convinced there was big money to be made. Around 1908, he bought a projection machine and some films and hit the road, more at ease in navigating the wide-open spaces of the Northwest than sitting at home. With Dot and Kathy still in Oakland and the rest of his family building industrious, civic-minded lives in Santa Rosa, C.C. returned to life as a nomad on the fringes of the entertainment industry. Finding himself in the Sacramento Valley of California, he bought the assets of a bankrupt stock company that included the scenery and script of a play called *Deadwood Dick* along with $56 worth of handbills for another play, *The James Boys of Missouri*. That both plays were instantly forgettable didn't faze C.C. in the least; he just merged the two productions, billing *The James Boys* but presenting *Deadwood Dick*. Nor did it stump him at all that the final curtain dropped as "Deadwood" killed Jesse James in an ax duel. For the most, the spectators seemed to like it, but in case they didn't, Pyle always presented this unusual historical drama on his last night in a town — and then left immediately.[48]

Without the manpower of a 12-person troupe — Margarita had moved on to a flourishing career in vaudeville — Pyle improvised. He performed *Uncle Tom's Cabin* with a cast of four. He presented *The Three Musketeers* with one musketeer — himself. At times, he had several actors, and they played five and six roles a night. Thinking his name could help sell tickets, he organized the grand-sounding "C.C. Pyle's Greater Lewis & Clark International Exposition," which opened in Moscow, Idaho, with the intention of traveling throughout the Northwest. But expenses were high, and interest was not. In Moscow, C.C. cleared exactly $7, and the international exposition was history. Back on stage, Pyle played General Custer in *Northern Lights*, but couldn't remember his lines. In one scene, when a messenger arrived with tragic news, Custer's line was to put his hand to his head and exclaim, "Good God!" But Pyle, his mind on too many things, sounded, "Good gracious!" The flub drew a big laugh — a sure sign to Pyle that it was time to try something new.

Standing on Main Street in Boise, Idaho, in 1910 and eyeing a big building, C.C. Pyle's mind was suddenly flooded with new promise and possibility. That he had run out of money and had to pawn his camera lens for a few dollars to buy food was no impediment. Taking a two-year lease on an old building at $100 a month — he would pay them later — C.C. had turned to a new, sure-fire way to make a mint. He would open Boise's first movie theater.

Directing a carpenter to build seats, a new front and a ticket booth, he barely paused when the man balked at the price of the lumber.

"Come with me," Pyle told the carpenter. The two men marched to the lumber dealer, where C.C. spoke up again. "Give this man everything he wants," he told the dealer. Who cared that Pyle had barely a dime to his name? C.C. figured he was onto something big, really big this time, and to make money he had to spend it too, even if it wasn't plentiful, at least not yet. Within a few days, Pyle's optimism was reinforced when a local businessman saw the theater and was so impressed at the magnificent renovations that he wanted a part of it. So C.C. sold him a half-interest for $2,500, paid off his debts, and had made a handsome profit in the process. Some weeks later, Boise had its first movie palace.[49]

Pyle invested his entire windfall into an amusement park and vaudeville hall, though things quickly went sour, thanks to a cranky mayor and Sunday blue laws. He lost his shirt and more. In need of a quick $750 just to pay his vaudevillians, Pyle faced a full-scale staff revolt when a stranger who could help suddenly appeared. The visitor was from a small town near Pocatello and needed a troupe of vaudevillians — quickly.

What a remarkable coincidence! But Pyle the strategist played it cool. The group could be had for exactly $750 down and a partnership, he told his visitor. It was a deal, and everybody left for eastern Idaho, where they enjoyed a successful week in the small town near Pocatello. After some harried wheeling and dealing, C.C. emerged without an actor, but somehow with $1,900 in his pocket.[50]

But Pyle was restless, and he couldn't see spending the rest of life in Boise, Idaho. Eyeing a bigger stage where he could be a really big shot, C.C. thought of where he could become a real movie mogul. That stage, he figured, was Chicago, at the time the capital of American silent movies where, four out of five films were shot. In 1910, C.C. left the West Coast, shedding his previous life, all except for one messy piece of remaining business — divorcing Dorothy. Separated for three years, Dorothy, with the toddler Kathy in tow, was living with her widowed mother in Santa Barbara, close enough to the film industry for her to still score occasional roles. In her lawsuit, Dorothy asked Pyle to end the marriage and to pay financial support. But in court, Pyle did some fast talking about his impossible wife who was capable of making a good living for herself and their daughter from the movies. By the time the judge had rendered a decision, Dorothy had her divorce but not a penny in alimony.[51]

Meantime, movie life for Margarita Fischer turned out well. She had met a young vaudeville actor named Harry Pollard, and together they launched their movie careers and hit it big. Working with the Selig Poly-scope Company in Chicago, they churned out a series of one-reel, silent movies, at least 18 in their first nine months, some starring Dorothy and featuring young Kathy. Married in 1911, Margarita and Pollard became a formidable entertainment team, and in 1913, starred in a version of *Uncle Tom's Cabin*. Produced by Independent Motion Pictures, this version included Harry playing Uncle Tom. Fourteen years later, he would direct another version of the film, that one a blockbuster two-hour affair.

In 1914, the Pollards moved to Arizona to be closer to the center of the growing movie industry. Margarita would go on to star in 30 more one-reel films, many directed by Pollard. In the spring of 1914, Fisher — by then the family had dropped the Germanic-sounding "c" from their last name — was voted America's most popular star in a write-in contest by *Photoplay* magazine, ranking her above such stars as Mary Pickford and Mabel Normand.

Fisher's star shone through the end of the decade. Most films of the era were on the lighter side, but Fisher shed her "Babe" roles of the past and developed a reputation as a serious actress. In 1916, she starred in *The Miracle of Life*, a film of protest against abortion. In 1917, she starred in *The Devil's Assistant*, which tackled morphine addiction. But she and Pollard faced problems of their own; they separated in 1919, about the time that Pollard lost his contract with American Studios. The couple eventually reunited and stayed together until Pollard's death in 1934.[52]

In Chicago, Pyle quickly established himself. He landed a position with the Essanay Manufacturing Company, a flourishing film studio founded in 1907 by George Spoor and "Bronco" Billy Anderson, which accounted for the studio name, a literal splicing together of "S" and "A." Essanay's first film, *An Awful Skate* starring Ben Turpin, was produced for a token amount and grossed thousands, cementing its reputation as a moneymaker. Shooting in Chicago and later in Niles, California, because of the better weather and wide-open spaces for westerns, the studio became a breeding ground of the silent film era's greatest stars. Wallace Beery, Tom Mix, Gloria Swanson and even Charlie Chaplin made films with the Essanay. The first American Jesse James movie, *The James Boys of Missouri*, in 1908, was an Essanay production, as was the first American *Sherlock Holmes*, in 1916. That same year, Chaplin departed the company, prompting a feud between Spoor and Bronco Billy, which hastened the dissolution of the company. But both Spoor and Anderson were lauded for their pioneering film work; years later, each man was recognized with an honorary Academy Award.[53]

At the studio, the freshly divorced Pyle wasted little time in setting his considerable charms on a new woman, who, like Dot, was an actress. Her name was Martha Lindsay Russell, a dark-haired vaudeville veteran who in 1911 and 1912 had cast her lot with Essanay and become a star. Earning more than $1,000 a week, Russell cranked out a slew of long-forgotten films, like *Her Hour of Triumph, The End of the Feud* and *Neptune's Daughter*. In April 1911, a year or so after his divorce, Russell became the second Mrs. Pyle, marrying C.C. in Indiana's Lake County.

As with his first marriage, Pyle's union with Russell appeared on the surface to be a real match. Assuming duties as her business manager and film producer, C.C. brimmed with ideas. He sent Martha on the lecture circuit to talk about life in the movies and build her popularity. In 1912, the Pyles traveled to Austin, Texas, where C.C. signed a pact with the Satex Film Company, the creation of two brothers named Paul and Hope Tilley, and the first outfit in the U.S. to make three-reel movies. Banking that people would pay to see their hometowns on the big screen, the Pyles and the Tilley brothers shot footage of towns and cities throughout Texas and Missouri and made a mint.

But never content with a healthy profit, C.C. set about to make it *really* big and convinced some investors to invest $25,000 with Satex. That allowed he and the Tilleys to make six films — they even crossed into Mexico to film guerilla leader Pancho Villa — but Pyle spent up a storm, mostly on a lavish lifestyle. Unable to account for nearly half of the original investment, the stockholders seethed and took legal action. By July 1913, Satex — and Pyle's latest job — were done.[54]

Spending lots of money and then some that he didn't have had become a confounding pattern for C.C. Pyle. Equally as mysterious were C.C.'s marriage traumas. About the time that Pyle was getting into his latest financial fiasco, his marriage to Martha was disintegrating. There is no record of why — "maybe it was the stress of the business falling apart," theorizes Geoff Williams. Whatever the reason, on December 5, 1914, the Pyles ended their marriage.[55]

By 1914, C.C. Pyle had lost two wives, a daughter, and wads of money that belonged to others. He had big ideas, but clearly was no businessman. He also had oceans of chutzpah and a knack for quickly getting back on his feet without looking back. How fitting that precisely 18 days after his second divorce, the 32-year-old Pyle married again, this time to Euphemia "Effie" B. Arnold, a 27-year-old divorcee from St. Louis, with two small children, Donald and Florence.[56]

Much as the death of John Fischer had done years before, C.C.'s current troubles appeared to signal a new part of his life, his latest "fresh" start. Back in Chicago, Pyle settled into a period of relative stability, for him anyhow. For much of the next decade, he wandered from job to job, working as a clerk and then selling insurance, but doing so as more of a homebody. Around 1918, Pyle took a job where he was most comfortable — back on the edge of entertainment, this time as a salesman with the Barton Musical Instrument Company, which made elaborate pipe organs for movie theaters. Founded in Oshkosh, Wisconsin, the Barton Company produced organs that were mounted in a theater's orchestra pit and operated by a pit drummer who played from a keyboard on a stand that swung above the keys of a piano. As theaters grew bigger, so did the organs, which became more elaborate, and in some cases came adorned with several cases — one for orchestral pipe ranks and the other for percussions and various sound effects. The biggest Barton organ of all was installed in Chicago Stadium, which had six manuals and more than 800 stop tabs. Tunes from the big organ would become a memorable sideshow of attending Black Hawks hockey games at the old ramshackle arena. Sadly, fire destroyed the organ in 1996.

The Barton Company built about 250 theater organs until its demise in the early days of the Great Depression. But Pyle didn't last anywhere near that long at the company, leaving after a year or two in the murkiness of more financial shenanigans. With demand booming, Barton began using contractors to build some of its organs. Whether Pyle was a part of the deception isn't known, but when the practice was revealed, he moved on. Though even less of Pyle's next position, as vice president of the Disco Security Company, is known, C.C. would eventually landed on his feet — again — this time in 1920, thanks to a new partnership that would lead him in just five years to a fateful meeting with Red Grange.[57]

"Publicity means only one thing — controversy," C.C. Pyle once preached. Nowadays, it's hard to fathom the howls of protest that accompanied the decision by Red Grange to leave college and turn professional. In criticizing his decision, college officials polished out all the tired clichés that Grange was soiling the purity and the sanctity of the college game.

Leading the bandwagon of defenders was the great University of Chicago coach Amos Alonzo Stagg, a former divinity student who in the 1880s had turned down offers to play pro football, claiming "the whole tone of the game was smelly." Apparently, he still thought so, and he slammed professional football as "cases of the debauching of high school boys" by promoters. "To cooperate with Sunday professional football games," Stagg warned, "is to cooperate with forces which are destructive to the finest elements of interscholastic and intercollegiate football and add to the heavy burden of the schools and colleges in preserving it in its ennobling worth." Stagg thought that anyone earning a college degree and a football letter should have what he called the "equipment of character" to get a "man's-sized job" instead of playing pro ball.[58]

The sanctimonious outcry obscured the real concern that professional football posed a threat to what by the mid–1920s had become big business. What if the loss of Red Grange started a trend of other big collegians lighting out for the pros? Left unstated but tolerated was the college ranks' common practice of using "ringers"—players enrolled at school to play football and attend class in principle only. A notable example was Notre Dame's George Gipp, a young man who Knute Rockne strung along for a time and then expelled, only to reinstate at the insistence of South Bend businessmen, who argued that a good football team attracted big crowds and was dynamite for business. Gipp spent more time carousing and gambling than going to class, but at least Rockne knew where to find him, which was usually at a South Bend pool hall. The great 1932 Marx Brothers film *Horsefeathers* satirizes the whole charade of using ringers. "Are you suggesting that I, the president of Huxley College, go into a speakeasy (to look for football players)," Groucho Marx asks Zeppo, who plays his son, "without even giving me the address?"[59]

A 1905 investigative series by *McClure's* magazine revealed a college game riddled with professionals and outright corruption. Such shenanigans were particularly rampant in of all places the upper-crusty Ivy League, where a Princeton player made a good living off his baseball earnings, and another, Andrew Smith, somehow managed to play for the University of Pennsylvania and Penn State in the same season. Apparently, the Yale All-American, J.J. Hogan, had been at it for quite some time — he was 25, a little aged to be a collegian, and was making a handsome living from football and from his investments in the American Tobacco Company, according to the magazine report. Elsewhere, a number of Harvard players played semi-pro baseball under assumed names.[60]

Magnifying the controversy in the first years of the twentieth century was an outcry against college football's violence. Football players of the era seldom wore helmets or much padding, leading to devastating injuries and occasional fatalities. In 1905, 23 deaths were attributed to playing college football, and newspapers commonly pictured football men with blood streaming down their faces.

Football violence became a national issue after President Theodore Roosevelt called for reform. An ardent football fan and a champion of the active life, Roosevelt feared that football, like prizefighting, was simply too brutal to continue without substantial changes in the rules. The president had a particular interest in seeing the game cleaned up: His son, Theodore Roosevelt, Jr. had broken his nose playing for the Harvard freshman team against Yale, though word was the Yale men had intentionally tried to hurt him.

In early 1906, college officials adopted a number of rules designed to curb the rash of injuries. The newly created Intercollegiate Football Rules Committee prohibited backs from hurdling the line and disallowed tackling beneath the knees. It specified lines to have at least six men and created a neutral zone at the line of scrimmage. They also enacted a number of rules to modernize and open up the game, among them requiring that teams advance 10 yards in three plays for a first down.

Most eastern universities adopted the new rules, and the number of fatalities fell. But three years later, the number again soared, and in the ensuing publicity, the *Washington Post* wondered "(if) any more proof (is needed) that football is a brutal, savage, murderous sport?" Not the superintendents and presidents of West Point, Loyola University, Georgetown and the University of Virginia, who in mid–November 1909 abruptly cancelled the remainder of their games. Adding their concern were Stanford's David Starr Jordan, who called the game "rugby's American's pervert," and Princeton's Woodrow Wilson, who argued that the deaths had "swallowed up the circus" of the game.[61]

A new set of rules in 1910 restored some order to the crisis in college football. These latest rules stacked seven men on the offensive line, outlawed interlocking pushing and pulling, and set four 15-minute quarters. The number of fatalities dropped somewhat, and so did the controversy. By 1912, it was mostly forgotten, thanks in part to a rule that liberalized the forward pass, which opened the field up and added excitement, and the emergence of a formidable new talent, the great Jim Thorpe.

At 6'1" and weighing 185 pounds, the 25-year-old Thorpe wasn't a particularly overpowering physical presence. He was merely magnificent at every sport he tried, from football to track, baseball and even tennis, golf and bowling. Born on a farm in what was then known as Oklahoma Territory, he was a mixture of French, Irish, Sac and Fox Indian, and went by the Native-American name "Wa-Tho-Huck," or "Bright Path." Thorpe's early years were difficult. At 10, he lost his twin brother, Charles, due to pneumonia, then his mother two years later and his bootlegger father just three years after that. Sent away to government-run Indian vocational schools in Haskell, Kansas, and then Carlisle, Pennsylvania, Thorpe rose to prominence in 1907 as the centerpiece of the tiny Carlisle Indian School's powerful college football team. That spring, he was walking by the track where college high jumpers were trying — and failing — to clear 5 feet 9 inches. As the story goes, Thorpe was dressed in school clothes, gave the high jump a shot on impulse, and easily topped the bar on his first attempt. In doing so, he set the school record.[62]

After a two-year layoff, Thorpe returned to Carlisle in the fall of 1911 and helped the football team become a national power. The school upset Harvard, 18–15, with Thorpe accounting for all of his team's points on four field goals and a touchdown. Coached by Pop Warner, who invented the single wing, the Indian School beat Army, Penn, Pittsburgh and Syracuse. Against Army, Thorpe ran 92 yards on a touchdown that was called back on a penalty. Handed the ball on the next play, he ran 97 yards for a touchdown that wasn't called back.

"Except for (Thorpe), Carlisle would have been an easy team to beat," recalled Army halfback Dwight Eisenhower. "On the football field, there was no one like him in the world." Trying to stop him, the *New York Times* wrote, "was like trying to clutch a shadow." Carlisle went 23–2–1 in 1911 and 1912. Thorpe was an All-American both years, and during the course of his Carlisle career, earned 11 letters in 11 different sports. He even won an intercollegiate crown in ballroom dancing.

But Thorpe saved his greatest performance of all for the 1912 Olympic Games in Stockholm, where he won both the decathlon and pentathlon, the only Olympian to ever do so. Thorpe's victory in the 10-event decathlon was extraordinary enough — he had never competed in a decathlon nor hurled a javelin until two months before the games. But his convincing win in the five-event pentathlon was stunning, considering it required skills like shooting, which he had only recently tried. In fact, Thorpe amassed so many points in the pentathlon that his performance would have earned him the silver medal at the *1948* Olympics. At the award ceremony for his second gold medal, King Gustav V told him that "Sir, you are the greatest athlete in the world."

"Thanks, King," said a grinning Thorpe. He would describe the compliment as the proudest moment of his life.[63]

Returning to the U.S., Thorpe was lauded with a ticker-tape parade down Broadway in New York. "I heard people yelling my name," he said, "and I couldn't realize how one fellow could have so many friends." But in

"Sir, you are the greatest athlete in the world," King Gustav V of Sweden told Jim Thorpe (pictured left) on the victory stand at the 1912 Olympic Games. Here, Thorpe trails top middle-distance runner Thomas McLaughlin of Boston. The race, date and place are unknown. From the Bain Collection (Library of Congress, Prints and Photographs Division).

early 1913 came the shocker that would plague Thorpe for the rest of his days: news that in the summer of 1909 he had received $25 a week to play minor league baseball for Rocky Mount of the Eastern Carolina League. Unlike other college athletes who played for money and used aliases, Thorpe hadn't thought to use anything but his real name in Rocky Mount, attracting the wrath of the International Olympic Committee that prohibited professionals from competing in the Olympics.

On January 27, 1913, the Amateur Athletic Association stripped Thorpe of both his Olympic gold medals as well as other awards he'd received from track. Thorpe begged the AAU for understanding, admitting his guilt but saying he should be "partly excused by the fact that I was simply an Indian boy (who) did not know about such things." The only bright spot of the whole episode came when both Hugo Wieslander, second in the decathlon, and Ferdinand Bie, second in the pentathlon, refused to accept the gold medals that the International Olympic Committee sent to them. Thorpe never criticized the decision publicly, but the pain was deep and lasting, and he campaigned in vain until his death in 1953 for the decision to be overturned. Only in 1982, nearly 30 years after Thorpe died, did the International Olympic Committee overturn the ban and restore Thorpe's victory while returning the medals to his family.[64]

So Thorpe turned to baseball, the era's most established major league sport, though it was far from what he did best. Signing a contract in 1913 with the New York Giants, he was a big name but just another journeyman on the field — fast, of course, and blessed with a strong arm but never able to effectively hit a curveball. Thorpe stuck around for six years as a big leaguer, playing with the Giants,

It is almost an understatement to call Jim Thorpe the greatest athlete of his time. The college football All-American, NFL pioneer and C.C. Pyle's friend excelled at any sport he tried, even ballroom dancing. He is pictured here at the Polo Grounds as a baseball player with the New York Giants in 1913, a year after winning — and losing — two Olympic gold medals. From the Bain Collection (Library of Congress, Prints and Photographs Division).

Cincinnati Reds and Boston Braves, batting a respectable .252 and participating in the famous Round-the-World tour of 1914. But Thorpe was too good an athlete to keep from playing other sports, and long past his prime, he still barnstormed in one thing or another, from football to track and basketball. Uncovered in early 2005 was an old ticket stub for a 1927 exhibition basketball tour through Pennsylvania featuring Thorpe, then 39, and "His World Famous Indians."[65]

Thorpe's first love was always football, which by 1914 on the college level was becoming the biggest and most lucrative happening on American campuses. Both Yale and Princeton opened huge, cavernous stadiums that year, filling them most Saturdays. Meantime, the popularity of football was spreading, to California, where the Rose Bowl had become a big event, and to the South, where teams from the universities of Alabama and Georgia had quickly emerged as powers.

At least Thorpe could always pick up a few extra dollars playing pro football, which was still struggling to shake its rag-tag, sandlot feel. Though pro football had been around since its first game was played in 1892 in Latrobe, Pennsylvania, near Pittsburgh, its history was unsteady, with collegians under assumed names occupying many early pro rosters. By the start of the World War I, the pro game had expanded westward to Ohio, with many major towns fielding semi-pro teams comprised of men who earned perhaps $10 a game on Sundays, supplemented with regular railroad or mill jobs during the week. If the quality of play was spotty, teams compensated with some nifty nicknames. Teams included the Columbus Panhandles, named for a division of the Pennsylvania Railroad, as well as the Toledo Maroons, Cleveland Erin Brauts and the late, not-so-great Youngstown Patricians.

Thorpe hooked on with the Bulldogs — the Canton Bulldogs — and quickly made them tops of the Ohio League, thanks in part to two of his former Carlisle Indian School teammates, fullback Pete Calac and halfback Joe Guyon, who joined him. Playing for the Akron Pros was former Brown University All-American running back Fritz Pollard, pro football's first prominent African-American player and a future member of the Pro Football Hall of Fame.[66]

By 1920, semi-pro football was expanding both north and west, into New England, and Illinois and Indiana, too. The great names endured, like New England's best team, the Providence Steam Roller, based on a comment that they would "steam-roll" their opponent. In New York, the Staten Island Stapletons became an accomplished semi-pro team, as did the Hammond All-Stars in Indiana, where two of the team's standouts, George Halas and Paddy Driscoll, bided their time before taking prominent roles in the early days of the NFL. Big gates, however, were still a long time in coming.[67]

By 1920, things were also looking up for C.C. Pyle. With a Champaign, Illinois builder named Almon W. Stoolman, he decided to build a lavish movie theater in the central Illinois college town where the University of Illinois, its ranks swelled by returning veterans, now had 9,000 students. On the surface, it seems incomprehensible that the rackety Pyle would go into business with Stoolman, who was a builder of considerable repute and exuded genteel respectability. Stoolman had built the railroad station in nearby Matoon and several fraternity houses on the university campus, including the Beta Theta Pi, Kappa Sigma and Sigma Alpha Epsilon houses. The station and three fraternity houses are all on the National Register of Historic Places.[68]

As with most things involving C.C., the theater shot up with few expenses spared. Named the Virginia Theatre, after Stoolman's daughter, and designed by noted theater architect C. Howard Crane, the movie palace was built in the Italian Renaissance style on its outside, to resemble a Florentine palazzo, and in the Spanish Renaissance style on the inside, to look like a courtyard of Old Castile. The Virginia featured arms of Spanish royalty, Baroque plasterwork, busts of Ferdinand and Isabella, a ceiling dome covered in silver leaf, and a big Hope-Grand orchestral organ.

Opening December 28, 1921, in grand style, the Virginia Theatre featured a live stage show of the hit mystery *The Bat* by Mary Rinehart and Avery Hopwood. The next night, the Virginia showed its first silent films — including *The Boat* starring Buster Keaton — as the big organ boomed and the theater's live symphonic orchestra played at intermission. Both films and live theater became staples at the Virginia; Keaton would perform there, as would Charlie Chaplin, W.C. Fields and the Marx Brothers.[69]

Pyle was flourishing. Managing the Virginia and the Park in Champaign, he expanded his enterprise in the next few years to six midwestern theaters, including a couple of others in Chicago and Kokomo, Indiana. It was a living — no one ever accused Pyle of dogging it — but C.C. would have traded it all in for a shot at the big time. Every so often, C.C. gave it a shot, as back in 1912, he offered new Olympic hero Jim Thorpe $10,000 to go on a baseball exhibition tour. Thorpe was tempted to accept, but on the advice of Pop Warner, his football coach at the Carlisle Indian School, turned Pyle and all the other promoters down. Warner said they were "exploiting Jim's new-found national popularity," which was true. But so was Warner, who was hoping Thorpe would return to Carlisle in 1913 to play football for another season of huge gate receipts. Besides, Warner argued, why rush? With another year of gridiron victories and triumphs under his belt, Thorpe would be able to command an even bigger paycheck the following year. But once Thorpe lost his medals, the offer was forgotten.[70]

As a result, C.C. Pyle would have to wait for his shot at the big time. Not until the evening in October 1925, when Red Grange walked into the Virginia Theatre to see *The Freshman,* would Pyle finally launch his meteoric ascent in sports promotion. A month or so after that, he would be among the best known, most flamboyant showmen in America.

3

"One of the Finest Men
I Have Ever Known"

Talk of a truly "national" football league had been bantered about for quite some time during the months that C.C. Pyle went into the movie business in Champaign, Illinois. On August 20, 1920, Ralph Hay, a cigar-chomping 30-year-old car salesman and owner of the Canton Bulldogs, hosted representatives of teams from Cleveland, Akron and Dayton for a meeting at his dealership in Canton. Hay had ambitious goals. He wanted to start a regional football league with teams from Ohio and Indiana, as well as from Buffalo and Rochester, New York.

It was a start. A month or so later, a larger group of 14 team owners gathered at Hay's dealership. This time they met in the showroom (the group was too big for an office) where they drained beer from buckets and finalized the outline of this new more "national" football league. Newcomers included Rock Island, Illinois; Chicago; Muncie and Hammond, Indiana; and the Decatur, Illinois Staleys, represented by George Halas. Teams from Buffalo and Rochester would join later. Calling their new conglomeration the American Professional Football Association, the owners shrewdly elected Jim Thorpe as league president, not for any particular managerial skills, but because of his celebrity. Indeed, most newspaper reports headlined news about Thorpe while paying scant attention to the formation of the league.

Owners appointed a three-man committee to create a league constitution. They met with a representative from the tire division of the Brunswick-Balke Calendar Company about a silver loving cup to be presented to the championship team. In doing so, they created a structure, and eventually at Halas' urging, a more memorable name: the National Football League. There was a $100 membership fee, although according to *Pigskin*, Robert Peterson's authoritative book on the origins of the NFL, not a single original owner ever paid that much. Said Halas, "I doubt there was a hundred bucks in the room."[1]

Those founders may have had little capital, but they had vision, drive and a bona fide entrepreneurial streak. Boldest of all may have been Halas, all of 25 years old and a 1918 civil engineering graduate from the University of Illinois. Six feet tall, Halas was fast and used his speed to become a multi-sport star with the Illini, where he caught passes for Bob Zuppke's football team, captained the basketball team, and played outfield on the baseball team. Commissioned in early 1918 as an ensign in the U.S. Navy, Halas was assigned to the Great Lakes Naval Training Station, where he joined the football team that defeated the Mare Island Marines in the 1919 Rose Bowl in which he was the most valuable player. That spring, Halas gave pro baseball a try by joining the Yankees, though he quickly found he couldn't hit big league pitching. Farmed to St. Paul of the American Association, Halas opted to leave baseball; his big league career had lasted all of 12 games, during which he hit .091. Back in Illinois, Halas went to work in the bridge design department of a railroad company and play end on weekends for Hammond.[2]

In March 1920, the Staley Starch Company of Decatur hired Halas to organize and coach a company football team, and play for its baseball team, coached by former big league Giants legend "Iron Man" Joe McGinnity, a future Hall of Famer. But Halas had loftier goals than spending the rest of his days in central Illinois, and lobbied to move the team from Decatur some 180 miles northeast to the big time: Chicago, his birthplace. Halas and company owner Augustus Eugene (A.E.) Staley, who considered his "Staleys" good advertising, clashed, went to court, and eventually compromised. The Staleys could go to Chicago provided it keep the team name. So in 1921, the Chicago Staleys, with $5,000 of Staley's seed money, won the first of Halas' six NFL titles, and even turned a handsome profit. In his autobiography, Halas insisted the team scraped by and earned all of $7.70 that year, but that wasn't quite right. According to football historians Dan Daly and Bob O'Donnell, Halas and his partner, Dutch Sternaman, cleared nearly $22,000, with $7.70 the amount left over in interest after the two owners had divided their profits.[3]

Football of the early 1920s, both the pro and college versions, didn't look much like today's game. Compared to the wide-open game of today, offenses were conservative, running the ball on most plays and rarely passing. When stuck deep in their own territory, teams often punted on first down, hoping to send the ball down the field by surprise and catch their opponent in a mistake. Passing was problematic in part because the ball was bigger and rounder, thereby harder for a quarterback to grip. Receivers as well were at a considerable disadvantage since linemen were prohibited from heading downfield to block for them.

There were other differences. Coaching from the sidelines was illegal. Substitutes were not allowed to bring in a play or even speak up on entering the game, which put more importance on audibles. For the most part, the quarterback or team captain called plays on the line of scrimmage, though that would soon change, thanks to Bob Zuppke's recent innovation, the huddle. In 1921, the Illinois coach was the first to incorporate huddles regularly into college games.[4]

Most teams of the early NFL fielded 16-man rosters, with men going "both ways," playing both offense and defense. For the most part, the starters, particularly the linemen, played at least three quarters and often all four since teams were permitted to carry only five substitutes. There were few specialists; generally, the quarterback or a back also kicked and punted. Other than top draws like Thorpe or Paddy Driscoll, the quarterback of the Chicago-Racine Cardinals, who reportedly earned $300 a game, most early NFL starters made about $150 a game.

Players of the era were on average considerably smaller than those of today. According to Peterson, the average size of a lineman on Halas' Staleys in 1921 was 206 pounds, and in the backfield, 174. The game's reigning big man, the 6'2", 234-pound tackle Ralph Scott, was soon to become Pyle's friend and coach. Owing to the college reforms of the previous few decades, most of the equipment — crude by today's standards — were effective in preventing serious injuries. Generally, teams provided the leather helmets, socks and jerseys; players bought their own shoes, shoulder pads and knee pads.

The NFL limped through its first few seasons. With an 8–0–3 record, the Akron Pros were champions of the inaugural season, outscoring opponents 151–7. On the other extreme were the unfortunate Muncie Flyers, which lost its first game, 45–0, and disappeared. Newspaper accounts seldom included accurate attendance figures, which were provided by the home team and usually inflated. Given the difficulties of compiling accurate figures, football historians have rounded off the average attendance in 1920 to 4,241, with the largest crowd, 17,000, gathering in Philadelphia to see Thorpe's Canton Bulldogs.[5]

Joe Carr succeeded Thorpe as president in 1921; the famous football star had little interest in administration. Carr was a good choice and issued a host of organizational improvements that gave the NFL more stability. He established territorial rules that prohibited teams from scheduling games in another team's region. He issued standings and worked deftly behind the scenes to attract former college stars and bulk up the more valuable big-city franchises. Paul Robeson, the great African-American All-American from Rutgers, joined Fritz Pollard in 1921 as a member of the Akron Pros, guaranteeing a new gate attraction and positioning the NFL miles ahead of other pro sports leagues as a racial pioneer. Carr also oversaw what proved to be a lucrative move — the Staleys' relocation to Chicago, where crowds of up to 10,000 typically descended on Cubs Park to see the team, soon rechristened the Bears.[6]

Those Bears, along with their cross-town rivals, the Cardinals, and the Green Bay Packers gave the NFL its only stability in those early years. Other teams, like the unfortunate Muncie Flyers, the Minneapolis Marines and Louisville Brecks, vanished almost as quickly as they appeared. Indeed, NFL life could get wacky and even downright vaudevillian in the case of the late, not-so-great 1922 Oorang Indians of La Rue, Ohio, a hamlet of 900 near Marion. Team owner Walter Lingo had the best of intentions. An admirer of Native Americans, he brought in Thorpe, now 35, as player-coach, as well as Guyon and Calac. But Lingo was interested primarily in staging lavish halftime shows to earn publicity for his trained Airedales and a mail-order puppy business. His first show featured a live bear trailed by the Airedales, and Oorang player Nikolas Lassa wrestling the bear. But Lingo figured the Airedales weren't enough, and in game two, created a exhibition of a World War I battle that featured Red Cross dogs and U.S. Indian scouts.

The Airedales would get the rest of the season off. The Indians spent the rest of the 1922 season on the road and disbanded. Marginalized as an NFL footnote, the Oorang Indians and their eclectic halftime shows underscored a larger reality. Next to baseball and the crowds that typically filled the 65,000-seat stadium of big-time college teams, "people who patronized professional football," wrote John Underwood of *Sports Illustrated*, "were thought to be of a caliber you now associate with Roller Derby." By 1925, pro football was still a minor league sport and in need of something big — like the coming of Red Grange.[7]

As college presidents spoke out against Red Grange's decision to turn pro, sportswriters pursued another question. It wasn't the sanctity of the college game, but something far more practical that concerned them. What possible use, the writers wondered, would the world's first sports agent even serve?

"About the only thing in the sports line that leaves me consumed with curiosity is why Red Grange needs a manager," wrote *Daily News* columnist Paul Gallico after the Illinois running back's professional debut at the Polo Grounds. "What does this manager do that entitles him to what — if I have read the papers correctly these last few days — is a 50 percent cut. But more fascinating still is the problem of what it is he does that a supposedly wide-awake young man with some years of college education is unable to do for himself?"

Gallico's comments are outdated in this age of millionaire player-agents. Grange could never negotiated such a wealthy contract. And hadn't boxers used managers for years? Gallico conceded that most fighters were virtually uneducated and needed help. But however flawed their arguments, sports-writers continued to admire the shy football star from the heartland while reserving their venom for the man who had rocked the sports world: C.C. Pyle.[8]

But Grange never wavered in his admiration of his manager. From the get-go, Red looked up to Pyle. He respected C.C.'s drive, dress and big shot demeanor, and remained a fierce defender and devoted friend until the end. Grange admired Pyle's $200 tailor-made suits and his sense of style — the way he commanded respect in his ever-present derby and gray spats with fashionable pearl buttons, the way he usually carried a cane and attracted the attention of women. Red even admired Pyle for his attentiveness to grooming; he received daily rubdowns and a lot of haircuts and mustache trims. It was as if C.C. Pyle was everything that Grange wasn't.[9]

Most of all, Grange admired Pyle's unwavering self-confidence. If people sneered about C.C. behind his back or in print, they listened when he opened his mouth, which was often. Pyle played the role of the worldly sophisticate, a man who may have grown up in a small town, but seemed right at home in the big hotels and big cities. "My dear boy," he would call Westbrook Pegler, sounding positively Gatsby-esque before offering him and all the other reporters a nip from his ever-present stash of Prohibition-era alcohol.[10]

"He was a fellow you would like," Grange said of Pyle. "The greatest mixer, a great storyteller. He loved to sit around and have a drink with any-one. A lovable guy. I never met any one who did not like Charley Pyle... They don't make 'em that way anymore."[11]

Pyle had arranged a grueling, two-part barnstorming tour for Grange and the Bears. It would begin Thanksgiving Day in Chicago, and then head east for 10 games in only 18 days — virtually a whole season crammed into less than three weeks. After an 11-day holiday break, the team would head

"He was a fellow you would like," Red Grange (left) said of his friend and manager, C.C. Pyle (right). "The greatest mixer, a great storyteller. He loved to sit around and have a drink with anyone" (Red Grange Collection [SC-20], Special Collections, Buswell Memorial Library, Wheaton College).

south to Florida and west through Louisiana to California and Oregon for another nine games in 38 days. The schedule included five games against NFL teams along with a host of games against makeshift teams of semi-pros, local stars and collegians in St. Louis, Washington, D.C., and Pittsburgh. That Pyle had scheduled so many games showed that he "clearly knew very little about pro football," wrote Grange biographer John Carroll, adding that Bear owners Halas and Sternaman "should have known better."[12]

On Thanksgiving Day 1925 at Cubs Park, Grange opposed the Cardinals and became a professional. Sentiment favored the Bears and their new star running back, but the Cardinals were one of the premier teams of the early NFL. Behind former Marquette star Red Dunn at running back, the Cardinals had dropped their first game and then reeled off nine straight wins, all at their home ground, Comiskey Park, including a 9–0 drubbing of the Bears, which drew only 13,000. With everyone anxious to see Grange, there

was considerably more interest in this game, with all 40,000 or so tickets —
increased by a quarter to $1.75 — long gone. The tickets had been snapped
up the previous Monday in three hours, leaving another 20,000 fans without tickets to roam about the park and battle police in an effort to get inside
the gates.

By game time, the atmosphere was electric. Outside the ballpark, cars
were parked bumper-to-bumper for 10 blocks, with neighborhood kids earning a small fortune in makeshift parking fees. Closer to the stadium gates,
scalpers did a brisk business in selling counterfeit tickets, most of which were
crudely printed and the wrong color. In the locker room, Grange sorted
through a few of the hundreds of supportive telegrams, including one from
a group of Milwaukee icemen who were "glad to see one of our boys get in
on the big money." Tethered to a peg and restless in front of the Bears dugout
was the team's mascot, a young bear cub.[13]

The crowd cared not at all that Grange had practiced with the Bears
for only three days and barely knew the signals. Red was their hometown
hero. They cheered his every move and booed when Paddy Driscoll of the
Cardinals purposely angled punts away from him. "It was a question of which
of us would look bad — Grange or Driscoll," Paddy said later. "I decided it
wouldn't be Paddy." The game ended in a scoreless tie — frigid weather and
swirling winds didn't help matters — but Grange ended the day gaining 92
yards and everyone seemed satisfied. When the game ended, thousands
streamed onto the sloppy field to try to reach Grange, who needed a police
escort to reach the locker room.

"The Cards weren't out to help Red celebrate an iceman's holiday,"
wrote Dan Maxwell in the *Chicago Tribune*. "They were out to show him up.
They couldn't do that. But they did prove that a pro game can be a game worth
watching.... It was Grange — Grange — Grange. The day of heroes isn't over."[14]

If the fans were satisfied, George Halas was ecstatic. The hard-nosed
Bears co-owner was said to have cried tears of joy while counting the gate
receipts — far above what the team usually earned in drawing an average of
5,000 a game. To him, the packed stands was a promising sign that pro football had a future and a fighting chance to achieve lasting popularity. "There
had never been such evidence of public interest since our professional league
began in 1920," Halas said. "I knew then and there that pro football was
destined to be a big-time sport." So did Paddy Driscoll's wife, Mary. "Isn't
it terrible the way people booed Red?" her husband asked her after the game.
"Paddy, they were not booing Red," Mary said. "They were booing you for
(punting away and) not giving him a chance."[15]

The Bears sold out their second game three days later, on Sunday, November 29, although a blizzard held the actual crowd to 28,000. Against the winless Columbus Tigers, which played their entire schedule that year on the road, the Bears escaped with a 14–13 win. On the surface, Grange played an average game for him, accumulating 79 yards from scrimmage on an icy field and accounting for nearly 140 yards in offense. He was starting to feel comfortable, however, as the Bears headed east into the meat of their schedule.[16]

Three nights later in St. Louis against a team of local all-stars sponsored by a mortician, Grange began displaying his considerable gifts. Only 8,000 had shown up in bitterly cold 12-degree weather and saw him score four touchdowns, run for 84 yards and lead the Bears to a lopsided 39–6 win. But there was no rest for the weary, with upcoming games Saturday in Philadelphia against the Frankford Yellow Jackets and Sunday at the Polo Grounds against the Giants.[17]

Pyle's contract required Grange to play at least 30 minutes of each game. The grind was oppressive. Other than a day off in New York after the Sunday game against the Giants, the Bears had few respites, either playing a game or traveling, and wearing the same mud-splattered uniforms day after day. The pace and the damp, dirty uniforms got to all the players, including Halas, who played end. But the conditions didn't faze Pyle. "This tour will make you so wealthy," he told Halas, "that next year you'll be able to afford two sets of uniforms."[18]

The pace was about to catch up to Grange. Playing Tuesday in a Washington snowstorm, he gained only 11 yards on eight carries against a team of sandlot all-stars. Traveling to New England for Wednesday's game, Grange's arm swelled up to go with his two black eyes and a bruised nose. "I'm played out, pilled," he told a reporter. "It's not all as easy as I thought. I went into this thing for all I could get. I'm getting it — in the neck."[19]

Adding to Grange's trouble was the fact that opposing teams were ganging up on the Bears' new star, piling on and tackling him late and often with malice. In time, NFL players would develop an unwritten code of ethics — an unofficial understanding of "hard, clean play," as Grange put it. But that wasn't the case among Washington's semi-pro players, one of whom named Lynch was fingered by Grange: he would "claw me, twist my ankles and try to unscrew my head with an insatiable curiosity to learn how this newspaper hero was put together."[20]

Frigid conditions created hard slogging for everyone. At Braves Field in Boston, where the league game against the Providence Steam Roller had been moved to accommodate a bigger crowd, the game-time temperature was 6 degrees below zero and the field was frozen. To build interest, the Steam Roller had hired a group of former All-Americans, including Jim Crowley and Don Miller, two of the Four Horsemen of Notre Dame, along with hometown favorite Fritz Pollard, the former running back from Brown. Grange did his best, but he was playing hurt and was ineffective. So were the Bears in a 9–6 loss. That the home team upset the mighty Bears didn't please the home folks, who, according to the *Providence Journal*, "booed and hissed and jeered" when Halas lifted Grange in the third quarter. The jeering continued after the game as Grange headed to the locker room "and the mob pressed in on him," as the paper reported, "mocking the fellow whose name was something of a national boast a few weeks ago."[21]

After an all-night train trip to Pittsburgh, the Bears were so desperate for healthy players for the next night's game that they suited up their trainer, Andy Lotshaw, who was big but had never played football. Lotshaw lasted at tackle for half the game, which was longer than the weary Grange made it. After re-injuring his arm, Red left the field, again to cascading boos, this time from a Forbes Field crowd of 18,000. Grange's injuries were serious — he had torn a ligament and broken a blood vessel in his arm — and the listless Bears lost, 24–0.[22]

That was it for Red Grange's great eastern tour. With his arm in a sling, Red wore his raccoon coat and sat on the bench for the last two games prior to the holiday break. The Bears dropped both games, on Saturday, December 12 in Detroit to the Panthers, 21–0, and the next day in Chicago to the Giants, 9–0. In Detroit, ticket sales had been brisk, but after Panthers owner Jimmy Conzelman told reporters that Grange wouldn't be playing, interest dropped off. Even so, Conzelman had been encouraged when just prior to game time he noticed long lines outside the Navin Field box office. "I remembered thinking to myself, 'What a great sports town; Grange isn't playing but they're still lining up to buy tickets,'" Conzelman said later. "Then I got the news from the ticket man: They were lining up to get refunds." Only 6,000 showed up.[23]

And so ended part one of the great Grange tour, which despite the continued outcry of the collegians, the injuries, the punishing pace and the plummeting attendance at its end, was a smashing success. "The general public has heard, vaguely, of professional football as played in different cities of the country for years, and with some success, but the game had not made much headway," Damon Runyon wrote in the *New York American*. "It had been slowly gathering momentum, however, and during the past season it began attracting more attention than ever — and more customers. It invaded new territory, including New York City, and it commenced getting valuable word-of-mouth advertising as a thing worth seeing.

"But it needed a Jumbo," Runyon wrote. "Professional football needed a Jumbo, and it got its Jumbo when it landed Red Harold Grange of the University of Illinois. He attracted nationwide attention to the professional game. He put it on the front pages of the newspapers.... Red Grange (has) done more for professional football than (Babe) Ruth did for baseball, because baseball was an institution when Ruth began, while Grange has probably made professional football an institution."[24]

Pyle had succeeded after all. But at the end of eastern swing, he wasn't even there. C.C. was in Los Angeles, where he was arranging the southern and western swings while growing testy at the prying questions of reporters. Foremost on their minds was whether Red really received $300,000 from the movie company. And did C.C. actually see the amount deposited in the bank?

"It's just a pack of lies about the $300,000 contract being a fake," Pyle said. "Yes, I saw the check and it is in the Champaign bank."

So how much had Grange earned so far? "I don't discuss figures," said C.C.

"Was it more than $500,000?" inquiring minds wanted to know.

Pyle: "I won't answer that question."

Somewhat more forthcoming about Grange's health, Pyle insisted his football prodigy star was in fine fettle. "Why, it's not half as hard to play regular games as it is to scrimmage everyday," he said, dancing around the question. "They send football players through hard workouts every day and think nothing of it. Red has not been playing in the last two weeks as he did regularly while practicing and playing in games at Illinois."

As for the rumors that Grange was so banged up that he wouldn't be able to continue the tour in California, Pyle said that was a lot of "bunk."

"Wait until he comes out here and you will see he is in perfect physical shape," C.C. added. "A few days rest will give him his old-time pep. I am not a man-killer and certainly would not let Grange play another game if we were not right."[25]

Meantime, a weary Grange went home to Wheaton — considerably richer but disappointed at his performance. He had nothing to be ashamed of, having played well in eight of the 10 games in which he appeared despite the back-breaking pace of the tour. Most sportswriters agreed with the analysis from Frankford coach Guy Chamberlin that "more was asked of (Grange) than any human being could perform." Red admitted that 10 games in 17 days was too much, "a killing pace under any circumstances, but especially so when considering the team carried only 18 men."[26]

Both Pyle and Halas took note. With the tour to resume on Christmas Day in the Miami suburb of Coral Gables, Florida, Halas signed a half-dozen new players. Pyle ensured that part two of the great American football tour would be as stylish as possible. Gone were the all-night sleepers, replaced by the equivalent of first class. So on December 21, the Bears pulled out of Chicago on their own Pullman car nicknamed "Bethulla," with a personal porter assigned to handle their luggage. Once in Coral Gables, he presented them with sparkling new sweaters emblazoned with "Bears" on the front, matching pants and knee socks.[27]

For the time being, C.C. could afford the new uniforms and the luxurious train. With the money rolling in, C.C. spared little expense to befit his new status. In New York, Pyle took an office at the swanky Hotel McAlpin on the southeast corner of Herald Square, often lunching at the hotel's renowned Marine Grill, noted for its expansive grotto of flowing, polychrome tetra cotta interior, and a destination for a generation of well-heeled New Yorkers. Pyle spent $25,000 to create thousands of glossy, autographed prints of Grange that he handed out for free. More dollars went to lawyers to create the contracts needed for each game on the tour. "He was no hand to carry a little red notebook and jot down every nickel he spent," Grange said. "He spent more of his own money than ours."[28]

It took more than a few dollars to secure a stadium in south Florida. Arriving December 23 in Coral Gables, Pyle found the area in the midst of a big land boom, a place crawling with wheeling-and-dealing real estate speculators exchanging lots and vast amounts of money at the drop of a hat. But the Bears had their own housing issue, including no stadium and a practice field that was nothing more than a big, open field of sand. But Pyle had seen to it, and just like that an army of 200 carpenters and workmen descended on the field, and in *three days* of frantic, round-the-clock construction, threw up a wooden stadium seating 25,000, finishing just in time for the game. Tickets were costly, ranging from $5.50 up to $18 — the price set by local promoters responding to Pyle's $25,000 guarantee. Only 8,000 saw the Bears beat a team of Pennsylvania collegians, 7–0.[29]

The break had done Grange well. Back in Wheaton, he bought Garland a new Roadster, gave his father a check for $1,000, and even paid off his raccoon coat, which he eventually gave to his brother. His arm had improved, and in Coral Gables, Red gained 98 yards and scored the game's only touchdown, a short plunge over the goal line. But any happening on the football field paled in comparison to the continued feats of the stadium workmen. The day after the game, the army of carpenters were back and tore down the makeshift stadium. "You'd never know a ball game had taken place," said Grange.[30]

The Bears moved cross-state to Tampa for some fun and sun before their next game, on January 1. During a week off, Grange stayed busy. On New Year's Eve, Red was enjoying himself perhaps a tad too much when he was arrested for speeding. Taking Pyle's advice, he and C.C. took a crack at the Florida land boom and invested $17,000 each in local real estate. A hurricane later destroyed much of the land — and their investment.[31]

At least Grange and the Bears had little trouble in handling the Tampa Cardinals, a hastily assembled group of collegians who included the great Jim Thorpe, now 37 and well past his prime. Though the Bears drew just 6,700 — some of whom were said to be turned off by ticket prices peaking at $8.50, about four times the average NFL rate — Pyle had a field day. He pocketed a $20,000 advance — in cash.[32]

The Bears won the next day, January 2, in Jacksonville, 19–6, against yet another team of all-stars, featuring former Stanford great Ernie Nevers. Headed to California, the team stopped in New Orleans to play a team comprised primarily of former Tulane University players. To build attention, Grange and his teammates went to Fair Grounds Race Track to watch the feature race, "The Red Grange Handicap," where they crowded inside the winner's circle as Red presented the first-place jockey with a large pink floral football. The stunt didn't do much good at the gate; only 6,000 went to the game, which the Bears won, 14–0.[33]

With Pyle already in California drumming up publicity ideas, the Bears piled back into their Pullman for the 1,800-mile rail trip to Los Angeles. C.C. took to the glamour and glitz of the town, and in the week before the game, made sure Grange and the rest of the Bears took full advantage of the Hollywood publicity machine. Red posed for photographs with movie stars, including Mary Pickford and Harold Lloyd. He and several teammates went to the roof of the 13-story Biltmore Hotel —150 feet above ground — and flung footballs into a crowd of 5,000 below, with those managing to catch the balls winning $25 in prize money.[34]

Helping the cause were local writers and a few national syndicated columnists for whom the presence of C.C. Pyle and the Bears was a genuine news story. Most prominent of the lot was the great Damon Runyon, who typically spent a month or two in the California sunshine to escape the winter weather back east, while filing a steady stream of pieces on boxing, horse racing and his longstanding hatred of golf. Among America's foremost syndicated sportswriters, Runyon was a fixture at big sports events, having covered everything from the daily New York baseball and football to trials, political conventions, revolutions, war and doings on Broadway.

Runyon's versatility and brand of humor earned him stardom on William Randolph Hearst's *New York American* and the right to cover what he wanted. Runyon had particular affection for the characters of New York's nightlife — the Broadway actors and dancers, the bouncers, gamblers, hustlers and wise-guys. By the mid–1920s, Runyon had left the full-time baseball beat and taken to cruising the coffee shops and nightclubs of New York in search of color and characters he'd write about in his columns and memorable short stories with titles like *Guys and Dolls, Blue Plate Special* and *A Slight Case of Murder*.

Runyon's joint of choice was Lindy's, the well-known Broadway restaurant he immortalized as "Mindy's" in stories. It was there that many of his acquaintances met, only to find themselves worked sometime later into a short story. No longer a drinker, Runyon would occupy a set at Lindy's for long hours, consuming vast quantities of coffee and hosting a steady stream of characters. Said one regular after reading a Runyon piece, "It ain't hard to spot the guys in the stories."

In Runyon's world, men were "guys." Women were "dolls" and money, "potatoes." The objects of Runyon's attention were for the most part those in entertainment, sports and on the margins. They were characters with swagger and an edge — a role that the smooth-talking C.C. Pyle fit perfectly.[35]

Runyon and Pyle had hit it off in New York and reacquainted themselves in Los Angeles. Both men recognized the mutual benefits of their friendship. To Runyon, C.C. was a story, and to Pyle, friendship with the writer was a path to coverage in dozens of papers nationwide. When Pyle signed the former University of Washington star George "Wildcat" Wilson as part of a collegiate all-star team opposing the Bears at Memorial Coliseum, Runyon and his colleagues took it from there in building the upcoming tussle into the latest "greatest game" ever, a dramatic contest of west and east, between Wilson and Grange.

"My favorite amusement this past fall was reading statements of football experts and coaches that somebody else was a greater football player than Mr. Red Harold Grange," Runyon wrote. "Twenty years from now, when we all have long gray whiskers, we will be harking back to Mr. Red Harold Grange as one of the greatest that ever lived."[36]

Before a professional football record crowd of 75,000 on January 16 at Memorial Coliseum in Los Angeles, Wilson out-gained Grange, 118 yards to 33. But a healthier Red played virtually the whole game, scored two touchdowns in a 17–7 Bears win, and was still the best player on the field. "There is no doubt that Wilson can do more things on a football field than Mr. Red Harold Grange," Runyon summed up. "He is a fierce line plunger, by far, and he can kick the old cowhide. But he is not as graceful in action as Mr. Red Harold Grange and I doubt that he is as elusive." Then Runyon threw in a kicker to reinforce his theory. "Grange, with a game at San Diego before him," he wrote, "probably endeavored to conserve some of his energy and muscle."[37]

Before leaving Los Angeles for the tour's last four games, in San Diego, San Francisco, Portland and Seattle, Grange tried mending some lingering resentments that had surfaced since he joined the Bears. Among the throng at the Coliseum was Bob Zuppke, said to be still sore that his star back had bolted Champaign for the big-time. But when Grange spotted Zuppke at a Los Angeles dinner hosted by University of Illinois alumni, he walked briskly across the room and shook his old coach's hand. It was a classy act that instantly diffused any lingering animosity between the two men.[38]

The Bears took three of their last four games, losing only to San Francisco. In the tour's second-half swing through the South and West, they taken eight of nine games while playing before modest crowds. But despite the uneven attendance, Red Grange's extraordinary professional debut was a bona fide financial success for the NFL, the Bears and C.C. Pyle. In the tour's first 11 games, 181,000 people had paid $342,000 to see him play. Immediately after the final game, Pyle wrote his second $50,000 check to Grange. And though Grange's colleagues had continued to be paid $100 to $200 a game, they too enjoyed a healthy payday thanks to 20 games, as many as some had played in their entire collegiate careers. The Bears also did well, clearing $100,000 from the tours and giving what Halas described as the team's "first financial cushion we'd managed to accumulate."

Pyle himself had made a killing — about $118,000, the equivalent of $1 million today, which sent his mind to thinking he could add to it. Cornering Halas and Sternaman on the long train ride back to Chicago, he revealed his plan to keep Grange in a Bears uniform for 1926. Citing the big crowds and the team's financial windfall, C.C. pitched the same 50–50 split of gate receipts for the next year, but provided Grange receive a one-third ownership in the Bears. Halas and Sternaman turned him down on the spot, arguing that no player should have access to that much power. In essence, they turned Pyle and Grange free to pursue other options.[39]

So just like that, the Bear owners had released the best football player of a generation. Pyle, meantime, had gotten a chance to zero in on a new obsession. What C.C. *really* wanted was his very own 1926 NFL franchise in New York starring the one and only Red Grange. C.C. had it all worked out, securing an agreement with New York Yankees general manager Ed Barrow on a five-year lease of Yankee Stadium, provided NFL owners would give him their blessing at the league's February meeting in Detroit. The team even had a name. In deference to Barrow and the stadium where they were due to play, the team would be New York's "football" Yankees.[40]

The triumphant tour finished, players headed home to take a break. That was not the case for the ever-restless C.C. Pyle, whose immediate task was fulfilling the film contract Red Grange had inked back in New York.

Unfortunately, the Arrow Production Company that had reportedly signed Grange to a $300,000 contract had gone bankrupt. That was merely an inconvenience, C.C. said, because the contract had been signed directly with the company's president, which required them to make the film. Come again? In reality, neither Pyle nor the president, W.E. Schallenberger, had secured an agreement — that is until Joseph P. Kennedy, who had bought the Film Booking Office, decided he would give it a shot. Kennedy didn't give a hoot about Grange's acting ability; he had asked his two football-minded young sons, Joe Junior and Jack, whether they would like to see Grange in a film. When the boys responded with enthusiasm, Kennedy's mind was made up: Red Grange would become a movie star, after all.

With the film contract in hand, Pyle and Grange, accompanied by Lyman "Beans" DeWolf, Red's old football coach at Wheaton High, as traveling secretary, arrived May 14 in style aboard the California Limited at Santa Fe Station in Los Angeles, where dozens of film notables greeted them. As usual, C.C. spared little expense, renting two luxury suites at the swank Ambassador Hotel for the three of them. Grange would appear in a film based on a script written by Byron Morgan called *The Halfback*, later changed by director Sam Wood to *One Minute to Play*.[41]

The local papers pumped out prose on every aspect of the filming. "Screen tests taken some time ago indicated that the famous grid star will film well," wrote Braven Dyer in the *Los Angeles Times*, "and that it's a lead-pipe cinch that there'll be plenty of action throughout the story." While that much was true, the silent film turned out to be a plodder with a predictable story line revolving around Grange, as high school football star Red Wade, whose athleticism is considerably stronger than his grades. So Red goes off to college with strict instructions from his father to keep away from football and focus instead on his studies.

But a Red Grange film without football? Perish the thought! On the train headed to college, there is a scheduling mix-up and Red enrolls at the wrong school, Parmalee College, where he breaks his promise and plays football — that is until his disapproving father finds out and demands that he sit out the team's pivotal game against Caxton. But with dear old Parmalee facing defeat in the waning moments of the game, dad lets up. Red enters and, of course, scores the winning touchdown.[42]

Most of the filming was done at Pomona College, with the game scenes shot at the Los Angeles Coliseum, where Red had recently faced Wildcat Wilson. Attracting extras for the crowd scenes was a challenge, not only because *One Minute to Play* was a low-budget affair and couldn't pay them, but because the film was scripted for the late fall in the Midwest. Would anyone actually show up wearing an overcoat in the middle of a sizzling July in Southern California? Not a problem, said Pyle, chiming in with yet another ingenious solution: an ad in the newspaper guaranteeing free admission to anyone dressed in fall apparel to see Wildcat Wilson's team take on Grange's team. As if on cue, some 15,000 die-hards appeared in felt hats, overcoats and scarves, giving the on-screen appearance of a day that could just as easily have been a frigid Saturday in Ohio or Illinois. Pyle could not care less that several thousands had been conned into thinking they were about to witness a real game. C.C. had pulled off another fast one, a fact that impressed Grange. "He always figured the angles," Red said of Pyle. "He wasn't anybody's chump that way."[43]

Meantime, Pyle and Grange poked their way around Hollywood. Guided by Pyle's old friend and colleague Bill Pickens, they joined movie stars at parties, shopped and went to the beach at Santa Monica. Picking out a tweed suit at an exclusive haberdashery partly owned by Douglas Fairbanks, Jr., Red bumped into the movie star himself, who promptly offered to flip a coin double or nothing for the purchase price. Grange won the toss, which earned him the second suit in which Fairbanks wrote on the inside label, "This suit is on you, but it's on me." Grange proudly kept the suit for nearly 15 years. Joining former heavyweight champion Jim Jeffries at his alfalfa farm in nearby Burbank, Grange, the Illinois farm boy, took considerable interest in the old boxer's thriving vegetable garden. When Red admired Jeffries' healthy crop of onions, the old boxer gave him some to take back to the hotel. He did, but the next morning the stench from the offending vegetables were overpowering. It turns out that the vegetables weren't onions, but garlic. Pyle, Pickens and Jeffries yucked it up for days at Red's expense.[44]

Grange took a particular liking to Sam Wood, the *One Minute to Play* director, who, he said, would have made a great football coach "because he could get a lot out of you the easy way." Even so, Grange remembered the four weeks of filming as "the worst drudgery I'd ever experienced." For the football scenes, Red spent 10 straight 90-degree days, from sunup to sundown, in a full football uniform, leaving him drained and wanting to do little but go back to the hotel and sleep. The only break during the filming came when Wood let Grange leave early several afternoons to catch the Angels, the Los Angeles Pacific Coast League baseball team.[45]

Grange had little idea how the film or the story line was turning out. After the filming ended in mid–July, he went back to Wheaton to prepare for football season and didn't see the final cut until it premiered in early September in New York at the Colony Theatre, adorned for the occasion with pennants, a band and ushers donning football sweaters. During the climatic final game, the theater crowd whooped and hollered as if they were at the Polo Grounds, with cries of "Attaboy, Red," as Grange hit the end zone with the winning touchdown. Afterwards, Grange gave a few remarks in which he humorously held forth on the idea of wearing painted lips while in a football uniform.[46]

Despite his reticence about acting, Red had actually fared pretty well on the big screen — far better than other athletes like Babe Ruth, Ty Cobb and Jack Dempsey, all of whom had appeared in real clunkers. Reviews for *One Minute to Play* were decent, as in the *Chicago Tribune*, where critic Mae Tinee wrote that the picture ends "with an honest-to-goodness game that is considerable of a sensation." Of Grange, Tinee wrote that "if you've never seen (him) play, now's your chance, for he plays it like everything in this picture." Mordaunt Hall, the *New York Times* critic, agreed in touting the film as "skillfully handled" and Grange's acting ability as "pleasingly natural." Indeed, the film did well at the box office, so well that Joseph Kennedy urged Grange to consider leaving football to act full-time. Flattered by the offer, Grange politely turned him down. "I considered myself a football player by profession," he said, "and not an actor."[47]

Red Grange knew his role. He was a football player first and a critical cog of the Golden Age of Sports, which by the mid–1920s was in full flower. In a decade defined by fads, frivolity and fashions, sports heroes were no longer just athletes, but full-fledged personalities who were expected to act, make public appearances, and endorse products.

The heavyweight boxing champ, Jack Dempsey (left), at practice. From the Bain Collection (Library of Congress, Prints and Photographs Division).

In 1925, there were only three other sports figures even close to Grange in popularity—Ruth, the race-horse Man o' War, and heavyweight champion Jack Dempsey. Ruth was a personality like no other, but both Man o' War and Dempsey were tainted, however unfairly by the restraints of their sports having significantly shorter careers next to the Babe, and by the times.

Like Ruth, Jack Dempsey had grown up poor. The two men were virtually the same age, but there the comparisons stopped. Whereas Ruth was gregarious, quotable, approachable and rarely met a child he didn't like, Dempsey was a rough man in a rough sport. Born in a log cabin near Manassa, Colorado, he was the age's sports anti-hero. "Most boxers hope to demolish their opponent," wrote Geoffrey Ward in his biography of Jack Johnson. "Dempsey seemed bent on obliterating his." Beating Jess Willard in 1919 to win the championship, Dempsey knocked him down seven times, broke his jaw, cracked four ribs and ripped out six teeth.[48]

Dempsey's personal life was just as messy. Like other prominent athletes of the era, he had been exempted from the draft as his family's sole support, a role that drew howls of protest from his divorced wife and sportswriters that he was a draft dodger. A trial exonerated him, and Dempsey had, in fact, tried twice to enlist, but the damage to his reputation was substantial. Dempsey was called a "slacker" throughout his heavyweight reign, which lasted all the way to 1926 when he lost to Gene Tunney. In later years, Dempsey would serve in the Pacific during World War II and become a beloved figure in New York as the owner of his restaurant, "Jack Dempsey's," a Broadway staple.

Man o' War's reign wasn't nearly as long. Bred by August Belmont II, the race horse was foaled in 1917, won big in 1919, but by 1920 was nearly finished. Though remembered as arguably the greatest race horse of all time, Man o' War would retire in January 1921 to a horse farm in Lexington, Kentucky, and live another 26 years — remembered and certainly lionized, but hardly with the kind of daily scrutiny received by an athlete performing every few days.[49]

Yet with newspapermen producing their purple prose, new sports heroes could crop up seemingly out of nowhere, even for a moment. The play of U.S. tennis players at far-off exotic-sounding places like Monte Carlo and Wimbledon were always good for headlines. And so was the improbable tale midway through 1926 of Gertrude Ederle, the 23-year-old New Yorker who rocketed overnight to international stardom as the first woman to swim the English Channel. Plunging into the chilly waters at Cap Gris Nez, France, in a two-piece bathing suit, slathered in grease and wearing watertight leather and rubber goggles she designed for the grueling task, Ederle battled 35 miles of treacherous tides and frigid waters before emerging at Kingsdown, Great Britain, 14½ hours later, having broken the existing *men's* record by nearly two hours.[50]

What Pyle could have done with Gertrude Ederle! The young swimmer's accomplishment captivated the nation, dispelling conventional wisdom that women couldn't be great athletes. Dubbed "our American girl" by President Coolidge, Ederle arrived back in the U.S. three weeks after her swim to a hero's welcome, having gone to Germany to see her grandmother immediately after the trip. In New York, some two million people lined Broadway and gave her a ticker-tape parade. Sitting in his office at the Hotel McAlpin and dispensing wisdom as he got a shave, Pyle expressed great regret that he hadn't been able to represent Ederle. "If I had that girl, I would have buried her aboard the first boat for home," C.C. told Westbrook Pegler. "There would have been no visit to grandma.... I would have opened an office and I would have said, 'Gentlemen, the line forms on the right and anyone with any propositions of less than $5,000 will please go away. The penny arcade is two blocks south, gentlemen.'"

Pyle says he would have sold the rights to Gertrude Ederle bathing suits, bathing caps, slippers, beach robes and swim goggles, and then negotiated a movie in which she would star. "It is really a shame that poor girl went to visit her grandmother," C.C. thundered. "I would have had Trudie write her grandmother a nice souvenir postcard ... But here this girl wastes two weeks, and by the time she gets home nobody will remember whether Trudie Ederle is the one who swam the English Channel or the one who rode the pig past the place where the preacher and that lady were undergoing murder."

Pyle estimated he would have earned $200,000 as Ederle's manager. Maybe. Shy and withdrawn, Ederle was never comfortable with the attention and would probably have scoffed at the opportunities. A few years later, she lost most of her hearing from swimming and became a recluse, living out most of her years quietly in the Queens section of New York City and teaching deaf children to swim.[51]

On May 20, 1927, less than a year after Ederle's epic swim, a boyish-looking 25-year-old former air-mail pilot, a Minnesota native named Charles Lindbergh took off aboard his specially made single-engine monoplane from Roosevelt Field on Long Island and flew to Paris, the first solo, nonstop flight across the Atlantic. The journey took 33 hours, and when Lindbergh emerged from his cramped quarters, he was engulfed by jubilant crowds and crowned the world's most famous man, its first true mass media celebrity. Back home, reporters asked Pyle, by now the PR man with the answers, what Lindbergh should do next. Why, he should make as much money as he could, Pyle counseled — or, as a reporter put it, "salt it." You could argue that as quickly "Lucky Lindy's" celebrity grew, so did the supposed know-how of one C.C. Pyle. The one-time grocery clerk from Delaware, Ohio, was rapidly emerging as one of the voices of the Jazz Age.[52]

So just what triggered this decade of ballyhoo, the fat and happy years of the Jazz Age, of speakeasies, flag-pole sitters, F. Scott Fitzgerald and sloe gin fizzes? More than anything, it was a collective feeling of America wanting to let loose after some hard years. The decade of the 1920s dawned less than two years from the end of the Great War, followed by the county's deadliest flu epidemic in history and crippling labor problems. The "good old days" were not always kinder, simpler times as depicted in the movies.

America hadn't planned on entering the Great War. But in 1915, a year or so into the fighting, a German U-boat sunk a British luxury ocean liner, the *Lusitania*, off the Irish coast, killing 1,198 — 159 of them Americans — and triggering a national outrage. In 1917 Germany declared unrestricted submarine warfare in the Atlantic. A week later, the U.S. cut diplomatic ties with Germany, and three months later, declared war. By July 1918, more than one million American troops were in Europe, which hastened the end of the war by the fall. Though U.S. casualties were minimal next to the carnage suffered by Europeans, more than 53,000 Americans were killed in action, with another 63,000 dying of disease.[53]

Even more devastating was the "war" back home, a fast-moving, lethal strain of influenza, which was believed to have started in the army camps and swept through the country, laying waste to staggering numbers of Americans. By 1918, the flu had sickened more than 25 percent of the U.S. population and killed 548,000—indescribably targeting the youngest and healthiest and devastating populations, from the biggest cities to the smallest hamlets. The death curves in the great flu epidemic were "W-shaped," with peaks for three groups in particular: babies and toddlers; the elderly aged 70 to 74; and young adults, between 20 and 40. The navy estimated than 40 percent of its servicemen caught the flu in 1918; the army said that 36 percent of its soldiers became ill.

It was as if the Black Death had taken root in early-twentieth century America. Every family seemed to have a father, a child, a brother, or an aunt who perished from this grisly illness in which the lungs filled with fluid, essentially drowning its victims. That so many victims were young adults was especially devastating, leaving untold hundreds of thousands of orphaned children as well as families without a breadwinner. That it hit in the closing days of World War I was perceived by many as yet another wartime nightmare, the equal of terrors faced by soldiers in the trenches. And then, as mysteriously as the flu appeared, it went away, having killed more people in a few months' time than any other illness in American history.[54]

Nor did the war's aftermath prove easier for many of the country's labor force. While on one hand, the rise of unions gave factory workers a new start in the post-war years—by 1920, almost 20 percent of industrial workers belonged to a union—the rise of union activism had consequences. Between 1919 and 1922, some eight million workers went on strike for better wages and conditions, four million of them in 1919 alone. Strikes that year ranged from the California citrus fields to southern cotton mills, El Paso laundries, Tampa cigar factories and into the silk factories of Paterson, New Jersey, telephone companies in New England and even Boston's police force.

With labor's increasing powers came complex conflicts of assimilation.

When in the summer of 1919 race riots erupted in cities throughout the U.S., many African Americans formed their own unions dedicated to socialism and black liberation. And with the growing radicalism of unions came the U.S. government's repression of radicals, much of the effort targeted to immigrants deemed "un–American."

Early in 1920, Attorney General A. Mitchell Palmer deployed federal agents in 70 cities across the country to arrest and detain 10,000 people identified in department files as aliens and Communists; of those arrested, about 500 were deported, with the rest turning out to be citizens or immigrants without radical ties. By 1921, 32 states had outlawed what was called "criminal syndicalism" — advocating illegal labor tactics or being a member of organizations that encouraged them. More than 100 detective agencies gave companies the operatives to spy on employees suspected of union-organizing, identify activists for firing, start fights at union meetings, and gang up on strikers. All tactics were aimed at disrupting the growth of unions.[55]

America in 1920 could have used a dynamic presidential candidate in such an atmosphere, but neither candidate would help matters much, even as women prepared to vote for the first time after the passage of the nineteenth Amendment. After eight years with a Democrat in the White House for the first time since the Civil War, the Republicans were solid in their dislike of Woodrow Wilson. Rejecting Wilson's far-sighted vision of a League of Nations, they unified around everything the Democrats weren't: isolationist, anti–Bolshevist, and anti–Semitic. No wonder their candidate was an affable but bland U.S. senator, Warren G. Harding, a former Ohio newspaper publisher most notable for his ability to shake a lot of hands. Though he fashioned his campaign after another Ohioan, William McKinley, Harding did not measure up to anything remotely presidential. Lacking self-confidence, he stumbled when delivering a speech, saying, "I never saw this before.... I didn't write this speech and don't believe what I just read."

Conveniently overlooked was Harding's true passion — sexual dalliances with his mistress Nan Britton, who he even stopped to see at a friend's apartment after securing the nomination, and had born him an illegitimate child. "His private life was one of cheap sex episodes," wrote Frederick Lewis Allen in *Only Yesterday*. "An ambitious wife had tailored and groomed him into outward respectability." Overlooked as well was Harding's lackluster record as a senator — he had managed to miss two-thirds of all roll-call votes. But in an odd way, Harding was exactly what America wanted at the time. How

President Warren G. Harding (second from right, front row) takes in opening day in 1923 at Yankee Stadium. Yankee owner Jacob Ruppert is in the second row (center, in bow-tie). Albert Lasker, the advertising magnate and Chicago Cubs owner, is front and center. From the Bain Collection (Library of Congress, Prints and Photographs Division).

people loved it when he proclaimed, "America's present need is not heroics, but healing; not nostrums but normalcy."[56]

The strategy worked, and Harding won the White House in 1920 in a landslide. The country prospered, and Harding did as well, for a time. But when a scandal erupted around the leasing of oil wells in his administration, things got rocky for Harding, who complained of the culprits, his former friends who "kept me up walking the floors nights." The president was urged to come clean and expose the scandal, but Harding refused, fearing political repercussions. He would never find out, for in 1923, he died of a heart attack, succeeded by Vice President Calvin Coolidge.[57]

The former Massachusetts governor and a man of few words, Coolidge was even duller than his predecessor. Sitting next to Coolidge at a dinner party, a woman confided of her bet to squeeze at least three words of conversation from the president. "You lose," Coolidge shot back, not even looking at his guest. Walter Lippmann said Coolidge owed his political success to effectively doing nothing. "This active inactivity suits the mood and certain of the needs of the country admirably," he wrote. "It suits all the business interests which want to be let alone." That was so, and in 1924, Coolidge was easily elected president.[58]

No wonder Americans were happy to focus on Red Grange, Babe Ruth and other sporting heroes of the age. They were just the tonic the country needed.

4

"Football for All and All for Football"

"Anyone who gets three or four of these stadiums will control sports in America," C.C. Pyle was telling a roomful of Los Angeles reporters. That would be a 70,000-seat domed stadium, complete with a retractable roof, escalators instead of steps for aisles and even a helicopter landing. For the most distant seats, C.C. had created a special glass — a magnifying glass with a crank to roll it up or down.

Halfway through 1926, C.C. Pyle had paid an engineering firm $5,000 for a set of blueprints to his latest, jaw-dropping plan — the sports stadium of the future. In telling people about it, he had drawn a crowd, which by now he was doing on a regular basis. It barely mattered that C.C.'s stadium of the future would cost millions and was *way* too expensive to build, or that he had called a press conference to announce another pie-in-the-sky idea. "It's impossible," he said in frustration. "It's impossible because it would cost three million dollars."[1]

So it went for C.C. Pyle, a man who in less than a year had risen from a small-town theater owner to a national figure. Creating a business out of the ether, Pyle was succeeding beyond his wildest dreams. In doing so, he had shaken up the stuffed shirts of academia and the sports establishment, and earned their attention. After many stops and starts, he was finally the big shot he had always wanted to be by commanding attention, and being trailed by reporters in search of a story. The world's first sports agent had become a presence.

Best of all, Charles Cassius Pyle was at last a big shot. He dressed well, stayed in the best hotels, rode the fastest trains — and in his restlessness, wanted more. Catching up with Pyle and Grange at the Morrison Hotel in Chicago, Damon Runyon introduced them to Harry Greb, boxing's middleweight champion, and Greb's manager, Red Mason, and sat back for the insightful exchange.

"Our last shot was in Phoenix, Arizona, with a tough bird named Owen Phillips," Mason was saying. "He gave Harry the best fight of any of those beezarks that he met on the trip. We got $2,500 there, and the house was nice and fat. You wouldn't think it, would you?"

Pyle was all ears. "What's the name of that town?" he demanded with penetrating interest while removing from his jacket the little red notebook to jot it down. "Phoenix, eh? Well, well, well, well!"

When Mason mentioned that Greb had earned a hefty payday in the town of Fremont, Ohio, Pyle penciled that into his notebook as well. "You say the name of that town is Fremont, eh?" asked C.C., his mind firmly planted on future ventures. "I'll not forget it."

"No, don't forget that one — and Phoenix," said Mason, "There's a lot of towns around. I'll send you a list."

Grange probably got closer than anyone else to the essence of what drove C.C. Pyle. "Charley made a million three or four times over and lost it," Red said. "Money meant nothing to him. But he did like to hear his name mentioned. He would go to the six-day bike races and sponsor $300 sprints just to hear his name mentioned over the loudspeaker. He rode the 20th Century Limited between Chicago and New York quite a bit, and whenever one of the waiters would say, 'Mr. Pyle, how are you?' he would leave a $10 tip. If the waiter didn't know his name, Charley wouldn't tip him a nickel. He loved the acclaim."

And Grange genuinely liked Pyle, and enjoyed his company. "He was a fellow you would like," Red said. "The greatest mixer, a great storyteller. He loved to sit around and have a drink with anyone. A lovable guy. I never met anyone who did not like Charley Pyle."[2]

Not quite. Despite the fact that Pyle may have taken the New York Giants off life support and given them a glimpse of professional football's potential in late 1925 when he helped pack the Polo Grounds with nearly 70,000 spectators, Giants owner Tim Mara was unwavering in his fierce loathing of C.C., viewing him as a rival, a threat to building his New York football empire.

Professional football in early 1926 was still a struggling business. Even when Mara's Giants drew well — an estimated 25,000 had seen them play Philadelphia's Frankford Yellow Jackets — the interest paled next to the college game. At the Polo Grounds, both its college tenants, Fordham and New York University, continued to outdraw the Giants, even though to attract fans, the pro team charged far less; seats were priced from 50 cents to $2.75. And upwards of half the crowd got in for free.[3]

Mara was still learning the football trade. After cheering a sweep that had gained a grand total of three yards, his son, Wellington, had to explain to his father that it hadn't been such a good play after all. But as a businessman, Mara recognized a threat when on February 6, 1926, at the start of the NFL owners meeting in Detroit, Pyle showed up with his intention to place a football team, the Yankees, at Yankee Stadium, a half-mile at most from the Polo Grounds. Invading a city that Mara saw as belonging to him didn't sit well with the Giants owner.

Striding into Detroit's Hotel Statler for the owners' gathering, Pyle and Grange were the odd couple of the proceedings. For one reason, Grange, though he was there with Pyle, was a free agent and still eyed by many as the NFL's future savior. As a result, the owners, many of whom were vying for his services, glad-handed the shy football star, with "his modesty and All-America demeanor charm(ing) everyone," wrote football historian Bob Carroll.

"Money meant nothing to him," Red Grange said of C.C. Pyle, pictured aboard the liner, France, probably to welcome Suzanne Lenglen to America in 1926. "But he did like to hear his name mentioned." From New York World-Telegram and the Sun Newspaper Photograph Collection (Library of Congress, Prints and Photographs Division, NYWT&S Division).

Then there was Pyle, for whom the football owners, fueled by Mara, directed particular scorn. To them, C.C. was the outsider trying to horn in on their enterprise with a franchise that they thought would unsettle things, create instability, and spilt the gate in the league's major market. If Grange was the likable hero, Pyle was considered a threat to the health of the fragile young league, a man with a bull's-eye on his chest, "a diabolical Svengali leading the trusting Redhead to ruin," as Carroll wrote. "In picturing

Grange as an innocent dupe and Pyle as evil incarnate, they underrated Grange and over-indicted Pyle." In reality, Pyle managed the one player the owners craved. And for everyone C.C. charmed, there were just as many who took his schmoozing, breezy manner for arrogance. But "that was fine with (Pyle)," argued Carroll. "He was there for money, not love."[4]

Pyle introduced Grange and got right to the point. First, he announced that he and Grange had already secured a five-year lease on Yankee Stadium from Yankee general manager Ed Barrow for all the Sundays and holidays from October through the end of the year. Then, he proposed that the NFL owners give him a team, to be called the Yankees, and painted rosy predictions of the vast crowds descending on the world's most majestic stadium to see football's greatest star.[5]

Was there room for two professional football teams in New York? Pyle would say that 19 of the 20 club owners, everyone but Mara, thought so and were on his side. But in public, at least, those other owners were forced into a corner of sorts, having to stick by fellow owner Mara, who would never agree to the presence of a new team, not just in the same city, but right across the Harlem River in the Bronx. In Mara's bleak view, this new team would hardly be a shot-in-the-arm for pro football, as Pyle argued, but a move guaranteed to steal attention, crowds and ticket sales from the Giants. Such a scenario, argued Bill McGeehan in the *New York Herald Tribune*, would look "very much as though next winter's professional season in this vicinity would settle down to a game of freeze-out."[6]

Mara jokingly bet Grange $100,000 that when the Giants played the Yankees, neither would "make a nickel." But he reserved a deep reservoir of venom for Pyle — in particular for how in his view, C.C. had bulldozed his way through the negotiations during the Grange tour. Here was Pyle again in all his persistence and arrogance, and "treating (Mara) as a tiresome obstacle to a New Dawn," as Carroll put it. So profound was Mara's hatred, according to an eyewitness at the Hotel Statler, that he came close to lunging for Pyle.

Pyle versus Mara was a face-off, one strong personality against another. Beyond the animosity, Mara's line in the sand was fueled by business. The Giants owner felt that a league franchise was of little value without exclusive territorial rights, and he figured that by giving into Pyle's Grange-led Yankees, his team would quickly become New York's second-class team.

Each man dug in. Pulling a snit of his own, Pyle thundered that "no blasted Irishman is going to keep me out of New York!" Seeking a solution, several NFL owners tried to broker a compromise in which the Yankees would join the league, with the Giants relocating to Ebbets Field, home of baseball's Dodgers in Brooklyn. They arranged a meeting between Pyle and Mara to discuss the issue. Both men refused to attend, and in the end, the owners had little choice but to side with Mara and against the Grange-led Yankees. In doing so, they cited precedent — a recent decision in which NFL president Joe Carr suspended the Pottstown, Pennsylvania franchise for playing an unauthorized game in Philadelphia, home turf of the Frankford Yellow Jackets.[7]

Absorbing the news, Pyle was disappointed, but hardly beaten. He still had a lot of money. He still had Grange and an agreement with the baseball Yankees to use their ballpark. If the NFL didn't want him, Pyle would go on to Plan B, which was bigger, bolder and brassier than anyone could have imagined. So Red Grange and the Yankees were shut out of the NFL? He would beat them at their own game, announced Pyle. He would start his own new league.[8]

Racing back to New York, Pyle worked feverish to throw together his new football league, to be called the American Professional Football League, or the AFL. It was the kind of action C.C. relished: talking big as he huddled in hotel rooms with this group and that group and working on deals that would beat the establishment at their own game. Aided considerably by plenty of publicity-seeking businessmen anxious to secure franchises, Pyle built his new league with lightning speed.

On February 17, 1926, all of eight days after his negotiations with the NFL had broken down, Pyle announced that his new organization would field 10 teams and start play in the fall. There would be the league's centerpiece, the Yankees, which C.C. co-owned with Grange, to be joined by franchises in Boston, Newark and Milwaukee. That there were in fact only four confirmed teams to this point was a minor concern to Pyle, who would rather paint an upbeat picture of a league on the verge of thriving. Hinting that teams from other major cities would soon be in as well — one from St. Louis, backed by Cardinals' great Rogers Hornsby, another from Cincinnati to be owned by Reds owner Garry Herrmann, and a West Coast team to be headed by former University of Washington All-American Wildcat Wilson — C.C. outlined a league in robust health. Besides, he said, five groups from Chicago and another three from Brooklyn wanted to be a part of things.[9]

On March 6 at the Commodore Hotel, Pyle announced that former Princeton University All-American "Big" Bill Edwards had signed on as AFL commissioner. It was a bold stroke that gave the fledging league a whiff of legitimacy. An imposing figure as a leader on the football field and in

Big Bill Edwards (left) pays a visit to the Big Man of the Bronx, Babe Ruth of the Yankees. With them is the not-so-big Yankee mascot. From the Bain Collection (Library of Congress, Prints and Photographs Division).

municipal government, Edwards made his name at Princeton, where he starred as the starting right guard for three years and two as captain, including the 1899 team that won the national championship. Big Bill then coached at Princeton, Annapolis and the University of Michigan, and officiated college games.[10]

At 300 pounds, "Big" Bill had earned his nickname, not to mention the enduring gratitude of New York political leaders for hard work and a heroic incident 16 years before that harkened back to his football days. In addition to launching an insurance business, Edwards had served a series of high-profile political posts in New York City, starting with Deputy Street Cleaning Commissioner and then as commissioner, which earned him top marks for his department's prompt and efficient snow removal. But nothing matched the rave reviews Edwards earned from an incident August 9, 1910, in which he became a bona fide American hero by saving New York mayor William Gaynor from an assassination attempt. Visiting the liner *Kaiser Wilhelm der Gross* at Hoboken, New Jersey, to wish the mayor well on a trip, Big Bill put his football instincts to good use when he tackled a disgruntled, recently fired dock worker named James Gallagher, who had just fired a pistol at the mayor. Though the mayor had been seriously wounded, Edwards subdued the shooter with a low, hard hit, pinning him to the deck.

In the struggle, Big Bill took a bullet in the arm, but recovered quickly to earn both a Carnegie Hero medal and the assurance of future political appointments for his quick actions. In later years, Edwards would contribute to Woodrow Wilson's two winning presidential campaigns and be named collector of the New York branch of the Internal Revenue Service.[11]

Edwards accepted a three-year contract as commissioner for $25,000 a year. He was given broad powers similar to former federal judge Kenesaw Mountain Landis, the grandly named iron-fisted baseball commissioner, whose five-year reign set the standard for how to run a professional sports league. Comparisons between Big Bill and Landis started immediately. Mr. Edwards ... becomes to professional football what Judge Landis is to professional baseball," the *New York Times* reported, "and Will H. Hays is to the moving picture industry." But sportswriters knew the Big Bill was a figurehead and more of a prestige appointment because C.C., serving as league vice president, was the man who would really be running things. Some wondered privately — but not in print — whether Big Bill would ever see even a dime of his promised salary.[12]

Overjoyed to be back in the game, Edwards kept the tone at the press conference upbeat, announcing right away that the new league would follow the NFL's lead and not sign an undergraduate football player until his class had graduated. Then, he grandly pronounced that the American League would work to preserve the tradition of the game — "a clean, red-blooded sport, a great character builder." Though Big Bill represented professionals, his players, he assured reporters, would play with a big dose of old-fashioned college spirit.

"Men play this game in college because they love the game, not merely

Big Bill Edwards, seen here marching with Boy Scouts in New York, was a bona fide American hero who joined C.C. Pyle's fledging American Football League as commissioner, lending his prestige. Despite a $25,000 salary, Big Bill is thought to have never earned a cent for his services. From the Bain Collection (Library of Congress, Prints and Photographs Division).

for financial reasons," Big Bill proclaimed. "No one wants to see our great game of football preserved more than myself. The good qualities of the game and the tremendous public interest combine to make the game the property of the public, and it must be played by others than college men and schoolboys. There is a great public demand, therefore, to see the game."

Then Edwards announced a 15-game schedule for each team, which would play twice a week from the close of the World Series in mid–October through December. To show that Pyle had learned the lessons of too many games, there would be no "barnstorming" or post-season exhibition tour. There would be, however, training tables and treatment for injured players at every game.[13]

In mid–July, Pyle gathered his owners for five days of meetings at the Commodore where they hammered out details of the new league. For starters, the American League would have nine teams and not 10 as first thought. Joining Red Grange's Yankees in New York would be the Brooklyn Horsemen, named for its two stars — Elmer Layden and Harry Stuhldreher, two of Notre Dame's "Four Horsemen." Other franchises took nifty nicknames as well, including the Newark Bears, Chicago Bulls, Cleveland Panthers, Boston Bulldogs and Philadelphia Quakers. Another AFL team, the Rock Island, Illinois, "Independents" were just that — NFL defectors — while the Los Angeles Wildcats, named for its star, George "Wildcat" Wilson, were actually a traveling squad due to play every game on the road, yet nowhere near the West Coast. Pyle had even lured several NFL standouts to the AFL, notably Bears quarterback Joey Sternaman. And taking over as owner, coach and quarterback of the Chicago Bulls was Joey's brother, Dutch.

Announcing the new league's slogan was "Football for All and All for Football," Big Bill Edwards used the occasion to launch another long-winded speech. "The formation of our league will enable hundreds of thousands to sit in and watch the heroes of college and school days play the great games they are capable of," he said. "Happy indeed is the great college star who can play his own game with freedom away from the restraint of college coaches. When men graduate from college they are just beginning to know how to play the game. For those who love the game and want to continue, this league offers such men a chance."

In fact, they had that chance and more, given the NFL's response to fight the new league by expanding instead of extracting. To counter Pyle's threat, the NFL established new teams in Brooklyn, Hartford and Racine, Wisconsin, and added two more, in Louisville and Los Angeles, as road teams based out of Chicago. With 22 teams in all — an all-time high that stood until 1970 — the NFL had taken on more teams than it could support. Meanwhile, both leagues faced an expensive, potentially ruinous war for talent.[14]

As the more established league, the NFL appeared to have the upper hand. The NFL Brooklyn franchise, dubbed the Lions, snared the lease at Ebbets Field, sending the AFL Horsemen to play most of their games on the road. Hoping to sign Ernie Nevers, the former Stanford University All-American and star of the 1925 Rose Bowl, both leagues offered him a salary of $15,000, with Nevers choosing to join the financially strapped NFL franchise in Duluth, which had thrown in a percentage of the gate receipts. The deal netted Nevers more than $50,000 for the season in which he earned every penny. That season, his Duluth Eskimos, whose players featured a design of an igloo on the front of their uniforms, played a back-breaking schedule of *29 games*, 27 of them on the road, including one eight-day period of games in five cities. Along the way, the Eskimos became a fan favorite — Grantland Rice called them "the Iron Men from the North" — and the team finished its long season by playing 10 exhibition games on the West Coast to take full advantage of Nevers' popularity.

Pyle responded by trying to sign as many top players as he could. Flush with cash from his Grange experiment and by an encouraging, new foray into professional tennis, Pyle focused on securing top talent for its two marquee franchises, the Yankees and the Wildcats. C.C. offered all-pro tackle Ed Healy of the Bears $10,000 to coach the Yankees, an extraordinary amount given he had was earning $150 a game in the NFL. But Healy turned him down flat, choosing to stick with the Bears in what appeared to be a sour reaction to Pyle's glitz and flash.[15]

C.C. was at the Morrison Hotel in Chicago when Healy dropped by to discuss the offer. Grange was there, as was tennis star Suzanne Lenglen and, in the adjoining room, a woman who, as Healy put it, "did not answer to the name of Mrs. Pyle."

By offering him the money on the spot, C.C. floored Healy, so much so that he said he needed to think things over.

"Charley," he said. "I'll give you an answer on that today."

"Oh, you don't have to answer me today," C.C. said.

"Well, this *is* shocking," Healy answered. "I've never really been up against anything where I had to make a decision with reference to leaving people I'm established with."

Healy left and marched across the street to the Conway Building, where Halas manned the Bears office. Telling him about Pyle's lavish offer, Healy managed to secure a salary increase from the Bears, but nothing that approached the Yankees' offer. Then he trudged back to Pyle's suite at the Morrison Hotel and declined the deal, saying because the Bears had treated him well, there was no reason to leave.

Besides, Healy found Pyle a little shady. He didn't trust him. "One of the things that prompted me to make such a quick decision," Healy said later, "was ... I figured that any man that could be married and divorced three times and come up with a woman in another room, I didn't have any business working for him." (Healy was almost correct; at the time, Pyle was twice divorced, and married to Effie Arnold.)

"If I had gone with him to New York, he might have taken care of my situation," Healy said. "Then again, he might not have."[16]

Eventually, Pyle hired Bears tackle Ralph Scott to coach the Yankees for an undisclosed sum. A former University of Wisconsin All-American and a World War I veteran, Scott went to New York and would later accuse Pyle of not paying his full salary.[17]

But at the outset of 1926, the football Yankees looked promising. Armed with a backfield that included Grange and such other former college heroes as Pooley Hubert of defending national champion Alabama, Eddie Tryon of Colgate and Harry Fry of Iowa, the New Yorkers opened at Cleveland's Luna Bowl against the Panthers, drawing a healthy 22,000, the city's largest crowd to see a pro game. Though the Yankees, attired in bright red jerseys, could muster little offense and fell to the Panthers, 10–0, they would rebound a week later in Rock Island, trouncing the Independents, 26–0.[18]

Only 5,000 showed up to see the game in Illinois, the figure held down by a rainstorm. It was an ominous sign for the fate of the new league, which would become largely determined by an unfortunate spell of lousy weather that seemed to happen that fall on most Sunday afternoons at game time. In later years, Grange couldn't recall much about his AFL days except for the downpours that dogged the teams all season. "I'll never forget that it rained every Sunday all fall," Grange said. "I don't think we had one sunny Sunday."[19]

Meanwhile, the Yankees faced another obstacle. With their baseball brethren facing the St. Louis in the World Series, Yankee Stadium remained off-limits for the footballers until late October. After playing their first four games on the road — splitting wins before mostly small crowds — the football Yankees finally made it to Yankee Stadium October 24 for the team's home opener, a marquee match-up against Wildcat Wilson and the team, which in name at least, was from Los Angeles. Pyle expected a crowd of up to 60,000, but only 20,000 appeared — a figure held down by a steady, all-day rainstorm that created a field of mud. Slipping about in the slop, the two teams could barely find their footing; several times Grange appeared poised to cut through the Wildcat defense, only to loose his balance and fall. Two cheerleaders adorned with a "Y" for Yankees on their sweaters gave a few half-hearted cheers before thinking better of it and sensibly finding the dryness of the baseball dugout.

At least the Yankees won, thanks to Eddie Tryon, who found a hole in the second half and mucked 80 yards for a touchdown. The Yanks took it, 6–0, which was the extent of Pyle's good news for the day; by game's end, only a handful of fans were still around. C.C. could take small comfort in the same water-logged condition that held the Giants' attendance down too; they drew less than 10,000 to their game at Polo Grounds.[20]

A week later, the Yankees finally got some dry weather and found their footing against the Quakers in Philadelphia, winning 27–0 before 30,000 at Franklin Field. Had it really been a year since Grange had threaded the

Penn defense in the mud and mist of the same stadium? But just when the team's fortunes seemed to turn more promising, bad weather hit again. Back in New York the following weekend, the Yankees eyed a big payday against Newark. But then it rained so hard that the city's subways were paralyzed and Yankee Stadium flooded. The game was cancelled.[21]

The competition with the NFL and the crowd-draining soggy weather took a fearful toll. Halfway through its inaugural season, Pyle's new league was having a full-fledged financial crisis. Newark would never get a chance to make up its game at Yankee Stadium or any other game for that matter; the team folded. Franchises in Cleveland and Boston did as well. Meantime, the Horsemen merged with the NFL Brooklyn Lions, improbably renamed the "Horse Lions." On the road with his professional tennis tour, Pyle hurried back to New York and tried to sort things out at league headquarters at the Hotel Astor.

Pyle engineered a quick fix, and just like that, dropped most of the league's teams. By early November, the American Football League had become a four-team league comprised of the Yankees, Philadelphia, Los Angeles and Chicago. Rumors were rampant that the two pro leagues were about to merge. Nonsense, countered Pyle. The AFL was "intrinsically strong; we have had bad luck on the weather but that kind of thing can't go on forever," he said. Reporters panned Pyle, saying his league would never survive. But recognizing a good story, they still wrote about him, in part because they genuinely liked his company. One in particular was Westbrook Pegler, the *Chicago Tribune* reporter who took to visiting Pyle in his office, and was devoting more space than ever to him in his syndicated column. Fortified by C.C.'s open liquor cabinet, a real draw in Prohibition times, he would then turn around to write columns, which as Grange recalled, would "call Pyle everything he could lay his tongue to that could go in the paper."

"Charlie sometimes would complain," Grange said, "but Westbrook would say, 'Just as long as I keep your name singular, don't holler. I'm writing about you.'"[22]

Meanwhile, the "Grangers," as the headline writers had taken to calling the Yankees, had taken six games in a row, inserting themselves by mid–November to the top of the standings in the four-team league. But then the Yankees dropped three in a row, including one to the Wildcats, a game in which both Grange and Tryon were injured, and two to Philadelphia. That dropped the team out of the league lead, which combined with the foul weather, dropped any interest in the team to a smidgen. When the Quakers clinched the league championship in that second win against the New

Yorkers, beating the Yankees, 13–6, at Shibe Park in Philadelphia, few back in New York seemed to notice. The *Times* ran a short piece on the game on page seven of its Sunday Sports Section — on the same day it devoted page after page to the Army-Navy game that drew 110,000 to the dedication of Soldier Field in Chicago.[23]

On the next day, with the Yankees set to play Chicago at Yankee Stadium, it didn't rain. But it was cold, really cold, and Grange was hurt and out of action, which limited the crowd to 2,500, who saw the New Yorkers beat the Bulls, 7–3. After the game, Mara, who lost $40,000 that season, challenged Pyle to a December 12 game. It was an attractive offer, but a date that Pyle had to turn down because of a previous commitment — the Yankees' scheduled game that day in Chicago. In hindsight, it was a another lost opportunity, Grange said later. "If a Giant-Yankee game had been arranged, it certainly would have attracted a huge gate," he said. Instead, he and the Yankees completed their season on a muddy, ice-covered field at Comiskey Park, beating the Bulls, 7–3, with only 10,000 bothering to show up.

That final game just about bankrupted Joey Sternaman's Chicago franchise. On the same day, the Giants took on the Philadelphia Quakers, which had accepted Mara's offer, and embarrassed the AFL champions, 31–0, before only 5,000 who braved more unfortunate weather — this time, a snowstorm. No one but Pyle knew how much he'd lost in trying to prop up his football league. All Grange would say is that he "lost a bundle."[24]

As it happened, Grange and the Yankees had enjoyed a respectable season, finishing 10–5 — not one team completed the 16-game schedule — while averaging nearly 15,000 fans a game. But the magic of Grange's name had dissipated, and both leagues had regressed to its sandlot root of small gates and an old-fashioned semi-pro feel. At least Pyle could take some satisfaction that his AFL consistently outdrew its rival leagues; the Giants drew an average of only 3,000 to 4,000 a game, making the Polo Grounds a lonely place on game days, and costing Mara $40,000. Looking through his binoculars, Mara would scan the stands and say, "There's no one over there either."[25]

Conventional wisdom would suggest that the AFL's overwhelming losses would be enough to sink C.C. Pyle and send him back to managing movie theaters in the Midwest. However, encouraged by his successful work with Red Grange and an emerging interest in his experiment in professional tennis, Pyle was anything but discouraged. A hard man to keep down, he was bursting with ideas.

First came the delicate matter of trying to recoup losses from the football season. Similar to the way the NFL had dispatched Ernie Nevers and the Duluth Eskimos on a tour of the West Coast, Pyle sent Grange and the Yankees off for a 10-game, post-season barnstorming tour of Texas and California despite his earlier pledge not to do so. Most players earned up to $200 a game; Grange earned more, a lot more, so much that he managed to regain some of his regular-season losses incurred as a team co-owner. Meeting the Yankees in Los Angeles, where he had gone with his professional tennis tour, Pyle turned to another new idea, perhaps his most outlandish promotion yet: hockey.[26]

In Los Angeles, C.C. joined Grange and Los Angeles boxing promoter Tom Gallery to announce the formation of a four-team California ice hockey league. In launching the league, they bought the Winter Garden Ice Palace in Los Angeles, made plans to spend $220,000 to build a rink in San Francisco, and prepared to recruit top hockey players from the East Coast. Putting Grange's old chum Beans DeWolfe in charge of the hockey operation, C.C. barely caught his breath and said he was revamping the American Football League, which would be comprised of six teams for next season.[27]

As with the domed stadium, Pyle's hockey league was mostly bluster. West Coast sports fans took scant interest in hockey, and although the amateur teams like the Hollywood Millionaires and the Los Angeles Richfields had a few spirited games, the league would die out by 1933. California's hockey high-water mark was probably the western swing in late 1927 made by the National Hockey League's Chicago Black Hawks. In addition to games at the Winter Garden against the Richfields and the Winter Garden Maroons, the Black Hawks' exhibitions featured the usual vaudevillian Pyle touches, like speed-skating competitions and lots of chances for spectators to gaze upon Grange.[28]

Red didn't mind. Always gracious, he was willing to do whatever Pyle asked of him. He and C.C. had become friends as they dabbled in movies and had a high old time in Los Angeles, living like fraternity boys with DeWolf and Yankee football coach Ralph Scott in a spacious 10-room house they rented on fashionable Gramercy Place in Hollywood. There, they enjoyed weekly poker games, dined on Scott's fried chicken dinners — the Yankee coach was an accomplished cook as a result of his ranch-hand days in Montana — and caught up with C.C.'s old speed-demon friend, Barney Oldfield. A real highlight of their stay were the regular Sunday evening parties at the home of Gallery's former wife, actress ZaSu Pitts.[29]

Meantime, Pyle had signed Grange for a new film venture, *Racing Romeo*, to be directed again by Sam Wood. "Romeo" was Red, a down on his luck, small-town garage owner who wants to marry Jobyna Ralston, the same actress Grange had seen in *The Freshman* during his fateful meeting with Pyle at the Champaign movie theater. But when Romeo can't seem to earn enough money racing cars to impress her wealthy aunt and win her hand, the aunt insists that Grange ditch racing if he intends to marry her precious niece. Romeo agrees, but sneaks back on the sly to the race track and speeds through the countryside to beat all comers to win both the race and Jobyna's hand.

This time, Red thoroughly enjoyed himself during the five-week shoot. For starters, he did his own driving, most of it fast around the track at Ventura Fairgrounds. But problems plagued the film from the get-go. Wasps stung Grange and Walter Hiers, who played his mechanic. A stunt driver was killed in a car wreck at the track. Then Pyle got into a nasty, prolonged scrap with movie executives over the percentage of profits from Grange's previous film, *One Minute to Play*. Film executives grew so exasperated with Pyle that they barely publicized the film; despite solid reviews, it quickly died at the box office.[30]

No wonder Pyle and Grange became anxious to get back to the East Coast, where NFL owners had gathered in New York to plot strategy for the 1927 football season. Realizing that the AFL would find it difficult to field even a six-team league, C.C. took stock of the bundle he had already lost in the "Grange" league, and sent an olive branch to the NFL by proposing a series of merger discussions. NFL owners had already taken drastic actions to achieve fiscal solvency, having lopped off 12 of their franchises.

This time, the NFL owners were willing to talk with Pyle. In July, the NFL added a team in Dayton, to be called the Triangles, bringing the league to an even dozen franchises. And in early August, the two leagues reached a peaceful compromise, with the NFL announcing that it had absorbed the few remaining AFL franchises. It sounded like an even swap, but in reality, Pyle had little leverage. The NFL owners dropped the AFL's Los Angeles and Chicago franchises, and finally made C.C.'s Yankees a part of the NFL, though granting them only four home games at Yankee Stadium. All were dates when the Giants were on the road.[31]

At least the Yanks looked like a team to be reckoned with in the 1927 season. Most of its 1926 team was back, supplemented by new offensive weapons like back "Wild Bill" Kelly from the University of Montana and a pair of ends, future Pro Hall of Famer Ray Flaherty of Gonzaga and Red Badgro from Southern California. Grange and the Yanks took their first game, 6–3, against Dayton, and a second, 13–7, against the Cleveland

Bulldogs, which featured the dynamic rookie Benny Friedman, the former three-time University of Michigan All-American who liked to shock the purists by passing on first down. The Yankees won the third game as well, an easy 19–0 victory over Buffalo on Columbus Day, and looked eagerly toward their next game, a showdown against the Bears at Cubs Park.[32]

The game marked Grange's first game in Chicago since he'd played for the Bears back in 1925. Like the Yankees, the Bears were undefeated, prompting a larger than capacity crowd of 40,000 or so to storm Cubs Park, with thousands more breaking through the center-field gates and taking positions around the perimeter of the field. Pyle couldn't stand that some people snuck into the park without tickets, knowing he was missing out on some extra dollars. "It literally broke (his) heart to see all those people get in for free," said Grange, only half-kidding. The Bears jumped to a 12–0 lead, which is where the score stood in the game's final furious minutes when Eddie Tryon threw a desperation pass to Grange, who leapt high in the air, collided with the Bears George Trafton, and landed awkwardly on the ground, his cleats caught in the soil. Tumbling into Grange, Trafton severely twisted Red's knee, leaving him sprawled on the field in excruciating pain. Play stopped, and Grange, too injured to walk, was carried off the field and through the parting thousands into the locker room. Some said that Trafton, known for playing rough, had deliberately hurt Grange. Not so, Red insisted of his former teammate, who helped carry him off the field. It was an accident, pure and simple.[33]

Grange had a torn ligament, a serious injury. Today, football players commonly undergo surgery to repair damaged tendons. But that wasn't the case in 1927 when doctors failed to recognize how badly Red was injured, and actually cleared him to play the following week in Green Bay. Without Grange, Pyle's Yankees were just another team and hardly a draw. Even as Pyle pumped out optimistic reports that Grange would be back soon, Red's knee remained swollen and discolored, and he spent weeks on crutches. Years later, Grange confirmed what had been an open secret in the early days of pro football — that team officials routinely covered up injuries to its best players, usually to protect the gate. "No one knew it at the time," he said, "but they had seen 'the Galloping Ghost' gallop for the last time."[34]

For a time anyway, Pyle's deception worked. Expecting to see Grange in action the following Sunday, the largest crowd to ever watch a pro game in Green Bay cheered when Grange, in full uniform but walking with a cane, limped to the sideline. But he didn't play a down, and the listless Yanks lost, 13–0 to the Packers. Nor did Red play the next week in Chicago, or the week after in Cleveland, where only 2,500 appeared in inclement weather to see Benny Friedman beat the New Yorkers, 15–0. With the team tanking, its star player out and attendance plummeting, the Yankees faced a dismal future as they prepared to face the Chicago Cardinals at Yankee Stadium.

Days before the game, Pyle announced that Grange would not be in the starting lineup, but would play. He stuck to his word, and at the start of the second quarter, Grange jogged toward the huddle "amid tumultuous applause which lasted for fully three minutes," the *Times* reported. Red played the rest of the quarter, rested in the third and played the fourth, having little impact on the result. Ray Flaherty had a good game, though, and scored three touchdowns as the Yankees coasted, 20–6.[35]

In retrospect, Pyle's insistence on keeping his badly injured meal ticket in the lineup was wrong, though par for the course in the era. "Pyle's economically motivated but reckless scheduling methods ... (didn't) aid Grange in making a gradual comeback from his injury," wrote Grange's biographer John Carroll. Red had only missed three games, but his devastating knee injury essentially ended his career as pro football's big attraction and first great broken-field runner. "From then on, I was just a so-so football player," Grange said. "I was strictly a straight runner.... The woods are full of straight runners." Red would spend the next eight months on crutches and visit doctor after doctor, one of whom placed his swollen knee in a barrel of ice and another who put it in a cast. But nothing worked.[36]

Grange soldiered on anyway. On Thanksgiving at Yankee Stadium against Cleveland, the Yankees jumped to a two-touchdown lead, but with Red never able to get on track, saw it slip away. Cleveland won going away, 30–19, for the Yankees' first home defeat. "I was in bad shape and I knew it, but I couldn't give up," Grange said. "No one in the stands that day knew I left my cane in the dressing room before coming out on the field."[37]

The Yankee season ended in virtual anonymity. The team went 7–8–1, was shut out by the Giants, and dropped far more money than in the previous season. Just as distressing to Pyle was the stellar performance of their cross-town rivals. By winning their last nine games, the Giants won their first NFL championship, compiling an 11–1 record and giving Tim Mara an emotional victory over C.C. Pyle for supremacy of New York's professional football world.[38]

Grange played out the string in pain, but still decided to accompany the Yankees on what had become a traditional post-season barnstorming tour of the Pacific Coast. Playing those extra games only aggravated his injured knee further, so much so that Grange, football's most electric player, wondered if he might be forced to retire at the age of 24. "It became apparent I had done irreparable damage to the knee," Red said. "For the first time since I was hurt, nearly four months before, I began worrying over the possibility that I might be through as a football player."[39]

Accompanying his New York Yankees to California, C.C. Pyle also faced an uncertain future. His football team had gone from promising to mediocre, and his star player, Red Grange, seemed finished, a point he seemed to confirm with the announcement that he was looking to buy a ranch and settle in Southern California. But Pyle, always the last man to brood, was keeping any ideas of failure to himself and looking on how to build on his latest and greatest venture. Actually, he'd been at it for some months already and it was starting to look like another winner.[40]

5

"People Will Pay to See Anyone They Hate"

Damon Runyon was edgy. On a rainy day in February 1926, he was sitting in the lobby of the Biltmore Hotel in Los Angeles, brooding about the great story he was missing. Even as he continued to prowl about the West Coast for columns about boxers and other athletes and promoters, Runyon would rather had been some 6,000 miles away on the sun-splashed French Riviera, scene of the era's greatest women's tennis match, one pitting the great French champion, Suzanne Lenglen, against her American counterpart, Helen Wills.[1]

Despite its elitist, country club roots, 1920s-era tennis in the U.S. was exploding in popularity, thanks in large part to the emergence of new stars like Lenglen and graceful American Bill Tilden. Colorful, temperamental and quotable, they moved about like movie stars, with sportswriters and society columnists clamoring for scraps of on- and off-court news regarding their exploits. At the pinnacle of era's tennis world were the "big three" tournaments — Wimbledon, which took place in the southeast outskirts of London; the U.S. Nationals at Forest Hills in New York City, and the French championships in Paris. Played on clay and thrown open to non–French players the previous year for the first time, the French Open underscored this new sporting craze, which generated headlines and bouts of patriotic fandom. Throw in the worldwide attention given to the annual Davis Cup competition, while British and American women competed annually for the Wightman Cup, and the tennis revolution was in full swing.[2]

Lording over the tennis world were its imperious ruling bodies, the national tennis associations like the U.S. Lawn Tennis Association and the International Lawn Tennis Foundation (ILTF), based in London. The top tournaments and cup competitions were for amateur players only, with amateurs

C.C. Pyle asked both Suzanne Lenglen (left) and Big Bill Tilden to join his professional tour. Lenglen agreed, while Tilden, citing his interest in playing in the Davis Cup, refused. From the Bain Collection (Library of Congress, Prints and Photographs Division).

prohibited from accepting prize money or teaching tennis, forcing many top players to scramble earn a living. Tilden earned a significant amount from writing tennis novels for young adults, with the loosely fictionalized hero, modeled after himself, always coming through with a victory and an important life lesson. For the most part, Tilden and other top players depended on under-the-table payments from promoters and from income drawn from the "pro-am" circuit in which they played with teaching pros or regional-level amateurs.[3]

Tilden and Lenglen dominated tennis through the decade, and had out-sized personalities and egos to match their talents. As the leader of the powerful U.S. Davis Cup team and a perennial U.S. Open winner, Tilden was the more popular of the two outside France. Nicknamed "Big" Bill for his powerful 6'4" frame, Tilden turned tennis into performance art. Entering the court like a model on a runway, he always put on a show, often falling behind lackadaisically before fighting back with his booming serve and cat-like quickness to win narrowly and with drama. Big Bill's role model was

Mary Garden, an opera singer and a close friend who called Tilden a "tennis artist," advising him that "artists always know better than anyone when they're right." A product of the Philadelphia Mainline, Big Bill, at least on the surface, was a graceful sophisticate equally at home mentoring younger players or moving among the café society and Hollywood set with close friends like Charlie Chaplin and Douglas Fairbanks, Jr. The world had yet to catch on to Tilden's dark side as a troubled megalomaniac, a lonely, disturbed man, and the emotionally starved sexual predator of adolescent boys.[4]

The temperamental Lenglen was a complex mixture of ego, élan and emotion. Born in 1899 in Paris, Lenglen had been rigorously molded by her autocratic father, Charles, into a player of unsurpassed accuracy and grace, the premier player of her day. "She can draw you into position despite everything you do to avoid it," said a rival, the American Mary Browne. "She can make three or four plays and tell you when she will end the point." To Commander George Hillyard, secretary of the All-England Club, which ran the Wimbledon tournament, Lenglen's play was "the outcrop of genius."[5]

Like Tilden, Lenglen was a diva who basked in the applause and attention. Hardly beautiful in a conventional sense, she was striking and slightly exotic — a birdlike woman with prominent buck teeth and prone to stylish white silk dresses and a head-wrap. A right-hander, Lenglen rose to public acclaim quickly and decisively in storming her way through the Wimbledon Challenge Round in 1919 while wearing a high-necked dress that swept the floor. In doing so, she easily handled the seven-time champion, 40-year-old Dorothea Douglass Chambers. After the second set, the Parisian calmed herself with a sip of brandy before rescuing two match points to secure a dramatic 10–8, 4–6, 9–7 victory.

The torch had been passed. Lenglen became the tennis world's first international superstar, sweeping Wimbledon six times from 1919 to 1925 and dominating her sport. Like Tilden, she saw tennis as performance art, once describing her ability to reach shots that others could not as "a cat walking on hot bricks." She became one of her country's greatest sports heroes, lionized throughout France as the "Goddess" and joined by the flamboyant René Lacoste and the Four Musketeers, the very top of the era's French tennis dynasty.

"My method?" Lenglen said with an air of diffidence. "I don't think I have any. I just throw dignity to the winds and think of nothing but the game. I try to hit the ball with all my force and send it where my opponent is not. I say to myself, 'let the other one do the running.'"[6]

But like Tilden, Lenglen carried inner demons. Driven by her overly

Convincing French tennis star Suzanne Lenglen to tour America was one of C.C. Pyle's greatest sports triumphs. She was a six-time Wimbledon singles winner. From the Bain Collection (Library of Congress, Prints and Photographs Division).

protective father, Lenglen was often an emotional wreck. Petrified of losing, she had tantrums and dissolved into periodic bouts of tears on the court. Losing badly to American Molla Mallory in the fourth round of the 1921 U.S. Open, Lenglen wept openly, had a sudden coughing fit, and then withdrew. Her Wimbledon streak ended with a similar dose of drama in 1926 when she outraged the British by keeping Queen Mary waiting in the Royal Box after a match. Though her tardiness was due to an error in communication and not a snub, the British were outraged and piled on the criticism. Lenglen dropped out of Wimbledon, and never returned.[7]

This mix of genius, artistry and drama was delicious fodder to talented writers like Runyon and Grantland Rice. For them, Susanne Lenglen was a prima donna, a magnetic personality and a bona fide star with whom the right promoter could make a mint. Imagine Lenglen touring America! So sitting in the lobby of the Biltmore, Runyon turned to the man sitting next to him, promoter Bill Pickens, who promptly belted out the name of the one man who could turn the pipe dream into reality: "Pyle!"[8]

It was no irony that Runyon should bring up his idea with Pickens. At 52, William Hickman Pickens, known as "Champ," was the man to know in Hollywood. A Birmingham, Alabama, native, Pickens had used his southern charm, powers of persuasion and passion for fast cars and flying objects to build a thriving Los Angeles-based public relations business. Need something in California? Pickens was your man, an eternal optimist with a flair for the unexpected and a mastery for spin. An event that went badly may have lost money but was always "an artistic success" in Pickens' world. It almost didn't begin that way, for Pickens started his career in Birmingham by standing on a street corner with a primitive Edison phonograph, featuring music heard through ear pieces after dropping a nickel in the slot. But when megaphones ousted the ear pieces, Pickens turned to promotion.

A bicycle racer in his younger days, Pickens had established himself earlier in the century by convincing Henry Ford to use Pyle's old biking friend, Barney Oldfield, to set a series of speed records in Ford's pre–Model-T "999." The records, most of them set on Florida beaches, enthralled the nation.

By 1910, Pickens was staging balloon and airplane races as well as contests pitting airplanes *against* cars. He staged shows of daredevil pilots in the early days of flight, billing the aerial circuses as "three miles long and a mile high," and became a sought-after expert on the future of flight. Billing Oldfield as the "Daredevil of the Ground," he had him taken on a dashing aviator named Lincoln Beachey, the "Demon of the Air," in a series of match races he called "The Championship of the World." Understatement just wasn't part of Pickens' world. In 1914, the duels ended during a stunt of upside-down flying when Beachey piloted his plane into San Francisco Bay.

That same year, Pickens scored a truly spectacular coup — a night air show over Washington, D.C., which he promoted by stocking salt bags on street corners throughout the capital with pamphlets that warned, "This is what would happen if an enemy were to bomb Washington." The attention worked; the U.S. Government soon began buying airplanes for war purposes.[9]

Pickens was able to engineer another airplane-related coup by inaugurating U.S. air mail service. In Santa Monica, he paunched dirt-track racing at Ascot Speedway and, as Pyle was well aware, had arranged the visit of the great Finnish distance runner Paavo Nurmi, the "Phantom Finn," after the 1924 Olympic Games to the Coliseum in Los Angeles, where he ran two races before 100,000 people.[10]

In some ways, Paavo Nurmi had a reputation as temperamental as Suzanne

Lenglen, making Pickens the choice to lure the tennis star to America. It really could work, Runyon insisted to Pickens. Besides, the writer added, playing tennis was a whole lot safer for its participants than flying airplanes indoors. "I wasn't much interested at first," Pickens said. "But Runyon kept ribbing me and finally convinced me that Suzanne would be a 'wow' in our big cities."[11]

Pickens happened to have just finished his stint as C.C. Pyle's front man during the West Coast part of the Red Grange tour. Pickens wasn't due to see Pyle in the near future, but Runyon was, in Chicago — and soon. Might want to mention the idea, Pickens told Runyon.

In late February in Chicago, Runyon met with Pyle, insisting that Suzanne Lenglen, like Red Grange, could take America by storm. The temperamental Lenglen starring in the U.S.? "No (way)," someone barked. "People hate her." Besides, they said, she was controversial, a tad too exotic and strange for mainstream America. Upon hearing that comment, Pyle knew instinctively that Runyon was spot on in his belief that a Lenglen tour would be a gold mine. "The fact that people hated her was enough for me," C.C. said. "People will pay to see anybody they hate."[12]

Just like that, Pyle decided to bring Suzanne Lenglen to America. As with Red Grange, he had a gut feeling, a hunch that getting the temperamental French star to turn pro and tour America could earn millions by peddling the personality more than the athlete.

It would start with Pickens. Pyle wired him in Los Angeles with instructions to take the next train to Chicago. From there, Pickens would set out immediately for New York for a ship to France, where with considerable persuasion, ego-stroking and the promise of a big check, he would attempt to secure her services to play a series of matches across America. The price could be steep, Pickens cautioned, possibly $15,000. But Pyle wasn't fazed in the least. "Sign her," he told Pickens. "Just sign her."[13]

Stopping in New York before setting sail for France, Pickens got a sense of just how difficult a challenge he faced. Edward Moss, secretary of the U.S. Lawn Tennis Association (USLTA), told Pickens that the organization would never agree to a professional promoter soiling the ranks of amateur tennis. In fact, the USLTA was negotiating to bring Lenglen on a U.S. tour of its own, a fact Moss neglected to share with Pickens and the real reason for the association's tepid reaction to Pyle's scheme. Pickens then caught up with French light-heavyweight fighter Georges Carpentier, a close friend of the Lenglen family, who said the French tennis star would never ever turn pro since the under-the-table money she earned as an "amateur" provided a handsome living.

Pickens sailed anyway. "I didn't mind Moss so much," he ruminated later, "but I had wasted a good cigar on Georges." Warned by a telegram from Moss that Pickens was headed across the Atlantic to sign her, Lenglen professed no interest in turning professional. "I play for my own pleasure and am completely free to do so when and where I desire," she said. "This is merely another one of the canards launched by the so-called sportswriters in the United States who always seem to take pleasure in inventing all kinds of unpleasant and untrue things about me, cooking up matrimonial prospects and similar nonsense every week."[14]

Considering Pyle proposed to pay Lenglen a pile of cash, one wonders what the USLTA told her about Pickens and Pyle. To Suzanne Lenglen's biographer, Larry Engelmann, "the USLTA position was clear: it was not about to split its profits with an upstart lowbrow promoter."

Pickens continued to forge ahead, doing his best to maneuver in as much secrecy as possible in what was developing into a major news story in both Europe and the U.S. Sniffing out a possible scoop, reporters caught up to Pickens in Paris, forcing him to invent some yarns about why he was really there, although everyone knew the real reason. He was arranging a European tour for Red Grange, he told them. No, strike that; he was trying to deliver an autographed football to the Prince of Wales. It took Victor Breyer, editor of the Paris-based newspaper *L'Echo des Sports* to spill the beans of Pickens' real intent, adding that he was shocked at the promoter's "temerity" in traveling halfway around the globe to sign Suzanne Lenglen. That sent Bill to the dictionary he kept in his vest pocket to look up the meaning of "temerity." "It meant 'gall,'" Pickens said, "which made me a millionaire in the 'temerity' business."[15]

French sportswriters joined the boxer Carpentier in telling Pickens that Lenglen would remain an amateur. But Pickens plunged ahead in full-fledged pursuit of the French tennis diva, thinking that if he could actually meet her face to face, he could convince her to change her mind. "Pickens ... found that every Frenchman he met claimed to know Suzanne Lenglen very well," wrote Engelmann, "and to understand her thinking well enough to predict precisely what she would do when confronted with the chance to become a professional tennis player."[16]

The presence of Pickens created an old-fashioned media feeding frenzy. Would Lenglen sign, or wouldn't she? Rumors flew, and so did opinions. The Paris edition of the *New York Herald Tribune* ran a prominent front-page photograph of Pyle, accompanied by a claim that Pickens was about to sign Lenglen for $200,000. The prospect of such a staggering payoff would be enough to humble most any athlete, but all it did was to send Lenglen's father, Charles, known simply as "Papa," into a full-scale, high-decibel tirade of anti–Americanism. "If I were a younger man, I would give a magnificent kick in the seat of the pants to all those so-disgusting American journalists who have written such filthy things insulting my daughter's honor," Papa yelled. "The American newspapers have printed such vile lies about Suzanne that I will not talk to any American reporter."[17]

It was reported that a Scottish promoter had offered Lenglen a lucrative contract. Asked by a reporter whether she had been offered $10,000 for a professional contract, Lenglen denied it, insulted not so much at the idea of turning professional, but at what she considered a piddling amount, unworthy of her considerable talents. And no, she added, there had been no offers from Scotland.[18]

Actually, Pickens had yet to even meet Lenglen or make a proposal. When he finally got around to calling Papa Lenglen to introduce himself as C.C. Pyle's representative, the testy coach hung up on him. Deciding that he had better deal with Suzanne directly, Pickens trailed Lenglen to Monte Carlo where she was playing an exhibition match. He tried seeing her before the match, but couldn't. Afterwards, Pickens was rebuffed again when Lenglen left the court, tossed her racquets to an attendant, and fled in a limousine that whisked her away to Nice. Pickens hurried to his rental car and followed the limo, hoping to catch her the following day at her hotel, only to find that Lenglen had abruptly checked out and left for a vacation.

Most would grow discouraged at all the brushoffs. But not Pickens, the old hand for whom the chase was all part of the job. Seeing Lenglen's performance — as getting a taste of her dramatic persona and the worshipful countrymen who cheered her every shot — convinced him that C.C. Pyle was right in his firm belief that the French tennis star could be an enormous hit in America. "The expensive gondola cheered me up," Pickens said, referring to the limo that had driven Lenglen away from the match in Monte Carlo. "Only amateurs with large incomes can afford those carts."[19]

Newspapermen continued to throw out impossibly large numbers of how much Pickens and Pyle were set to offer Suzanne Lenglen to play tennis in America. Westbrook Pegler reported that C.C. would probably offer her $200,000 — "a downright hilarious number of francs" — while keeping another $200,000 for himself. Others wrote that Pickens was set to offer Lenglen $250,000 for tennis and another $100,000 for the movies. Pickens called the Lenglens again, this time reaching Anias "Mama" Lenglen, who insisted that she was Suzanne's business manager, and listened carefully to

the proposal. It was a door opener, and earned Pickens a date to meet the
tennis queen and get down to business.[20]

They met. Pickens found Lenglen dressed for the big meeting in negligee
and lying on a chaise lounge while stroking a Pomeranian in her arms. It was
as if his real meeting was with Gloria Swanson and not a tennis player, but
Pickens was clearly impressed. Beyond the negligee, Lenglen was a woman of
steely character, someone who, even with her mother present, could speak for
herself, he thought. "I could see that she was no school-girl tennis star who
could be salved with one of those what-you-owe-the-sport arguments," Pickens said.

Pitching the idea of the American tour, Pickens shrewdly figured that
one of the obstacles had been Lenglen's moral opposition to the term "professional." So he never brought it up, stating that Pyle wanted to be her
manager in everything *but* tennis. The great Suzanne Lenglen, he declared,
would take the U.S. by storm as an artiste and not an athlete.[21]

Pickens' appeasement to the tennis diva's sizable ego pushed the right
buttons. Of particular concern to Lenglen was how she would be received
in America, given the disaster of her only trip there when in the 1921 U.S.
Open at Forest Hills, she had broken down on the court and been savaged
in the press as an unstable prima donna. An aberration, a one-time blip,
assured Pickens, who called it the unfortunate reaction of "the tennis cliques
of Long Island" and hardly the "real" America, where she would be hailed
as a star. In the heartland, Pickens told Suzanne, real Americans were waiting to shower her with both affection and their dollars. Recognizing his
place, Pickens then assured her that C.C. Pyle wasn't just another greedy
American publicist, but a real gentleman ready to cater to her needs and
ensure that the great American tennis tour was carried off in style. Best of
all, Pickens added, C.C. wasn't even a New Yorker.[22]

Pickens said that Lenglen would play tennis in America as an amateur
while earning income by syndicating her ghost-written newspaper articles
and marketing her novel, *The Love Game*. Saving his grandest pitch until
last, Pickens said that what he and Pyle really had in mind was putting
Lenglen, bad teeth and all, on the Broadway stage as the star of a musical
comedy. After that, Pickens suggested, stage stardom was a surefire path to
the movies, possibly a "romantic film story" in Hollywood.

Adoring crowds! Broadway! Hollywood! With stars in her eyes, Lenglen
was smitten. Maybe Americans weren't so bad after all, she told herself.
Maybe her dismal 1921 trip to Forest Hills really wasn't her fault, but stemmed
from the overreaction of those snobby New Yorkers. Pickens, the old hand,

called their preliminary discussions a form of "verbal shadow boxing" in anticipation of the real purpose of their meeting — money.

Lenglen threw out a figure — $200,000 — saying that she had been offered that amount to turn professional back in 1918, just after the Great War had ended. Though Pickens doubted that he and Pyle could ever raise that amount of capital, he figured his best strategy was to keep it simple by quickly agreeing to the amount, and to get it in writing. He drew up an agreement for the $200,000, and Lenglen, in the presence of her mother, signed. The three drank a toast to Suzanne's new career as a non-professional "artistic celebrity," and Pickens hurriedly pocketed the document and departed before anyone could change their minds.[23]

Back at the hotel, Pickens' telephone rang. On the other end was a frantic Suzanne Lenglen, saying that she had made a grave mistake by signing the contract and insisting they meet again. They did, with Lenglen accompanied by an American named Charles Willen, who she introduced as her manager. Demanding to review the contract, Willen pestered Pickens, but the wily p.r. pro refused to produce the document, creating the tall tale that it was being copied and could only be seen the following day at the earliest. In the interim, Willen demanded they renegotiate, saying he had been planning to accompany Lenglen on an American tour, "There is a lot of money waiting for her over there and I am not going to allow you or Pyle to put anything over on her."[24]

Pickens assured Willen that the contract was on the up-and-up, and that the funds due Lenglen would be deposited in time in "a weather-proof bank." Back and forth the talk went like a long tennis volley before the principals emerged with a slightly amended contract. But neither Lenglen nor Willen was a match for Pickens. The one major change: a requirement that C.C. visit France in August to close the deal.[25]

Pyle arrived in late July 1926, landing in Pourville, near Dieppe, and accompanied by his attorney, Colonel Bill Hayward. Not just any lawyer, Hayward was a bold choice — a member of a prominent New York family and a French hero who had been awarded the French Legion of Honor for a leading a National Guard regiment of African-American soldiers in the Great War. Known as the 15th "Heavy Foot," Hayward's men had withstood furious German assaults on the front lines with gallantry and courage, and then earned the enduring admiration of the French by laying tracks that rebuilt the railways. "Magnifique!" exalted a French officer as he watched Hayward and his men work their magic. All told, they spent 191 days in combat, longer than any other American units in the war. "My men never retire," Hayward said gruffly. "They move forward or they die."[26]

Hayward and Pyle were a formidable pair, a duo of dashing and charismatic Americans. Wasting little time, they headed immediately to Lenglen's summer house, where Willen would not be present, to finalize the deal. At the meeting, Pyle did most of the talking, and picked up where Pickens had left off by appealing to Lenglen's vanity. Resurrecting that dreaded word, "professional," C.C. was direct, and with his deep baritone and authoritarian air, created an appealing scenario: In America, getting paid to play tennis didn't carry quite the slight that it did in Europe. Being a pro in America, Pyle explained, would give Suzanne control of her own destiny and not cost her social status. Sign up, C.C. preached, and the wealth that she would earn in several months could provide a lifetime of comfort.

"You are not always going to be the star you are today," Pyle told Lenglen. "You won't always be sitting on top of the world. If your social standing and friends are such that you'll lose them by turning professional, you can console yourself with the thought that the money you'll get will be worth a hundred times more than the things you'll lose."

Pyle, ever the realist, knew that athletic fame was fleeting and athletes needed to get all they could while possible. "By turning professional," he told Lenglen, "you can insure yourself enough to enable you to live in comfort all the rest of your life. Ten years from now if you go into a smart hotel and order an elaborate luncheon, you won't be able to pay for it by reminding the head waiter that in 1926 you were an amateur tennis star."[27]

Reaching into his suit pocket, Pyle produced a contract that he left with Lenglen, with the promise that he and Hayward would be by shortly with the money. Once in Paris, the dynamic American duo took care of the overmatched Charles Willen, assuring him that everything was set, while conveniently overlooking the fact that they really didn't have the money. In Paris a few days later, Lenglen met Pyle for dinner and dancing, but no business talk.

For Lenglen, the flattery and attention from this dashing American promoter came at precisely the right time. It was that summer at Wimbledon where she stood up the queen at center court and was undergoing particularly venomous treatment from the British. That unnerved the fragile tennis diva even more than usual, so much so that she had withdrawn from the Irish Championships, one of the few European titles that still eluded her. And she was seeking medical help for her nerves back in France.

In securing Suzanne Lenglen for his tour, Pyle told Lenglen about the promise of America. Here was a new continent to conquer, he assured her, where most audiences were nowhere near as stuffy as those in Forest Hills or the hyper-critical Europeans. Back in Pourville, Pyle met Lenglen again and rewrote the contract, with so many people signing the document that it looked like a petition, Pickens said later. Pyle had even thought to invite a dutiful Red Grange to the signing. It was a shrewd move because adding America's greatest football star to photos of the announcement meant front-page news back home.[28]

Suzanne Lenglen's American tour would start in October at Madison Square Garden in New York, and then head over a four-month period to some 40 cities across the United States and Canada before finishing in Havana. As with the Grange football tour, the pace would be punishing, and reporters wondered if the schedule was too much. "All I am doing in commercializing tennis is what the tennis associations are doing," Pyle said. "Why, they even make the players pay entrance fees. The present system forces players to sneak a little money on the side. I am giving the player an opportunity to make money doing the thing he or she does best. Furthermore, tennis is a healthy game and more Americans should play it."

Pyle never revealed how much he actually paid Lenglen, but the figure was almost certainly nowhere near the $200,000 trumpeted in the press. "That is entirely between us," C.C. said of the precise figure, adding that it was his policy not to divulge financial arrangements. "The reports about the sums she is to receive have all been unauthorized." Not that there was any need to correct the figure, Pyle reasoned, since it made great press. For the moment, C.C. basked in the triumph of signing the temperamental star, a feat that few had thought possible. "I found her extremely affable and ready to cooperate," Pyle said of Lenglen. Asked about Suzanne's prospects of making it big in Hollywood, C.C. suggested she had first better get her buck teeth fixed. "For the movies, you know," he emphasized.[29]

Awash with attention and new riches, Lenglen seemed like a new woman. Yes, Suzanne insisted, she would deal with her teeth provided Pyle could find a good dentist. She had even overcome her phobia about the concept of professionalism, deciding the term suited her after all. "I have tried to be a real amateur," Lenglen said. "Now I'm going to be a *real* professional. I have given my life to tennis so far, and I feel I am entitled to derive something from the game."

Pyle agreed. "Now that she has become reconciled to the idea of turning professional," he said of Lenglen, "she is into it hammer and tongs."[30]

Tennis officials ridiculed the signing, saying there was no one on Lenglen's level, leaving her without suitable competition. That much was true; the only Americans anywhere in her league were Helen Wills, followed by Molla Mallory, the opponent when Lenglen withdrew from Forest Hills in 1921, and Mary Browne, the world's sixth-ranked amateur. Pyle kept mum amidst the criticism. "He allowed the officials and the sportswriters to nibble at this negative bait until he was all chewed up," Pickens said. "He had plenty of announcements to make, but he was milking one cow at a time."[31]

The reality was that Pyle was in a bind about finding a worthy opponent for Lenglen. He approached Wills' father, Charles, and offered $100,000 for Helen to turn pro and join the tour to play Lenglen. But Charles Wills turned him down flat, despite Helen's remarks to a reporter that such a large amount of money was tempting. "If some one offered me that much," she said, leaving out the fact that Pyle already had, "I'd have to do some serious thinking about the matter." Molla Mallory passed as well, setting $500,000 as her price for turning pro, knowing full well that was out of reach. "I'm too expensive," she said. Needing some top men to complement the women's matches, Pyle asked Frenchmen Henri Cochet and René Lacoste, both of whom turned him down. "I do not think much of the future of professionalism," Lacoste said. "Tennis must remain really a sport and not become a profession. Besides, amateurs are numerous, well organized and very firm on this point."[32]

Even before Pyle had sailed to France, he had approached Big Bill Tilden, who had demanded and secured at least $50,000 for the tour before changing his mind and turning the offer down. Big Bill said he would rather remain an amateur for the chance to help the U.S. regain the Davis Cup and then become a professional, reasoning he'd be worth twice as much.

"If any of the boys had won the championship for America this year, I would have been on your doorstep," Tilden told C.C. "But I do not think I am through as a tennis player (and) I have a peculiar feeling that I ought to win back the championship."

When Tilden suggested he join the following year instead, Pyle turned the tables and refused this time. "Hell no," C.C. thundered. "We need you now. Next year, professional tennis will be organized and we won't need you."

"Mr. Tilden," said Pyle, "(remaining an amateur) is a fine feeling, but it won't buy any bread and butter. I think you are a damn fool."

"Mr. Pyle," replied Tilden, "I think you are right."[33]

Finally, C.C. nabbed Mary Browne, who from 1912 to 1914 had won U.S. titles in singles, doubles and mixed doubles. A Santa Monica, California, native, Browne played the "Coast" game, combining an aggressive net game and a powerful serve, and captained the U.S. Wightman Cup team.

Though Browne was 35 and clearly on the downside of a long career, she was a name — quotable and smart, noted for her charitable work, and a remarkably versatile athlete in the Babe Zaharias mold. Browne had been playing golf for only a few years when at the 1924 U.S. Women's Amateur Championship, she almost won, taking second to Dorothy Campbell-Hurd.[34]

Browne signed with Pyle for $15,000 and 5 percent of the tour's gate receipts. At first, Browne admitted she felt "contaminated" at the idea of turning pro, but soon fell under C.C.'s sway and logic, admitting that making a living at the game she had played for two decades was attractive. Browne had been paid travel expenses, but the payments were so miniscule that she often dipped into her own savings just to get to and from tournaments. "It is necessary for me to make money," Browne said with bluntness, "and as I can play tennis probably better than anything else, I have come to the decision to play professional tennis."

In casting her lot with C.C. Pyle, Browne recognized that professional tennis was the wave of the future, and would actually help to clean up an amateur sport riddled with hypocrisy. "It will eliminate commercialism from amateur tennis and end the bickering that has been going on inside (the U.S. Lawn Tennis Association) over players writing for money. If we have two distinct classes of amateur and professional, as in other sports, the people who can afford to play tennis purely for the love of it will be amateurs and those who haven't the means will be professionals." The new tennis crowds were more democratic — "the masses rather than the classes," Browne explained — which made them anxious to size up new stars and see the old favorites knocked off. And Browne understood both her supporting role and Lenglen's appeal. "People will want to see Mlle. Lenglen once regardless of the tennis, but there must be competition between high-class players if professional tennis is to stay," she said. "Mlle. Lenglen, of course, is the greatest player in the world."

On September 23, hundreds of fans turned up at the dock to wish Lenglen bon voyage as she and Mama Lenglen left France aboard the *France*. Suzanne hadn't practiced much over the previous three weeks, having spent most of her time shopping for dresses on the Rue de la Paix in Paris and vacationing in St. Moritz, but wasn't concerned. "I never felt better in my life," Suzanne declared, "and I think I will be able to give a good account of myself after a little practice."

Who beyond Browne would she be playing in America? "I don't know," Suzanne said. "Ask Pyle."[35]

Lenglen was traveling in exquisite style, stuffing all those new dresses and the rest of her vast wardrobe into a dozen trunks and 20 hat boxes. Pyle had secured one of the best cabins on board for Suzanne and her mother, with fresh flowers and champagne placed each day in their room. From all accounts, Lenglen was in good humor and was looking forward to touring America; she even found time to free up space in one of her trunks — selling 25 Suzanne Lenglen dolls, each dressed like her and wearing a trademark headband.

Docking September 29 in New York, Lenglen's presence inspired an old-fashioned media stampede. Pyle was delighted at the hoopla. Some 25 reporters and a dozen photographers were on hand to record the ocean liner's arrival at the West 15th Street Dock on the Hudson River. Those expecting a sulking and surly star would have been disappointed, for here was Lenglen on her first visit to America since her celebrated breakdown at Forest Hills, and looking downright radiant.

"I am free," Suzanne said with a theatrical gesture for emphasis. "No more can tennis associations tell me that I must play here or play there. And want I want money to make myself and my family independent."

"Freedom, freedom!" she added, with an outward wave of the hand, a gesture that "banished all care," the *Times* dutifully reported. In coaching Lenglen about how to talk with the press, Pyle knew the themes that would resonate with Americans. Two themes guaranteed to get a rise — or at least a quote — were "freedom" from authority and the opportunity to make an old-fashioned buck.[36]

Dressed immaculately in a suit, bow tie and overcoat, C.C. led the welcoming committee at the dock. Watching as Pyle presented his celebrated guest with an oversized bunch of red roses, reporters wondered whether the promoter, who was single again, was wooing Lenglen with marriage on his mind. Did the contract, Lenglen was asked, include a non-marriage clause? Staring at Pyle, Suzanne was dumfounded at the question. But not C.C., who stepped in and handled it deftly with a sly smile creasing his face. "I do not feel that I know French women well enough," he said, "to ask for such a proviso."[37]

That got things back on track. Suzanne answered everything else thrown her way. Yes, she adored tennis, particularly when she won, she said. American tennis players were "terribly good," she said, before naming Billy Johnston — "Little" Bill to Tilden's "Big" Bill — as the best U.S. men's player. No, she didn't regret that Helen Wills, probably her ablest challenger, had decided against joining the tour. Mostly though, she talked about herself — detailing

Landing in New York in 1926 and not even off the ship before the start of her great American professional tennis tour, Suzanne Lenglen was a press sensation, and seemed to be enjoying herself. A few days later, C.C. Pyle would take Lenglen to the World Series for a lesson in how to control her famous temper. From the Bain Collection (Library of Congress, Prints and Photographs Division).

the perfume named after her and her brand of racquet as well — and smiled throughout.[38]

The reporters recorded every utterance and gesture as if Suzanne was the U.N. Secretary-General. They detailed Lenglen's wardrobe — a suit of beige wool crepe and a fawn-colored blouse, a coat trimmed with fox fur, suede slippers, and a large pearl ring and a pearl necklace, topped off by a beige hat, worn stylishly on an angle. Joining Pyle in the welcoming committee were Colonel Bill Hayward and Red Grange, who blushed when a reporter suggested that he and Lenglen square off at tennis. And with that, the shy Grange, turning "the color of his nickname," the *Times* wrote, slinked off to sit on a sofa aboard ship.

With the tour still a week away, reporters had considerable time and copy to analyze every aspect of Lenglen's game and personality. Because she hadn't swung a racquet since leaving Paris, they wondered if she would be in top form. And what if Lenglen, despite her relative humor on arriving in New York, self-destructed again as she had at Forest Hills? These questions were triggered by Pyle's admission of a "temperament clause" in the contract, which protected him from a loss of income should Suzanne have a meltdown.[39]

"Mr. Pyle does not go into any intricate definition as to what might be classed as temperamental," wrote Bill McGeehan in the *New York Herald Tribune*. "He merely says that he is satisfied that Mlle. Lenglen will not be temperamental. The proprietor of Red Grange and the greatest of the women tennis players seems to have come into possession of a secret that many handlers of opera singers and professional athletes would like to know."

There probably was no clause. Pyle knew that a continued emphasis on his client's combustible personality sold tickets, and that debate over the existence of such a clause would build interest. McGeehan was doubtful, saying that "all professional promoters ostensibly deplore temperament, but I do not think they mean it."

"Take the case of Mr. Babe Ruth of the New York Yankees," McGeehan wrote. "Mr. Ruth is classed as a temperamental athlete, and sometimes his outbursts of temperament cause considerable mental anguish to his owner ... and manager ... I maintain that if Mr. Ruth were merely a baseball player who could hit more home runs than other baseball players, he would not be what the boys call a drawing card. The temperamental Babe Ruth is the most lavishly paid athlete in the national pastime because he has been attracting customers, which is the objective of all professional sport."[40]

Reporters pondered that with Lenglen and Browne on board, what other top players would round out "Pyle's trouping team," as they were labeled. Still needing a top-ranked American male, C.C. sought out "Little" Bill Johnston, America's second-ranked male, behind only Vince Richards. Working through a Wall Street friend of Johnston's named Elmer Griffin, Pyle offered the 5'8" Johnston $50,000, but Griffin didn't believe his friend would ever see anywhere near that amount. "Billy," said Griffin, "I think Pyle's as crooked as the day is long, but he's willing to put the $50,000 in escrow."

Johnston seriously considered the offer for several days. He turned Pyle down, not because of the amount, but because the 32-year-old, two-time U.S. Open champion figured he was near the end of his career and didn't want to deal with the rigors of playing tennis in a different town every night for months on end.[41]

Pyle floated Helen Wills' name again, thinking she — or rather her father — might reconsider his earlier offer. Meantime, he signed a couple of other players; the rising Frenchman Paul Feret, a friend of Lenglen, and Americans Harvey Snodgrass, Howard Kinsey and Walter Westbrook. But in what was becoming his trademark, C.C. was saving his big announcement for a special occasion.

As with many things Pyle did in his colorful career, the news of his next "big" signing came with a carefully choreographed dose of drama. It happened on the evening of September 30 as C.C. hosted a banquet for 250 guests in the grand dining room of the *France* in Lenglen's honor. Amidst the sumptuous spread and what the *New York Herald Tribune* described as "a brilliant company of (200) men and women," the evening's toastmaster, Big Bill Edwards, rose with the promise that something major was about to happen. And with that, he gave the floor to Pyle.

"Ladies and gentleman," C.C. told the hushed audience, "I know that you will agree with me when I tell you that I have secured the services of one whom I firmly believe is the greatest male tennis player in world, Mr. Vincent Richards. He is now a professional and will joint with Mlle. Lenglen, Miss Browne and the other players in the series of exhibition matches that I have arranged."

Pyle paused for effect. Gesturing theatrically, he continued. "I have the honor, ladies and gentlemen, to introduce Mr. and Mrs. Richards."

On cue, trumpets in the ship's orchestra blared and symbols crashed. All eyes turned toward the back of the massive hall, where at the top of the ship's stairway, Richards and his wife, Clare, appeared, as if dropped in from a helicopter. Escorted by Colonel Hayward, they majestically descended the stairs into the banquet room and threaded their way through the stunned crowd to the head table.[42]

C.C. had snared another big name. "With the instincts of the real showman," wrote Fred Hawthorne in the *Herald Tribune*, "Pyle had planned his stage setting with the skill of a Belasco." The signing of Richards, the sport's reigning golden boy and the John McEnroe of his day, was a coup. Only 23, he had been atop the world's tennis ranking seemingly forever. Just like McEnroe, he was a brash New Yorker who had burst through as a teenage prodigy — in his case, winning a national championship at 15. At 19, Richards joined the U.S. Davis Cup team, and since partnered with Tilden as a three-time national doubles champion. Suffice to say that Richards and Tilden, along with Johnston and Richard Williams, comprised the "big four" of U.S. men's tennis.[43]

Pyle could have rattled on, but he knew to be brief and then sit down, letting Richards bask in the drama. With flashbulbs popping, someone cheered. It caught on soon the entire ballroom was awash with standing, applauding people. At the head table, Mary Browne was first to reach

Richards and pump his hands in congratulations; Lenglen and a host of others soon followed. The big news was another Pyle public relations coup, earning Richards major billing on the next day's sports pages, second only to news about the Yankees–St. Louis Cardinals World Series.

To reporters, who reached his table a few minutes later, Richards was forthright about his decision. "I have regrets that I will no longer be able to play amateur tennis (and) not help in the defense of the Davis Cup," he said, "but I have a first duty to my wife and little daughter.

"Mr. Pyle's offer was such that I felt I could not rightfully refuse it. After all, a man's first duty is to his family, and I have taken this step after full consideration. I believe that professional tennis, as Mr. Pyle is going to conduct it, has a great future."[44]

Red Grange was there, and what impressed him wasn't just that Pyle had lured another big-name athlete to turn professional, but that he had somehow pulled off the whole sumptuous affair at a minimal cost. "I regard that dinner as another stroke of sheer genius, for wouldn't you have thought he could square the bill for less than $10,000?" Grange asked Westbrook Pegler. "Yet, all he paid was the waiters' hire and maybe the cost of some stimulating beverage for his guests. He talked that party out of the steamship company on the ground that it would be great publicity for their boats. And the thought of an American outfumbling a Frenchman for a dinner check for 250 people leaves me awed and reverent."[45]

C.C. was careful not to steal Richards' thunder, and used the occasion to announce that following the close of the tour in January, he planned to hold a national open championship, either in New York or Los Angeles. Up for grabs would be $40,000 in prize money, or so Pyle said.

With Richards committed to the tour, the columnists got cracking, once more focusing their attention on how Pyle had managed to turn yet another American sports bastion on its head — "upsetting the apple cart," as someone said — and in this case, wreaking havoc for the U.S. Davis Cup team. But Pyle was simply ahead of his time — again — which some critics were starting to grudgingly acknowledge. By sheer will, C.C. was ushering in the modern age of sports, prodding another conservative governing structure to look to a new future.

"If Mr. Pyle continues to lure the tennis players from the paths of amateurism there will be no Davis Cup team worth mentioning next year, and that highly prized container certainly will go to France, where there are no Pyles to collect the amateurs," Bill McGeehan opined in the *Herald Tribune*. "Certainly, there is nothing unethical in an athlete turning an honest professional.... But one can appreciate the alarm that is felt by the USLTA if Mr. Pyle's venture should succeed beyond his dreams."[46]

That USLTA "alarm" was genuine. USLTA magazine editor Stephen Wallis Merrihew directed his venom at both the players who had turned pro and particularly at Pyle, "who knows nothing of tennis and simply wishes to make money," he wrote. Predictably, the USLTA banned its amateur members from participating in Pyle's season-ending open tournament. "They have made their bed," Merrihew rattled on. "Lie on it they must, however hard it may become, however scant the covering it contains."[47]

That C.C. name seemed to generate as much attention as the athletes he managed suggests how far this former small-town theater owner had traveled in less than a year, having sprung from nowhere into the national conscience and daily headlines. Fueled by the success of the Red Grange tour, Pyle had become a symbol of the big-time "golden age" of sports. If Grange had created Pyle's fame and reputation, C.C.'s "tennis troupe" sealed his influence.

Writers pondered Pyle's newfound celebrity, wondering just how far the star of America's first sports agent could rise. "Much will depend on how Mr. Pyle handles his troupe," McGeehan wrote. "If he puts it over there is little doubt that some of the others will begin to listen to the music that is played by his cash register. It is up to Mr. Pyle. He may make tennis an attractive business, and then the amateurs may be in the minority."[48]

In the fall of 1926, C.C. Pyle was at the peak of his powers. An indication of how far Pyle had traveled in such a short time was a September 1926 Associated Press dispatch around the time C.C. announced the signing of Mary Browne. Not only did Pyle have tennis on his mind, but he used a press conference in Los Angeles to hold forth on the start of training camp for Red Grange and the Yankees in Aurora, Illinois, and to express his disappointment that Olympic sprint champion Charlie Paddock had turned down his offer to run a series of three races that would have reportedly earned him between $50,000 and $70,000. Newspapermen were reporting every last scrap of news, including what Pyle *wasn't* doing, among them adding track and field to his growing stable of professional athletes. Paddock, the 1920 Olympic 100-meter gold medalist and silver medalist in the 200 meters at the 1924 Games, had decided to remain an amateur with hopes of reaching the 1928 Games. That was too bad for Pyle. Paddock, a Texas native, a California resident, and an actor and writer was among the most interesting athletes of the era. He was known for his trademark "flying finish" in which he would leap about 12 feet from the finish, and with his arms spread wide, break the tape. In *Chariots of Fire*, the 1981 Oscar-winning film about the 1924 Games, Paddock was portrayed by Dennis Christopher. Alas, Paddock would make his third Olympic team in 1928, but couldn't reach the 200-meter final.[49]

Continuing to focus on tennis, Pyle announced the tour would kick off the weekend of October 9–10 at Madison Square Garden in New York before heading across Canada and the U.S., first to Toronto, then to Montreal, Buffalo, Boston, Philadelphia, Pittsburgh, Columbus, Chicago, Denver and California. The cross-country barnstorming tour with its hectic pace was fast becoming a C.C. trademark. Like the previous fall's football tour, it would be a grueling schedule.[50]

On Saturday, October 2, Pyle, joined by Lenglen and Richards attended the opening game of the 1926 World Series between the Yankees and the St. Louis Cardinals at Yankee Stadium. It was a social occasion, a chance to be seen, and newspapers featured his name among the "sport magnates" to attend. But C.C. had a lesson in mind for Suzanne. Amidst continuing speculation about her history of on-court histrionics and concerns about antagonistic crowds, C.C. wanted her to see how baseball players sloughed off the razzing as an occupational hazard.[51]

They saw a master at work — the great Yankees' left-hander, Herb Pennock, who gave up two hits and a run in the first inning, and then settled down by yielding one more hit to beat the Cards, 2–1. That the powerful Yankees, with big hitters like Ruth, Lou Gehrig and Earle Combs in the lineup, couldn't mount more of an offense fired up the home crowd, which razzed its team, and offered Professor Pyle a bona fide teaching moment. Pointing to hometown hero Ruth as he was taunted by the Yankee brethren that expected more than the New Yorkers' six measly hits, Pyle drove home his lesson.

"*That's* what you have to expect in this country," C.C. explained. "The bigger they are, the harder they're razzed."

Caught up in the excitement, Lenglen was an eager student. Smiling, she nodded with apparent understanding. "Yes, I believe I know what you mean," Suzanne said. "If they tell me the 'razz,' I laugh, eh?"

"Well, we shall see," said Pyle. "But perhaps it would be advisable for the mademoiselle to put cotton in her ears or wear ear muffs before she goes on the court."[52]

Looking to keep his tennis stars sharp, Pyle arranged for a special Wednesday workout at a Manhattan court, inviting a contingent of reporters to cover the occasion. Set for noon at the Van Kelton clay courts at 57th

Street and Eighth Avenue on the West Side, C.C. was hoping to catch the lunch crowd and create a buzz.

It rained Tuesday night, making the courts muddy. But Pyle got exactly what he wanted — a real "scene," crowded with hundreds of stenographers and clerks peering from office windows at the court below, and a mob of untold others jamming the streets around the court, all of it described with minute detail by reporters in the next day's papers.

Lenglen stole the show. Even at practice, she was "a marvel of grace and lightness on her feet," Fred Hawthorne wrote in the *Herald Tribune.* Pyle took a back seat — sort of— and joined Pickens as a ball boy, as he worried that the slick condition of the court could cause the French tennis star to turn her ankle.

"Careful, Mademoiselle Lenglen, don't run," he instructed Suzanne.

"I don't want to run in this very sticky mud," she replied, flashing her freshly minted smile, another sure sign that the one-time ice goddess of tennis was enjoying herself.

Lenglen stuck to the script. She didn't run, instead gently volleying with Browne for close to 90 minutes. As she departed, a lone voice rang out from a group of sand-hoggers taking a break from their work in excavating the subway to watch the workout. "Hey there, Suzanne!" he yelled.

"Thank you!" she said, waving to the group, flashing another smile. If anything underscored Pyle's efforts to change a stuffy country-club sport's image and spread it to the working class, this was it.[53]

On Saturday evening, October 9, Pyle's professional tennis troupe got rolling. Ticket sales were brisk, but not at the level that C.C. had predicted. No, Madison Square Garden wasn't sold out, but 13,000 spectators filled up perhaps three-quarters of the spacious arena. In doing so, they paid $2.20 to $5.50 per ticket to see Suzanne Lenglen play in America for the first time in five years.

It was thought to be the largest crowd ever to watch a tennis match in America. New York Governor Al Smith and Mayor Jimmy Walker were there, as were Bill Tilden and golfers Walter Hagen and Glenna Collett. So were Ring Lardner and Lenglen's old friend, boxer Georges Carpentier.

Carpentier and fellow heavyweight Jack Dempsey had dined with Suzanne before the match and then posed for photographers, with Lenglen slipping in and out of selections of her 40 suits. All were designed by Patou, with whom she had a contract.

There were last-minute complications, all of which Pyle handled as best he could. Responding to his announcement that he had secured the services of two long-time tennis officials, Albert Gibney and Edward Conlin, the USLTA barred its linesmen and umpires from officiating, but waited until just before the match to make it official. That left Pyle in a quandary, having to delay the start of the match almost 45 minutes as he scrambled to find substitute. Nat Browne, Mary's brother, stepped in as umpire.[54]

Not that anyone in the crowd cared much. They were there to see a spectacle like no other tennis match in history. Pyle had installed a specially built court comprised of a dark green canvas stretched tightly over flooring built of cork under powerful Klieg lights, making it similar to what one observer called a "fairly fast clay court." The court was portable and could be easily dismantled and hauled around the country.

Pyle had taken on the stuffy governing body of tennis and added real flair to the stately old game. C.C. even came up with a new word to describe his technique: He was "circusing" the game, he said. Traditional tennis terminology was thrown out the window. Instead of the word "love" for a zero score, Nat Browne substituted "nothing." Ring Lardner thought the balls were extra lively, and criticized Pyle for what he called the "rabbit ball."

To keep the crowd energized during the delay, a brass band played the popular tune "Valencia" over and over. Popular baseball comedians and former Washington Senators Nick Altrock and Al Schacht did an impromptu routine, giving USLTA officials further bouts of heartburn. The matches moved briskly. Richards kicked things off by easily beating Paul Feret in a two-set match. Then, as the band struck up the French national anthem, *La Marseillaise*, Lenglen appeared, looking like a runway model. Dressed in a Riviera costume featuring an accordion pleated skirt, a sleeveless yellow sweater and a yellow bandeau, Suzanne was accompanied by Pyle, who looked a tad out of sorts as he stood, holding her ermine evening wrap.

It was the evening's most dramatic moment. Noticeably nervous and displaying little of her trademark sizzle, Lenglen got off to an uninspired start against Mary Browne. But when Browne dropped a shot just over the net and caught Suzanne flat-footed, the French star caught fire and played the rest of way with what Larry Engelmann described as "machine-like precision" to easily dispatch Browne, 6–1, 6–1, in 39 minutes.[55]

Paired with Feret in mixed doubles against Browne and Richards, Lenglen continued to dazzle. Rushing the net to win a dozen points, she sent reporters into a parade of superlatives from "the poetry of her motion" to her "dash and verve" and "acrobatic style." Even the USLTA's Merrihew was impressed, adding soberly that "there is not the slightest doubt ... these exhibitions have filled a want."

Mary Browne (left) and Suzanne Lenglen (right) were rivals and admirers. Their matches across America helped C.C. Pyle earn his second fortune in sports. From the Bain Collection (Library of Congress, Prints and Photographs Division).

Pyle grossed $24,000 for the evening, a solid start. Even the criticism was muted, with the *Times* taking Pyle to task for, of all things, Lenglen's almost unfair domination of the competition. "If Babe Ruth knocked a home run every time he came to bat, it is a safe conjecture that he would lose enormously in drawing power," the newspaper wrote. "With Mlle. Lenglen it is written beforehand that if she does not win 6–0, 6–1, she will win 6–1, 6–2." What was missing, the paper added, was "the freaks of chance."[56]

But the skeptics were resigned to the fact that Pyle had created a new future for tennis. "The attitude ... seemed to be, 'Oh, yes, it is interesting, but is it tennis?" wrote Bill McGeehan in the *Herald Tribune*. "To the customers with whom Mr. Pyle is concerned that does not matter much."

Only about 6,500 filed into the Garden for the Sunday exhibition. Lenglen and Richards again won easily on a day that proved more memorable for two people Pyle brought in to accompany the 40-city, four-month tour. William O'Brien joined as Lenglen's personal masseur, and became so taken by Pyle and his ways that a few years later he would launch his own professional tennis tour with Richards and Tilden. Meantime, Anne Kinosolving, a *Baltimore News* reporter, signed on as Suzanne's press agent, a task she came to regret once the tennis star reverted into her old irritable self.[57]

For now, though, Lenglen personified sweetness and optimism. In Toronto, she was welcomed with open arms, with journalists outdoing one another with adoring hyperbole. There, a few days later in Baltimore, then in Boston and again in Philadelphia, the crowds were exuberant and happy to see her. And at each spot, Lenglen easily overpowered Browne, who never managed to win more than two games in a set.

But in Philadelphia, Lenglen flashed her celebrated temper. Playing in an auditorium so cold that spectators could see their breath since the court had been placed directly over a hockey rink, she easily disposed of Browne, 6–0, 6–2. But with the conditions not to her liking, she seemed to be going through the motions, methodical and hardly smiling. Was the temperamental star growing weary of the grind after one week?

Pyle should have intervened, but busy counting his receipts, he barely seemed to notice. After six stops, C.C. announced that 41,000 had paid $83,400 to see "the international stars twinkle." But the fact is everyone in the tour was finding the pace too hectic. Moving on to Montreal, Buffalo, Cleveland, Pittsburgh, Columbus and Chicago, Browne grew despondent by her inability to win and exhausted by the travel. Pyle offered her a $200 bonus if she could win at least seven games in two sets and $300 for a set.[58]

In Chicago, Lenglen had another meltdown. At the Coliseum before

6,500 enthusiastic spectators, including officials from the French C
Suzanne posed for the usual pre-match photos, but then cursed a
ally took a swipe at a photographer who tried snapping a few more pictures
than she wanted. The crowd roared with delight, but the altercation completely unhinged Suzanne. She beat Browne, but only after dropping five
games in the first set and another two in the second, which at least earned
Mary the $200 bonus. After the match, Suzanne took out her frustrations
on Pyle, lashing out at him that she'd had enough with America and wanted
to return to France.

Meantime, the other players complained about Lenglen, who rarely
socialized with anyone and stuck close to her mother. "(Suzanne) was always
saying she wanted to go home," Snodgrass told biographer Engelmann. "She
would get all dolled up every night and then fight and argue with everybody. She was always throwing everything out of her dressing room, screaming that she wanted to go home. She was a real case."[59]

Facing a mutiny, Pyle took the high road. Spinning the unsteady temperament of Lenglen as a positive, he said her meltdowns reaffirmed his belief
that that people would focus on the personality and, most importantly, pay
to see someone they hated. "The whole problem was to keep them hating
her," C.C. told reporters. "Suzanne is charming when she wants to be, and
we had to repress that side of her nature. Every now and then, she would
go pleasant on us, and we would have to jog her a little, and have her make
faces at Miss Browne, or get unpopular with the local aristocracy by refus-
ing to meet them."

In Portland, Lenglen threw another fit. Screaming at Pyle that she was
finished once and for all with his tour, she dumped most of her equipment
in the hallway outside her dressing room. By then, others were venting their
wrath at C.C. as well. "I found him to be dishonest," Snodgrass told Engelmann. "He was really just a bunch of bullsh___, a con artist, always talking
about big things."

By the time the tour arrived in Portland, Lenglen and Snodgrass had
grown weary of Pyle's lofty talk and shared a genuine concern that they
might never be paid their promised salaries — $15,000 in the case of Snod-
grass. Triggering their worry was that Pyle, increasingly tending to football
matters, had disappeared shortly after the promising start in New York and
only reappeared in Portland, just in time for Suzanne's meltdown. As it
turned out, Snodgrass's concern was legitimate: Promised $15,000 for the
tour, he would be paid only $9,000 and have to sue Pyle for the rest.[60]

But just when it seemed Suzanne Lenglen was at her wit's end, she turned on the charm. Pulling into San Francisco Bay Terminal, she emerged from the train and looked radiant in a fur scarf while clutching an oversized bouquet of red roses. "Slender, animated, and a perfect actress ... all graciousness and affability," a *San Francisco Chronicle* reporter wrote of his first impression of the famous tennis star. It was as if the beauty of San Francisco had wiped away the tantrums and insecurities. Or maybe it was a gracious visit from Helen Wills, whose hometown was across the bay in Oakland, or perhaps it was Pyle, back traveling with the tour to soothe and service Lenglen's needs. A fawning press, content to outdo one another with platitudes about this vain French star, couldn't have hurt either.

Whatever the reason, Lenglen was once again the personification of graciousness in San Francisco. Pyle was sticking around this time, and assisted in promotion by his brother, Ira, made sure that Suzanne was coddled in as much luxury as possible. The Pyles put the troupe up at the Palace Hotel, the best in town. They directed the hotel kitchen staff to ensure Suzanne was given her favorite foods — an appetizer of celery sticks dripped in catsup, followed by lamb chops. As Lenglen's spirits picked up, so did her appetite. Joining Pyle for lunch before a press conference in San Francisco, she finished off her meal *and* his plate of oysters à la Kirkpatrick.

Pyle worked hard in California to get Lenglen's temper under control. Local reporters helped by penning glowing reviews about her workout wardrobe — "fetching black pajamas," as one wrote — and all aspects of her game. When Lenglen gave tennis lessons to underprivileged children at a youth center — set up by Pyle — the reporters covered her every comment, which continued to be upbeat. "(Lenglen) certainly can be a gracious lady when she wants to be," wrote San Francisco columnist Harry Smith.[61]

More than 5,000, including Helen Wills, turned up at Civic Auditorium to see her play. Reporters were delighted at Pyle's "circusing," theatrical embellishments like introducing the players and then having them skip out of the shadows into the bright lights of the court. Suzanne beat Browne easily, 8–6 and 6–2, as Wills watched from her balcony seat.

Wanting to pay a visit to Lenglen, Wills called her hotel but found that Pyle, to ensure privacy, had disconnected the telephone. Wills tried again a few days later at the Oakland Hotel in Oakland and got through, and the two reigning stars of women's tennis chatted amicably for more than an hour. That evening, Wills and 3,000 others watched Lenglen dismantle Browne, this time 6–2, 7–5.

The telephone chat of the two reigning tennis divas prompted talk of their epic exhibition in Cannes and whether they would ever play again.

Many hoped they would, among them Wills' coach, Pop Fuller, who had watched Lenglen play in San Francisco. Fuller was impressed, but concluded there was "no chance" Suzanne would ever beat Wills and fueled no hopes of a match.

Arriving in Los Angeles, Pyle faced the inevitability of another Lenglen slaughter of poor Mary Browne. To build interest, he spun the impending match into a kind of heavyweight title fight, a titanic battle of two warriors. Pyle had an angle — Browne was a hometown hero, having grown up in nearby San Monica — which he milked by saying she appeared poised to finally defeat the great Lenglen. Browne followed along, telling reporters that "my hour is near" in a statement written by Pickens. "Of all places in the world where I would like to turn the trick, Los Angeles is the one."[62]

Adding to the intrigue were days of newspaper articles, most of them full of pure hokum cooked up by Pyle and Pickens. Lenglen's old nervous condition was said to have cropped up, leaving her unable to practice. At Lenglen's swank quarters at the Hotel Del Coronado near San Diego, a team of doctors reportedly conducted a thorough examination of the tennis star and declared that she was exhausted and needed a long break.

Lenglen was said to be practicing and ignoring the orders of the physicians, while insisting her best tennis came when she was close to nervous collapse. Trotting Lenglen out for a press conference, Pyle portrayed her as a hero fighting the odds against tiredness, injury and illness. "If Mary K. Browne is counting upon besting the champion by catching her out of condition, she will have to try some other tactics," C.C. said. "Mlle. Lenglen is a champion because she never rests. It is her temperament that makes her a champion. She has the fighting heart that a title-holder of any sport must posses to remain at the top of her profession."[63]

Lenglen agreed, telling the *Los Angeles Times* in a bylined piece probably penned by Pickens that "temperament is a peculiar term and it covers a multitude of sins."

> It gives, for instance, to the dramatic soprano the right to throw soup tureens at her impresario's head, to the struggling poet whose genius is as yet unrecognized by imbecile editors, the right to wear his hair and his cravat long and flowing.... Not only do their temperaments confer certain rights upon these artists, but conversely it is their right to have certain temperaments.... What the brush is to the painter and the pen to the poet, the tennis racket is to me. My game is my art, and my medium of self-expression consists of a half-dozen rubber tennis balls, a net, a court, a racket and a gallery. Consequently, I have what is popularly known as a temperament.[64]

But in a rare moment of candor, Pyle revealed why he had signed Browne, and not Helen Wills, whose skills were more comparable to Lenglen's. "I realized even before I had her turn professional that if she were defeated by (Wills) she would terminate her tour and return home to her beloved France — heartbroken," he said. "She would have to listen to the equivalent of 'I told you so' in French."

Pyle's spin still worked splendidly. Adding even more spice to the matchup, he leaked a tale that Lenglen, so consumed by Browne's newfound confidence and poise, was actually stepping up her secret training to new levels of intensity. "Mlle. Lenglen is not what is know as a good loser," C.C. said. "Rather she is a hard loser and that is the reason she trains at all times for her matches. Even though the law of averages says that a champion who defends her title too often is bound to go down into defeat, Mlle. Lenglen does not concede anyone a chance."[65]

Falling for the bait, reporters for the *Los Angeles Times* built the matchup into a kind of slugfest of two heavyweights in a supreme battle that almost transcended sports. Susanne Lenglen was the tennis version of Ty Cobb, baseball's answer to an athlete who thrived on nerves, a *Times* reporter wrote. "It is this nervous energy, which gives her strength on the courts." Facing a determined Mary Browne would be "the greatest test of her athletic career," the paper added.[66]

Giving the match an extra dose of star appeal, Pyle installed 300 special ringside seats for Hollywood celebrities, many of whom had taken to tennis after installing courts on their estates. The star appeal worked, for sitting courtside among the crowd of 7,000 at Olympic Auditorium were Charlie Chaplin, Harold Lloyd, Douglas Fairbanks, Jr., and Mary Pickford.

But as throughout the tour, the build-up was the best part of the evening. The match was another mind-numbing drubbing, as Lenglen easily dispatched Browne, 6–0, 6–1. So much for the newfound determination of the hometown hero; Mary didn't take a single point in the first set. But once Pyle had counted his gate receipts for the evening, he could not have cared less; C.C. had cleared $21,000.[67]

Many believed Lenglen's overwhelming success would be a shot in the arm for the tour as it packed up in California for its last leg — a long haul back east, with stops in San Antonio, Dallas, Houston, New Orleans, Birmingham, Atlanta, and finally a series of matches throughout Florida and Cuba. Along the way, two significant things happened that would not only sour the rest of the tour, but ultimately drive Pyle from tennis and on to new endeavors.

Itching to get away from his temperamental tennis star and to focus on football, Pyle stayed in Los Angeles, leaving Pickens to handle the rest of the day-to-day management of the tour. But Lenglen didn't care for Pickens, who was far too blustery and nowhere near suave enough for her taste; only Pyle commanded her respect. And so she acted out again, this time egged on by a special, new friend, the exquisitely named Baldwin M. Baldwin of Los Angeles. A wealthy man about town, Baldwin was in his early twenties, married and with children. But after he met Lenglen in California, he had become so infatuated with her that he joined the tour on its eastern swing, advising Suzanne that she was worth far more than Pyle's meager thousands.[68]

Baldwin, the grandson of E.J. "Lucky" Baldwin, a colorful character who had earned a fortune in the stock market and California real estate, was an heir and an operator. Suddenly, his name was popping up everywhere in news releases and newspaper articles as Lenglen's "manager." But his real eye wasn't on Lenglen, but on the possibilities presented by her wealth, as if he didn't have enough himself.

With Baldwin along for the ride and carping most days that Suzanne wasn't earning enough, Lenglen spent much of the trip east in bed, claiming to be ill. She argued with Pickens, while Baldwin — newspapers were linking him romantically with the tennis star — worked to unravel any trust the tennis star had built with Pyle. Meantime, Pickens said the couple were engaged, which Baldwin's secretary strenuously denied. The tour had become a rolling soap opera, which hit bottom in New Orleans when Richards contracted jaundice, a condition that would plague him the rest of the trip. Suzanne continued to sulk, appearing more disinterested and listless with each passing day, so much so that in Havana, she even let Browne win a few sets.[69]

Back in the Northeast to finish up the tour, Lenglen said she was still too ill to play, forcing cancellations of exhibitions in Hartford and Newark. She played in New Haven and then Brooklyn, but only mixed doubles and appearing to be barely trying. She and Howard Kinsey beat Browne and Snodgrass in New Haven, but lost a match, finally, at the 23rd Regiment Armory in Brooklyn. At the tour's last appearance, two days later in Providence, Lenglen and Richards lost to a team of men, Kinsey and Snodgrass.

The tour was finally done, but the rancor endured. Pyle still owed his players a substantial amount, and Baldwin demanded that Lenglen receive a better contract should the tour head to Europe, as it was rumored. Chiming in was Papa Lenglen, who wired his daughter from France with news of new lucrative offers — and strict instruction to sign no new contracts, and

most certainly not one with Pyle. Getting in a shot himself, C.C. said he
wasn't about to concede control, souring his relations with Lenglen for
good.[70]

On February 16, C.C. announced he was giving up tennis. Speaking at
a news conference at the Hotel Vanderbilt in Los Angeles, he released the
tour players, leaving them free to negotiate with whomever they pleased. Fed
up and sounding tired, Pyle wanted no part of any tennis tour "until the
players make up their minds with whom they wish to play, and realize that
they are not entitled to increases in pay."

But there was C.C. the next day, filled with humor and reasserting himself as his old gracious self. "Mlle. Lenglen and I part company with nothing but the friendliest of relations," he said. "Mlle. Lenglen and Mr. Baldwin
have decided to map out her future professional program together. I am perfectly willing to step out of the picture."

Not that anyone needed to shed a tear for Pyle. Driven by gate receipts
and a considerable cut of Lenglen's endorsements, C.C. had cleared about
$100,000 from the tour, the equivalent of perhaps $1 million today, and his
second fortune in a little more than a year. Pyle also was growing reflective
that his skill was peddling a personality, not a sport. "I was in the Suzanne
Lenglen business, not the tennis business," C.C. added.[71]

So how much did Suzanne Lenglen earn from her deal with C.C. Pyle?
Pickens estimated she cleared $100,000—some $60,000 from the contract
and the rest from gate receipts. Richard earned $35,000, and Browne
$30,000, with 5 percent of the gate. Total receipts for the tour were nearly
$500,000.

Browne left immediately after the tour for Cleveland, where she planned
to retire from tennis and enter the sporting goods business. She had dropped
38 consecutive matches to Lenglen, and picked up considerable insight about
her opponent's greatness. Lenglen had unusually quick foot speed, a sparkling
tennis mind, and most of all, extraordinary tactics, Browne told a magazine
writer. Browne said that Suzanne's early training had stressed how to play
tough shots and reach balls others couldn't. Lenglen's shot wasn't as hard as
that of Helen Wills; what set her apart, Browne theorized, was her overall
skill level.[72]

On February 19, Suzanne Lenglen set sail from New York, again aboard
the ocean liner *France*, for home. Mama Lenglen was with her, as was Baldwin M. Baldwin, who would end squiring Lenglen about France, but not
marrying her. Talking with reporters as she was about to board the ship for
home, Suzanne was philosophical about her four-month American experience,

appearing to have regained her humor and customary flamboyance. "I am glad that I came to America," Lenglen said, adding that she was looking forward to drinking a lot of champagne during the crossing because all the smoking on board made her seasick. "I expect to have a bottle near me at all times," she said.[73]

Pressed for her views on America, Lenglen pronounced herself suitably impressed with many things, from its hospitality to its people. "Everywhere we went, north, south, east or west, we were received magnificently," she said. "No one appeared to be able to do enough for us." As for Americans in general, she added, "I had warned to look for booze and bunk, for boors and bores (but) I have found ice water and straight-forwardness, gentlemen and interesting people."

And what had impressed Lenglen most of all about the U.S.? "The height of the buildings, especially in New York," she said. "It makes one feel puny; it's simply crushing." Lenglen had grown attached to the telephone as well. "It takes less time to call up Chicago from New York than Asnières (a Paris suburb) from Paris," she said. And she pronounced pleased at having improved her English. "I talked English all the time now," Suzanne said, "even to my mother, who doesn't understand a word of it."[74]

Returning to the West Coast, Pyle was ready to move on. He had taken on the football and tennis establishments and shaken things up. He had made a lot of money — twice in a little more than a year — which gave him the capital to begin focusing on another new idea. With Suzanne Lenglen on her way back to France, C.C. Pyle was well on to his most fantastic and wackiest idea yet: a footrace across America.

6

"The Most Stupendous Athletic Accomplishment in All History!"

Early in 1927, as the story goes, C.C. Pyle was reading the newspaper when he stumbled on a small item about a 72-year-old man who had run 96 miles without stopping to deliver a message during the 1921 Riff campaign of Moroccan independence. "Wasn't that something?" Pyle said to himself, his mind filling with heroic images of courageous athletes running long distances with admiring people along the way shouting encouragement, all of it orchestrated by himself.

Similar tales of long-distance feats peppered history. According to legend, the Greek soldier Pheidippedes ran 25 miles from a battlefield near Marathon to Athens to bring the news of the Greek victory over the Persians in 490 BC. "Be joyful, we win!" the messenger is said to have called out before dropping dead of exhaustion. Though the story didn't appear in print for more than 600 years — making one wonder if it really ever happened — it is in the spirit of Pheidippedes that the modern marathon, resurrected in the 1896 revival of the Olympic Games and adjusted slightly in the 1908 Olympic Games to today's standard of 26.2 miles, is run. Pheidippedes is the product of a time-honored tradition of foot messengers who formed the most reliable way of sending announcements in the ancient world.[1]

In the U.S., romance was attached to those restless souls who crisscrossed the wilderness. Lewis and Clark, in the early nineteenth century, were probably the first to have made it clear across the continental U.S. to the West Coast. Then came the hordes descending on California in the late 1840s and 1850s in hopes of striking it rich in the gold rush, and settlers venturing west to stake out plots after the 1862 Homestead Act. Ministers, homesteaders, educators and assorted dreamers and schemers went as well, particularly after 1869 when the last spike was drilled into the ground at

Promontory, Utah, to mark the completion of the Transcontinental Rail-road, which made the two coasts accessible in days, not months. Some headed west for a new life, while others went for adventure, on a dare, or to fulfill a deep-seated restlessness. Legends built about the ones who made it — or those who went the other way, from west to east, like the improbable Nor-wegian mother of eight from Spokane, Washington, named Helga Estby. Behind on taxes and the mortgage, Helga learned that a sponsor would pay $10,000 to a woman who walked across the continent. In 1896, she and her 19-year-old daughter, Clara, did, crossing 14 states some 3,500 miles all the way to New York.[2]

But the Estbys were mere amateurs compared to Edward Payson Weston, who in 1860 had walked on a bet from Boston to Washington, D.C., for Lincoln's inauguration, and inspired by a congratulatory handshake from the new president, soon turned his habit of walking long distances or what was called "pedestrianism" into a national craze. In 1909, the 70-year-old Weston walked 4,000 miles from New York to San Francisco in 100 days; four years later, he walked more than 1,500 miles from New York to Min-neapolis in 51 days. Weston, who became a disciple of exercise and the dan-gers of how cars made people lazy and sedantry, would die of injuries after being struck by a Brooklyn taxi cab.[3]

In the early twentieth century, cross-country car trips had attracted significant press attention, like the 1908 "Great Race" in which a handful of auto enthusiasts set out to be the first to drive from New York to Paris. Though the six teams of racers — three French, and one each from Germany, Italy and the U.S. — ended up sailing from San Francisco to Japan, their race across three continents that included the Russian tundra in the dead of win-ter captured the world's imagination and later inspired the film, *The Great Race*, starring Jack Lemmon, Tony Curtis and Natalie Wood. Taking the 22,000-mile race in 169 days was the U.S. team headed by driver George Schuster, Sr. of Buffalo.[4]

In 1919, following the end of World War I, the U.S. Army was looking to see if the automobile and truck could replace the horse and the mule in military transport — and set off on an ambitious coast-to-coast military truck convoy. Starting in Washington. D.C., the convey, which included 34 heavy cargo trucks, four light delivery trucks, a wrecking truck, and a 25-year-old observer, Lieutenant Colonel Dwight Eisenhower, made it to San Francisco in 62 days. Averaging 58.1 miles a day — 6.07 miles per hour — over 3,251 miles of rutted, often unpaved roads with few gas stations, even fewer garages and a lot a mud, was a considerable achievement. And it was a journey that young Eisenhower would not soon forget; as president, he would use the experience as part of his inspiration for signing legislation that created America's Interstate Highway System.[5]

C.C.'s mind raced. An ultra-marathon fit right in to an age where frivolous feats of endurance like danceathons and marathon flagpole sitting had become popular. C.C's race would have a grand-prize winner, of course, but anyone making it that far would be able to bask in what would certainly be national acclaim. Such an event would be a big-time money-maker, Pyle figured, with runners streaming into towns clear across America, people coming from the hinterlands to see them, and stores, restaurants and hotels making a killing. Shops in all the towns would do a bang-up business, and so would C.C., with officials forking over sizable fees for the privilege of having the runners stop in their towns, which would be publicized through datelines sent across the nation. Officials would become so eager to host the running caravan that bidding wars would break out, driving the fees, all of them payable to Pyle, of course, ever upward. With the excitement would come endorsements — plenty of them from shoe sellers to foot-care products, snack foods and fitness drinks. And no spectator could possibly go without one of Pyle's programs, chock full of local advertising and costing only a quarter.[6]

What excitement! What a money-maker! Orchestrating this event of events would be the promoter of promoters, one C.C. Pyle, back to his carny roots in whipping up the small-town folk, this time as a stream of tired, gallant runners filled their streets like modern-day versions of Pheidippedes. It would be a foot race, a tent revival and a street fair combined, leaving the locals with something to talk about and remember for years. It would be the grandly named "C.C. Pyle's International Transcontinental Race," starting in Los Angeles and going clear to New York. There the runners, with their cumulative times tabulated and known to millions thanks to publicity they had generated all across America, would end up in a big finale at a New York stadium, cheered on by thousands. Then would come C.C. as he bestowed huge cash prizes to the top finishers, with a promise of more riches ahead in the subsequent nationwide tour of top runners. From sea to shining sea and coast to coast — some 3,422.3 miles — the race would be a spectacle for the ages and "the talk of the country," as C.C. predicted.[7]

Actually, the story of stumbling across the newspaper tale of the Moroccan messenger was C.C.'s imaginative version of having developed the idea himself. The reality is that the concept of a transcontinental race didn't even belong to Pyle, but to a Tulsa public-relations man named Lon Scott.

Hired by the Route 66 Association to drum up attention for the recent formation of this new highway reaching across 2,400 miles, three time zones and eight states, all the way from Santa Monica Boulevard and Ocean Avenue in Santa Monica near Los Angeles to the banks of Lake Michigan in Chicago, Scott had a vision: A footrace along all 2,400 miles, he suggested, to draw attention to the joys of traveling this glorious new superhighway.[8]

Today, Route 66 is a magical name, a piece of American lore captured in song and literature. In the 1930s, Route 66 was the "Mother Road," the path many natives of the devastated Oklahoma Dustbowl, their jalopies piled high with belongings, traveled to reach a new beginning in sunny California. John Steinbeck made that story — and the road — famous in *The Grapes of Wrath*. To later generations, Route 66 was a symbol of the American wanderlust, the ribbon of asphalt that allowed one to leave a conventional life behind and the highway that inspired Woody Guthrie, Merle Haggard and Jack Kerouac. For highway officials, the goals were more mercenary in nature — to attract tourists. To them, Route 66 was the "Main Street of America" where waitresses called you "hon" and served heaping slabs of blueberry pie, motor courts and motels had cute names like the "Blue Swallow" and the "Wagon Wheel" and there was always the promise of a snake farm or a pecan stand just around the bend. Historian and writer Michael Wallis calls Route 66 "an inspiration to literature, music, drama, art, and a nation of dreamers ... a highway fashioned from vision and ingenuity (which) has forever meant 'going somewhere' ... a road to adventure."[9]

Critical to the development of Route 66 — and to American life, for that matter — was the development of car travel. Virtually overnight, cars allowed workers to live miles from work and commute. Cars accelerated the development of suburbs, brought farmers in from the hinterlands, and provided a ready means of escape for those seeking a new life. Suddenly, a weekend trip to the beach, once hours away by railroad, or a trip into town was easy. Cars became a status symbol, a sign that one had made it, particularly after 1925 when Henry Ford, the Detroit automaker most responsible for the success of the American automobile, actually *dropped* the price of his Model T to an all-time low of $290. With cars more affordable to working people, America became a more mobile society. And states, once considered too isolated for development, became ripe for new industries.

Early highway travel was hard. Roads were often unpaved, a sea of mud when it rained, and badly marked. Restaurants were few and far between, as were gas pumps, which were usually built on sidewalks in front of stores. Yet by the early 1920s, traveling by car or "motor camping" had become one of the nation's top pastimes while triggering a boom in the construction of conveniences like tourist cabins, hotels, motels, garages and diners.[10]

Leading the campaign to put a road system in place was the Associated Highways Associations of America, led by Tulsa businessman Cyrus Avery, which included 42 member-associations across the country. The era's visionary of the American road, Avery put his knowledge behind development of an interstate highway system and insisted that easy-to-remember numbers be given to existing roads, with even numbers for roads running east and west and odd numbers for those going north and south. Among Avery's great strengths was mastery of politics and regional infighting, which he used to build roads that became the roots of America's transcontinental highway system. Patching together what became Route 66 from old Indian trails and local roads, Avery made certain that the road passed through his hometown of Tulsa as well as the state capital, Oklahoma City, giving a big boost to the economies of Oklahoma's two biggest cities.[11]

Of the almost three million miles of highways in America in 1920, only about 36,000 miles had surfaces strong enough to accommodate the weight and pressure of automobile traffic. With most roads built to handle little more than horse and buggy traffic, the government went to work paving vast portions of the countryside, creating a nationwide frenzy of construction and building. By 1926, when Route 66 was opened, only about 800 miles or one-third of its length was actually paved, with most of the remaining miles of roadway covered by graded dirt or gravel, bricks covered with asphalt, and, in some cases, wooden planks. Demand for better and faster roads had become a U.S–wide clarion call among vehicle owners, business owners, and politicians trolling for votes. Avery and his association knew the stakes, particularly in Oklahoma, where better roads would provide increased truck traffic and a real plus to the state's booming oil industry.

Lon Scott, the PR man, said the idea for staging the Route 66 trans-America footrace had originated at a civic leaders' dinner in Oklahoma City, prompted by a booster who yelled out above the din, "What are you going to do for U.S. Route 66 publicity?" Then as suddenly as the question was posed, as Scott put it, the answer shot out from another part of the room: "Put on a foot race!"[12]

Though Scott never could say for certain who had made the original recommendation, he suspected it had been Alec Singletary of the Oklahoma City Chamber of Commerce. Mulling it over, Scott was intrigued. If a band of hearty athletes could run halfway across the country and attract a lot of publicity in doing so, certainly the rest of America might consider taking in the glories of this wondrous new road — not on foot, but by car.

Most at the meeting laughed, thinking the idea for a race was ridiculous. "So many were flabbergasted and so utterly stunned with mirth," Scott recalled, "they were guffawing, 'Foot race, foot race, foot race,' and laughing as they walked out of the banquet hall. There were dozens of them — the finest gentlemen in Oklahoma, Missouri, Kansas, and a few from Texas. Our business, political, and religious leaders, our civic leaders, yes, our best citizens were red in the face from laughing."

But Scott wasn't the only one to think the idea was not so far-fetched. Reporters covering the event thought it had merit. "That foot-race idea, you'll want to be sure to dig into that, it's worth a lot to your highway," one scribe told Scott. "You'll reap more publicity for your southwest country than any other idea I know."

Several reporters suggested that there was a man to see, C.C. Pyle, should Scott want to pursue the idea. Scott called several New York sports desks looking for Pyle, who soon got word and called him at his Highway Associations' office in Springfield, Missouri. Recognizing a potential windfall, Scott and Pyle quickly got down to business: The association would give C.C. $60,000 to oversee the race, with the amount payable when the runners reached Chicago. Scott, meantime, would handle publicity — or so he thought.[13]

Scott envisioned a steady stream of press raves from reporters covering the derby about the joys of traveling Route 66. That appealed to C.C., but what he craved above anything was seeing his name in headlines as the one calling all the shots. In early 1928 while with his football Yankees in Los Angeles, Pyle turned his considerable energies to something completely different — not just a race along the 2,400 miles of Route 66, but one that would head from Los Angeles to Chicago, and then continue all the way to New York. There was a lot to do, from determining the logistics of housing and feeding the runners to drumming up headlines. Secure with the knowledge that $60,000 would be waiting for him when the race reached Chicago and confident there would soon be more, C.C. gushed with even more bombast than usual. Runners would vie for a top prize of $25,000, with $10,000 for second and $48,000 to be split among the rest of the top 10 finishers. "In fact, (the derby will be) about the easiest thing I've ever seen," Pyle said, brimming with confidence at the range of commercial possibilities, from town officials along the route vying — and paying — for the privilege of hosting the runners to program sales.[14]

"Chambers of Commerce are urged to put up the Pyle posters and to advertise bargain day sales in all shops on the day of the great event," wrote the *New York Times'* John Kiernan, with only slight sarcasm. "It is the expectation of the promoter that his thundering herd will make history with their forays through the hinterland. No longer will the oldest citizen say: 'That was before Prohibition.' Or: 'I mind, it was just a month after the Maine was blowed up.' No. The new style will be: 'It was eight years and three months, exactly, after the famous Bargain Day Transcontinental Foot Race passed through our town.'"[15]

It's not clear whether Pyle ever bothered to discuss with the Route 66 Association his plan to get the runners not just the length of the highway, but from Chicago to New York, too. Convinced he was about to launch the grandest sporting event in the history of the world, Pyle figured he would generate enough publicity to placate the association *and* enough income to ensure the runners made it all the way to the East Coast. Excitement would be intense, C.C. preached, with all those town officials bidding for the right to host the running caravan. And who couldn't resist a program featuring numbers of the runners and dotted with local ads? Pyle figured he would sell at least a million programs.[16]

Here is how it would work. "The first lap will be to Bingville, for instance," wrote Frank Getty of the wire service, United News, using a hypothetical name of a town. "Now Bingville has not been selected at random. C.C. Pyle does nothing at random. Bingville has paid $2,000 for the privilege of having the runners finish in front of the new courthouse and remain overnight. It has supplied food and shelter for the athletes. And then there are all manner of advertising concessions, for which — see Mr. Pyle. The hokey-pokey privilege, the lemonade stand privilege. Who controls them all? Pyle."

And when the great footrace had ended? "Those cities such as Minneapolis, Detroit and Buffalo, which because of their geographical location, have been deprived of the privilege of seeing the race, need not think that Pyle had forgotten them," Getty wrote. "The best of the trans-continental survivors will be taken on tour ... and will perform under the Pyle management wherever the jingle of cash is heard."[17]

Pyle was banking on technology to build and sustain a drumbeat of publicity for his runners. That the derby would generate headlines was a given, C.C. said. His ace in the hole to securing publicity, he assured everyone, was his own little technological concoction — the derby's own radio station, dubbed KGGM, to be manned in its own truck by a three-man California radio crew, along with teleprinters and teletypewriters, all of which would quickly and efficiently send the day's results to an eager public.[18]

C.C. Pyle (left) confers with Bunion Derby runner Thomas Ellis in El Reno, Oklahoma. Dressed in sweats, a hat and goggles, Ellis looks like he's ready for some mountain climbing (courtesy the El Reno [OK] Library).

C.C. was banking that his runners would benefit from the success of a new information age that already fueled a kind of cottage industry of new heroes, both large and small, whose exploits were eagerly lapped up by a hungry public. No, his athletes would never be as big as the era's really big names like the great Babe Ruth, who had hit a record 60 home runs in 1927, Red Grange or Charles Lindbergh. But they might squeeze into the next rung comprised of people like Richard Byrd and Floyd Bennett, who made the first successful flight over the North Pole, and ex-prizefighter Alvin "Shipwreck" Kelly, who perfected the new nationwide mania for sitting atop flagpoles for days at a time. "(They all) made 1928 a natural time for Pyle's (footrace)," wrote Route 66 historian Susan Croce Kelly, "a race guaranteed to make heroes out of ordinary people and an event so outrageous that it could not help but attract national attention."[19]

Bill Pickens jump-started the media push. "Authorities on crowds are unanimous in predicting that with proper local advertising, millions of persons can be attracted to various cities and towns along U.S. Route 66 Highway," he wrote, "to witness the titanic struggle between the greatest long distance runners of the entire world." Pickens and Pyle then mailed packages of press releases to top sportswriters; each featured the letterhead *C.C. Pyle's L.A.–N.Y. Race* and included a competitor's number for the scribes.[20]

As with most things involving Pyle, the reaction to the big race was mixed. C.C. would find out later just how greatly he antagonized Route 66 Association officials by inserting his own name into the title of the race and not that of the highway he was getting paid handsomely to promote. Shaking his head at C.C.'s audacity, Westbrook Pegler quickly dubbed the race "the Bunion Derby," and the name stuck. And writers soon pegged Pyle with a batch of derisive new nicknames, including "Cash and Carry" and, once the runners' injuries piled up, "Corn and Callus," both variations of his initials. But Pyle could not care less, knowing he was getting publicity for an event that stood to be his biggest yet. Winning the race, he declared, would be "the most stupendous athletic accomplishment in all history!"[21]

Looking for runners, Pyle placed announcements in newspapers throughout the country, stipulating that competitors pay a $100 entrance fee, a steep price at a time when the amount was a month's average salary for a factory worker. C.C. chose Ascot Speedway in Santa Monica as the starting line and March 4 as the start date because it rhymed with "mach force." Pyle required that the runners report to the speedway by February 12 "for final conditioning," though not everyone did. The official program would list 249 entrants, and only 200 or fewer reported for training.

Too bad for those who showed up early. Pyle ran the training like marine boot camp, giving no thought to a distance runner's need for rest, nor hard days followed by easy days. At training camp, runners rose at 6:00 A.M., and after breakfast, ran 25 to 50 miles in preparation for as many as the 75 miles or so a day they would be traveling in the derby. Dinner was at 6:00 P.M., after which the runners relaxed and were treated for injuries. Lights dimmed at 9:00 P.M. And then they would get up the next day and do it all over again.

At least the food selection was decent. Runners dined on a choice of eggs, cereal, toast and fruit for breakfast, with soup, salad, meat and vegetables for lunch and dinner, all of which reporters dutifully recorded. What didn't make the papers is that Pyle charged runners 50 cents a meal and 50 cents a night for lodging, which was a bunk in a tent city set up in the infield of the speedway.[22]

Some runners grumbled about the spartan quarters and having to pay for meals. But what really got them steamed was the sight of Pyle rolling up most mornings in his spanking new, custom-made double-decker coach in which he and selected guests would travel along the race route, like lords reigning over the serfs. Pyle dubbed it "The America," and proudly pointed out its Pullman-style seats, which could sleep two, reclining chairs made of blue mohair plush upholstery. Made by the Fageol Motor Company in Oakland, the vehicle was a 1920s cross between a Hummer and a luxury condo, with interior paneling made of hand-finished mahogany, carpeting, hot and cold running water, a bathroom and even a dressing room, along with heat and air conditioning. Behind the driver was an office featuring a collapsible table, writing desk, phonograph and radio receiver. Upstairs was seating for six, a collapsible awning and windows with windshields. The America set Pyle back $25,000, hardly a dent, he said, with $60,000 waiting for him in Chicago and millions more to be made in appearance fees.

Pyle was so happy with his big vehicle that he could barely contain himself. Visiting from Chicago, his wife, Effie, christened it with a bottle of grape juice, an event viewed by Pyle's daughter, Kathy, with whom he had happily repaired his relationship in previous years. Then C.C. hopped in the driver's seat and drove the two hours north from Oakland to Santa Rosa to show off his new vehicle to his mother, brother and sister.[23]

And if The America didn't gobble up enough funds, C.C. paid $25,000 for another bus, this one to carry race officials. So what if he'd already gobbled up $50,000 of the $60,000 that awaited him in Chicago? Between the fees paid by all the towns along the way and the advertising revenue, the

C.C. Pyle's America, the Hummer of its time, was a $25,000 custom-built bus that writers called the "land yacht." It was Pyle's home during the Bunion Derby as well as race headquarters. Meanwhile, the runners slept in tents, barns, under stadium bleachers and wherever else they could find shelter (courtesy the El Reno [OK] Library).

cash would soon be rolling in, he reasoned. But to pay that much on transportation alone at a time when the runners were sleeping in tents left a stench, making Pyle appear more like a plantation owner than a promoter. For a businessman with the gift of gab and a common man's ability to rattle the society swills, Pyle had gone a bit too far this time, or so it appeared. Even Red Grange, who Pyle recruited to be a race official and travel along as he recovered from a knee injury, was taken aback, saying, "(C.C.) couldn't go like the average guy." Grange was put in charge of making advance reservations and typically traveled behind The America in a handsome red roadster.[24]

To build attention, Pyle staged a series of events, ranging from 15-mile running to 10-mile walking races. And he secured more attention with the arrival of big-name international runners, thanks to the work of Hugo Quist, Paavo Nurmi's manager whose recruiting trip to Europe had been a success. Among the big-name entrants was renowned ultra-marathoner Arthur Newton. A 44-year-old British native and resident of Rhodesia, Newton was the holder of every record for distance running from 29 to 100 miles, a man who had never run an Olympic marathon because he considered the distance too short.

Meantime, Quist pressed onwards, attracting others, including 1920 Olympic silver medalist Juri Lossman of Estonia; Finland's Olli Wantinnen; and Englishman Peter Gavuzzi, a steward on the "Majestic" of the White Star Line and the recent victor of Britain's Newmarket Marathon. A couple of other top Finnish runners living in New York also entered — Gunnar Nilson and Willie Kolehmainen, a 2:29 marathoner and the brother of Johan "Hannes" Kolehmainen, the 1920 Olympic gold medalist.[25]

So at 3:30 P.M. on Sunday, March 4, under partly sunny skies, Grange ignited a bomb signaling the start of the longest footrace ever. With that, some 275 runners circled Ascot Speedway several times before an appreciative crowd of several thousand, and headed off on a route that would take the heartiest of them all the way to New York. Crossing Santa Monica Boulevard, the runners turned east on Route 66, cut across Los Angeles and disappeared into the mountains. Watching closely from their vehicles was a host of officials headed by Pyle, Pickens, Grange and a couple of new ones — race referee and former champion sprinter Arthur Duffy and timer Ralph Goodwin of Los Angeles.[26]

Newspapermen conceded that the Europeans — Kolehmainen, Lossman and Newton — stood the strongest chances of Bunion Derby success. Led by the great Nurmi, the Finns had enjoyed dominance in distance running for the last several Olympic Games, a standard of excellence that would endure for decades. Of the Americans, Nicholas Quamawahu, a Hopi Indian from the tiny town of Oraibi in northeast Arizona, was a relentless front runner and the winner of Pyle's 15-mile race back in February; he seemed strong. So did proven distance runners like August Fager from Ashtabula, Ohio, Harry Abramowitz from New York, and Bill Busch of Philadelphia. Another contender was John Salo of Passaic, New Jersey, a native Finn and a shipyard worker who had put in strong performances in marathons in Boston, Brooklyn and Philadelphia. And who couldn't resist the chances of Phillip Granville, a Jamaican who lived in Hamilton, Ontario, and held many Canadian distance records? To preserve his strength over the long haul, Granville had concocted an unusual strategy: He was planning to walk to Chicago — and then start running.[27]

Trailing the top runners was a motley collection of characters. Some had been good college athletes, established in sports like hiking, swimming and even wrestling. Others were eccentrics and charlatans, and a few were just unhinged. Moseying toward the Mojave Desert was 56-year-old Lucian Frost, a beaded, long-haired actor who played Moses in Hollywood productions, wore the biblical robes of his role, and had developed his distinctive limping gait after developing frozen feet while working as an Alaska mailman. There was a Hindu philosopher who chanted as he ran; another runner, from Italy, sang arias along the road; and Albert Rothschild of Los Angeles, a 54-year-old hiker, believed like Granville, that speed walking was the way to go.

Others had never finished a footrace, including a champion swimmer from Florida, and another who bragged that he was ready for the challenge, having once skipped rope 11,000 times in the same spot. Another entrant ran and walked as he played the ukulele and was accompanied by two hound dogs. The oldest entrant was a 63-year-old man who walked with a cane. And the youngest was a gutsy 16-year-old African American named Tobie "Cotton" Joseph, who was running for prize money to climb from poverty. A Louisiana native living in Los Angeles, Joseph was the oldest of five children whose father, an ex-auto mechanic, had been paralyzed in a garage accident. Joseph had talent — he once covered 25 miles in 3½ hours. His family was serious about the race; following him in an old Ford Star touring car were his father and two brothers.[28]

The Josephs shared one thing with several other runners: Given the extreme difficulty of the task ahead, some brought support staff, usually a family member or a hired trainer. Covering 40 to 60 miles with no days off, the runners could use every advantage they could find. A prominent physician, Dr. K.H. Begg, predicted that completing the derby would take five to 10 years off a runner's life. Pyle's slapdash arrangements didn't help matters. Each night, blankets and personal effects marked with each runner's number were dumped on the ground near the finishing line with little regard for order. And that was when the supply truck actually got there; distance and terrain often kept the trucks from reaching the checkpoint before the runners.

For the most part, Pyle continued to run things as he had in training camp — a little too much like boot camp to suit most runners. Baths and showers were infrequent, particularly for the laggers, who typically arrived hours after others had showered and used up most of a small town's hot water. According to newspaper accounts, blankets were seldom washed, and less so as the days wore on. Sticking to the morays of the day, runners were housed according to their nationalities and skin color, with the English and Canadians in one tent, Scandinavians in another, and Native Americans,

French and Germans in their own separate quarters. Excluded altogether were Cotton Joseph and other African Americans; Joseph at least had his family for comfort, with the others dependent on black communities along the race route for lodging and meals.[29]

Just how daunting a task lay ahead for the runners came through loud and clear on the Bunion Derby's first day. Figuring they would be averaging 40 miles or about a marathon-and-a-half a day, Pyle gave them a break, sort of, by sending the band of runners *only* 17 miles over the Hollywood hills, through Pasadena and, turning sharply southeast, into the tiny town of Duarte, which today skirts metro Los Angeles. That would be the last "easy" day for the entire race, with runners heading on day two nearly 35 miles to Bloomington, outside San Bernardino, in what would be a more typical idea of the change ahead. By the end of day three — some 46 miles through the winding roads of the San Bernardino Mountains to the edge of the Mojave Desert at Victorville — nearly 90 runners, or about one-third of the starters, had dropped out.[30]

By the end of day five, 16 more runners had dropped out. Conditions were inadequate. Stopping for the night in Mojave Wells, the 180 or so runners had to share a single working water spigot. Heading some 7,000 feet up the Cajon Pass, the air thinned, making it harder to breathe as the sun and the heat beat down relentlessly. Back on level roads, the winds howled, whipping up the sand and dust that stung the runners and seemed to lodge into their into every pore. A visitor recalled strolling about the tent in camp one night and hearing the agony — the cries of the runners nursing virtually every conceivable injury from ankle sprains to blisters, shin splits and sun burn.

For the moment, big names led the pack. Some 97 miles into the 3,400-mile route, Nicholas Quamawahu sailed along in the lead, followed by Nestor Erickson, a Finn living in Port Chester, New York, just north of New York City, and Arthur Newton. But odd things were happening daily. Three miles outside of Victorville at the start of a 36-mile stretch through unrelenting desert winds to Barstow, Willie Kolehmainen gave up, his feet wasted by swollen arches. That evening in Barstow, a few others dropped out, and the number of derbyites dwindled to 150. Even Quamawahu was having troubles; seized by cramps, he was rescued by a rub-down, and then resumed the race at a walking gait.[31]

At the end of each day, Pyle sent a bus back along the race route to collect the injured runners, with those quitting the derby collecting their $100 deposit for the trip home. In the beginning, those who had been hurt and wanted to keep going would be returned the following morning to the point where they had stopped. But with scores of runners already dropping hours behind the leaders, it was taking much too long to transport the athletes back and forth. So Pyle created a draconian rule, specifying that runners not reaching the day's checkpoint by midnight would have to leave.[32]

On day eight, Arthur Newton seized the lead on a 32-mile trek through the blistering sun to Mojave Wells. He would remain at the front for nearly two weeks — a man who said he had never run a standard 26.2-mile marathon because it was too short a distance for his taste, and seemingly born to win this longest race. Newton stretched his lead to one hour, then three, six and eight. But then, as the race passed the 600-mile mark around Flagstaff, Arizona, the derby took a dramatic turn when Newton sprained an ankle, came down with tonsillitis and dropped out. Just when the race appeared to be developing into a one-sided rout, Newton was gone, creating two new leaders. One, as expected, was Arne Souminen, a 28-year-old Detroit physician by way of Finland. The other, never considered among favorites by pre-race pundits, was just the man who could add some spice to the race: Andy Payne.[33]

A 20-year-old Native American — a member of the Cherokee tribe — who had grown up in northeast Oklahoma, Payne was a relative unknown, overlooked among the big names. As the oldest of seven children, Payne was destined to finish high school and take over the family farm run by his father, "Doc," a curious nickname given he was a farmer and rancher his entire working life, including a stint spent at the farm of Will Rogers' son, Clem. Andy had flashed some talent in high-school track; he was his district's top miler and half-miler, and typically ran the five miles back and forth from home to school each day instead of riding horseback as his siblings did. But leading the great Bunion Derby? Was an upset in the making?[34]

On the other hand, Payne had quite suddenly become part of an uncanny and proud tradition of Native Americans with an ability to run long distances — and not just marathons, but extraordinary distances. In June 1927, a 42-year-old member of the Oneida nation named Levi P. Webster, known as Chief Tall Feather, ran 88 miles from Milwaukee to Chicago in 19 hours, 47 minutes, easily breaking the previous record by more than two hours. A week later, a 55-year-old Karook Native American named Mad Bull covered the 480-mile Redwood Highway Marathon from San Francisco to Grants Pass, Oregon, in 7½ days — and celebrated by buying his first car, with his named printed on the door.

Payne didn't care much for analysis of such events or for conversation with reporters. "I thought I could do it," he said when asked why he had entered the Bunion Derby. "I just enjoyed running, and had a knack for being able to cover the ground on foot," he said. But his reserve hid a quiet self-confidence and gritty determination to win C.C. Pyle's big race. In a letter to his family, he revealed a bit more of what drove him. "I knew I could run and could stand just as good a chance as anybody," he wrote. Throw in a bit of the classic American wanderlust, and Payne seemed to have just the character and resiliency required to be a champion. For adventure and to pick up a few dollars after high school, Andy and his brother enjoyed hopping freights headed to California where they would work odd jobs and return home, well-armed with exotic tales of camping along the way in hobo camps.[35]

In contrast to the glittering records of the Bunion Derby's top marathoners, Payne's records were nothing special. He had never run a race at a distance even close to a regulation marathon. But in late 1927, when Payne saw the two-page ad about Pyle's race in his hometown paper, he wanted to enter, figuring the $25,000 top prize would pay off the mortgage on his parents' farm and help him to pay for his planned marriage to girlfriend Vivian Shaddox.

Vivian was Payne's former high school math teacher. The two were only a month apart in age, and liked one another immediately. But because Andy was her student, dating was out of the question. With some help from the Chamber of Commerce of Claremore, just south of his microscopic hometown of Foyil, and a loan from his father, Payne raised the steep $125 entry fee — actually, it was $25 with a $100 deposit. Hitchhiking to Pyle's training camp in Los Angeles, Payne worked odd jobs to pay for his room and board, while putting in the base of miles that would serve him so well on his long trek across America.[36]

The prospect of Andy Payne leading the race as the caravan approached his home state gave the Bunion Derby a much-needed dose of excitement. The race needed something, for as the days rolled on, C.C. Pyle's great transcontinental footrace was turning into a numbing grind unable to attract the kind of attention he had predicted. Pyle continued to churn out the press releases, and though the daily race notices were dutifully filed by the Associated Press and run in most major newspapers, the stories by the end of March were becoming notably more brief, particularly with baseball's regular season drawing near.

But for all of Pyle's big talk and bluster, he had overlooked the reality that there weren't a lot of people around to watch the derby in the desolate,

winding mountain passages and dusty, miniscule towns of Arizona and New
Mexico. This wasn't a race in the traditional sense — like a track meet where
runners went around an oval and were always in sight — but a long stream
of grim plodding humanity spread out for miles. Watching the day's finish
could take hours; interesting for a time, but hardly spectator friendly.

Nor were town officials as excited to bid — and outbid — other towns
for the right to host the runners, depleting Pyle of what he had expected
would be several hundreds and even thousands of dollars a day. It became
apparent that Pyle's finances, as James Harrison of the *New York Times* called
them, were a case of "plenty of outgo and no income." And that "outgo"
including considerable expenses for food for both the runners and the crew,
wasn't about to stop.

"This raises at least one question," wrote Harrison. "Where does Mr.
Pyle come off? It will hardly be possible to charge admission to the public
thoroughfares lining the course. The sale of programs would scarcely defray
the expense, and there would be no market for hot dogs and peanuts."[37]

Not a problem, replied Pyle, the man with an answer for everything,
and what he claimed was a surefire method of exciting the fair citizens of
the smallest, most isolated desert towns of the Southwest. All he needed,
C.C. insisted, was better advance publicity for his ace in the hole — a traveling sideshow that chugged into the small towns each evening to help welcome the tired runners. Get the word out properly, Pyle promised, and the
derby would quickly turn a profit, with spectators getting to watch the runners, meet a bona fide celebrity in Red Grange, and, for a charge of 10 cents,
attend C.C.'s fair.

The carnival was bizarre even for the era's traveling shows. In the polit-
ically incorrect language of the day, it had "freaks" like "Plug the Poison
Girl," who did an intricate snake routine, a fire-eater and a tattoo artist
named "Kay Ho." Pyle's show featured races with all kinds of barnyard wonders, among them a five-legged animal alleged to be half-pig, half-dog and
another said to be half-turkey and half-Guinea chicken. There was "Warf
Warf," the dog-faced man; "Wasko," said to be the world's most clever police
dog; and, a half-Guinea chicken with two distinct squawks. On the side were
all kinds of "games of skill," as Pyle grandly called the card sharks who tried
fleecing the natives of their earnings, except when were shut down by the
sheriff in Rolla, Missouri.

One of the more bizarre items in the sideshow was a mummy advertised as an "Oklahoma Outlaw," which was actually the cadaver of a one-
time train robber named Elmer McCurdy. One would think McCurdy's tale

would have ended in 1913 when he was shot and killed by a posse after robbing a train in Oklahoma and his body was taken to an undertaker in Pawhuska, Oklahoma. But when no relatives turned up to claim the body, the undertaker embalmed McCurdy, but used so much arsenic that he preserved and dried out the body, essentially turning it into a mummy. With nowhere to go, Elmer McCurdy's cadaver occupied a corner of the Pawhuska undertaker's office for years until it was claimed by somebody claiming to be a family member. Elmer's mummy wound up at a carnival sideshow in Los Angeles before Pickens figured it was perfect for the crowds the marathon.[38]

The strange tale of Elmer McCurdy was an apt symbol of C.C. Pyle's return to his carny roots. Surrounding himself with restless souls, even dead ones, was nothing new for this promoter of promoters. Nor were dwindling funds and an ability to talk his way out of a pickle. Perched aboard his luxury cruiser, C.C. was a gambler at heart, still in charge and convinced that the next big payday was just down the road. In a sense, Pyle's optimism paralleled Elmer's post-derby career, but only after another few ordeals. Returned to Los Angeles after the derby, Elmer became a Hollywood prop, but lost an arm when a stagehand bumped him. Trying to repair the "prop," the stagehands suspected the body might be human after all, which a coroner later confirmed. Jump ahead to the 1980s when an Oklahoma City artist named Fred Olds read about Elmer, who at this point was the feature attraction at an amusement park, and resolved to give the body a proper burial in Oklahoma. Olds did just that, taking Elmer back to his home state and burying him at a cemetery in Guthrie.[39]

7

"It Is a New
Racket Altogether"

C.C. Pyle's caravan of runners zigzagged slowly eastward through microscopic Southwestern towns, many of them bumps in the road with wonderfully poetic names. From Holbrook, Navajo, Lupton and Two Guns, Arizona, the runners shuffled into New Mexico towns like Gallup, Thoreau, Old Laguna Pueblo, Los Lunas and Seven Springs. Back and forth jostled the leading pack: Arne Souminen, on top since Newton had dropped out, followed by Payne, Erickson, John Salo and Peter Gavuzzi, one of the few pre-race favorites still in the running.[1]

Days started at 7:30 A.M. sharp, with Pyle calling roll through a megaphone from atop his the land yacht, as reporters had taken to calling the motor coach, and starting the runners off. Then he would roar ahead into towns 40 and 50 miles down the road. There he would ask for $1,000 from the mayors of towns and up to $5,000 from mayors of cities in exchange for the caravan to set up camp there that evening. He often veered off course slightly to wangle for a higher fee with officials from other towns, and sometimes turned down an offer altogether. When Albuquerque officials proposed paying Pyle $5,000, half of which would go directly to the runners in a public ceremony, C.C. brushed them off. Either the entire fee would be paid to him alone or they would bypass the city. When the town insisted on the split, Pyle directed the running caravan to veer off Route 66, which went right through the heart of Albuquerque, and make a semi-circle detour of many extra miles around the city. Other town officials drove an equally hard bargain, realizing that in the remote parts of Arizona and New Mexico they needn't pay C.C. a dime since there were few other places to go.[2]

Outside Navajo, Arizona, C.C. Pyle's great transcontinental race took on several unusual competitors — a pack of stray dogs, including one nicknamed

"Blisters," who was befriended by John Salo and would tag along for hundreds of miles. Pyle didn't care much for the dogs, which required food and water, and gave the scene a rag-tag feel. But to Salo and other runners, the dogs quickly became welcome companions who helped make a hard task a bit more pleasant.[3]

What a scene the Bunion Derby must have been! Having a 20-vehicle caravan suddenly appear was a bonanza to people who lived isolated lives. It was an instant fair and a lure for people to spend an evening in town to watch the end of the race, attend the carnival and patronize shops, restaurants and bars, which usually stayed open late with the runners in town. The sudden appearance of C.C. Pyle's troupe was a happening, starting with the convoy of vehicles that included the radio truck and a portable hospital manned by a doctor. Once there, townspeople could gaze upon the gaunt, hearty runners, who were starting to resemble members of a refugee camp — "the whiskered and incredibly lame and bedraggled troupe" as Pegler derisively called them. Townsfolk could say hello to the great Red Grange, the first genuine celebrity many had ever met. Beyond the fair were a host of other oddities like the corpse of poor Elmer McCurdy, particularly after it was embellished by a new, even stranger touch: the monologue of African-American runner Earle Gardner, pretending to be the outlaw as he spun the tale of his dastardly life. Pyle's land yacht was another favorite, and C.C. loved giving tours of the inside. And so was the Maxwell House Coffee advertising truck with its 300-gallon coffee pot on the back that dispensed free coffee to spectators and runners alike.[4]

That few town officials were willing to pay the appearance fees as the caravan moved steadily eastward toward more populated areas didn't seem to bother Pyle. Nor did the reporters who occasionally showed up to snoop around for a story beyond the leaders, only to find growing evidence of a weary, discouraged band of runners. C.C. was in his element, a picture of constant motion and very much the big-city big shot who did it all, from talking to everyone to orchestrating the night's activities. Without question all those residents of little towns where the Bunion Derby pulled up each night had never seen anyone quite like C.C. Pyle.

C.C.'s publicists did their best in trying to spice up the list of daily winners, overall leaders and composite times. Winning the 30th stage, a 34.3-mile trek into the eastern New Mexico hamlet of Tucumcari, some 1,071 miles east of Los Angeles, was Seth Gonzales of Denver, but formerly of New Mexico, which earned him a warm greeting from what was billed as a "throng of admirers." How big a "throng" turned out wasn't explained;

Tucumcari's population was only 6,000. Trotting in some hours later was Mike Kelly of Goshen, Indiana, who was dead last in cumulative time among the 93 survivors. Discouraged and with his feet in pain, Kelly gamely wired his mother: "My shoes are about gone; send dad's old ones."[5]

In New Mexico, the Bunion Derby lost another participant — Frank Johnson, a 39-year-old Granite City, Illinois, steelworker whose difficulties summed up the plight of Pyle's athletes. Collecting his $100 deposit, Johnson left for home and arrived several days later, suffering from an assortment of ailments, including a painful case of shin splints, a severely swollen left ankle, and lips cracked so badly that they bled when he tried to eat. Deeply tanned and bone skinny, Johnson was so hungry that he was "hollow from head to heel," his wife said. "I can't prepare enough food for him."

Johnson was discouraged. The shin splints, he said, had made it exceedingly uncomfortable for more than a week before he quit, and he was one of the runners without a trainer to help him. "I believe I could have continued if a trainer had been available to treat the blisters and stiffness," he said.[6]

Those who could afford trainers were fortunate. Among them was Payne, who had struck up a friendship at training camp in Los Angeles with Tom Young, a Florida drifter who considered running the derby before thinking better of it and hiring himself as a trainer. Attending to Payne and two others, Young followed the runners during the day on a motorcycle before tenderly addressing their aches and pains each night.[7]

Adding to the runners' considerable number of challenges was primitive footwear. Though track shoes had been around for years — the 1894 *Spalding Company Catalog* featured three grades of spiked footwear, each low-cut, made from kangaroo leather uppers, and with six spikes. But these specialty running shoes of the era were made for the cinders and were hardly durable enough to hold up on the roads. Judging by the few surviving photos of the Bunion Derby, most runners appear to be wearing either high-top basketball shoes or hiking boots, which would have easily become worn down as the miles ticked off.[8]

Frank Johnson's apparent hunger was emblematic of a problem serious enough to provoke the runners to a near mutiny. In Amarillo, Texas, several runners confronted Pyle, demanding that he improve both the quality and variety of the food, and double their daily food allowance of 40 cents, which, even in the America of the mid–1920s, was barely able to cover more than coffee and a roll. Angry that they had been served stew 10 days in a row on dirty dishes, they threatened to quit en masse unless Pyle changed his ways.

"No more stew!" a runner screamed at Pyle, who had promised filling, scrumptious meals in the pre-race literature. "Ten days in a row is more than we need. We need stick-to-the-ribs food served on clean dishes, not on plates and cups wiped off with a dirty towel."[9]

Making the runners especially testy was a swirling snowstorm they had diligently endured on a 37-mile stretch of the Texas Panhandle, between Vega and Amarillo. The hard slog claimed another runner, David Davies of Sandwich, Ontario, reducing the field to 90. The rest, many of them numb with cold, demanded better.[10]

Pyle realized he faced pressing issues. With towns reluctant to pay his "advertising fee," he had serious cash flow problems, forcing race officials to skimp on some of the basics, he said. Thinking quickly, C.C. announced he would increase the daily meal tickets to $1.20 — "right out of my own pocket, every single day from now 'til the end of the race, rain, shine or snow!" — which were redeemable at restaurants along the route. He did away with the tents, promising that derby organizers would ensure lodging every night for the runners, though most didn't have the cash to pay for a room. At least a few like Souminen, the physician, could afford it. So could Harry Gunn of Ogdon, Utah, whose millionaire father, Freeman Fremont "Dick" Gunn, had hired a sleeping bus and two trainers for Harry and was following his 25-year-son in his Pierce Arrow roadster.[11]

For most, conditions improved marginally. But restaurant managers soon got wise to the C.C. Pyle meal plan, and began serving the athletes with special menus marked "Coast to Coast," featuring overpriced helpings of ham and eggs. Runner John Pedersen, a native Swede and a jeweler from Spokane, Washington, complained that was "all we ever got," earning C.C. yet another nickname: "Ham and Eggs" Pyle. No wonder some runners had taken to hanging around the Maxwell House truck, which continued to distribute coffee on the house *and* peanut butter and jelly sandwiches. Even Red Grange felt sorry for the runners and could be counted on to rise in the dead of night to fetch them a cup of coffee.

Having rid themselves of the tents, Pyle and his race organizers made do with what they could find for the runners' lodging, which in most cases were Elks' lodges, school gyms, an occasional barn, and in Oklahoma City, the space under the grandstand at the fairgrounds. It was survival of the fittest, with the front runners of the pack getting their choices of the best and often the only rooms in town. But back-of-the-packers like Pedersen would arrive hours later and have to settle for another night on the floor of an Elks' lodge, a barn or an empty store.[12]

But just when things seemed grim, along came a thunderbolt and a reason to believe the derby might triumph after all. Heading into Oklahoma, Arne Souminen, the race leader for more than a month, dropped out with a pulled tendon, making Andy Payne the sudden front-runner with a lead of some 2½-hours ahead of his nearest rivals, Peter Gavuzzi and John Salo. It didn't matter that Payne was from Foyil in the eastern part of the state; Oklahomans east, west and everywhere considered him one of their own, a homegrown hero. Leaving Texas and pulling into Oklahoma's first rest stop of Texola, population 337, townspeople gave Payne a thunderous welcome.[13]

Now this was how it was supposed to be! Seizing the moment, Pyle rushed into print a special "Andy Payne" edition of the "official" race program, and dropped the price from a quarter to 10 cents. The program cover featured a photo right from central casting — Andy running through a gauntlet of spectators and cars as he crossed the state line into Oklahoma. Dressed in long johns under long-sleeved shorts, and a cap, Payne, runner number 43, seems to have an extra bounce in his step. No wonder, for appreciative Oklahomans had already passed the hat and raised $1,000, which they presented to Andy as the first Bunion-Derby runner to cross the state line.

So it went mile after mile across Route 66 in Oklahoma. People lined the streets of the towns and country roads to cheer on Andy Payne. Farmers left their tractors in the fields and headed to the fence to shout encouragement as he ran past. Motorists blared their horns, and in the towns, people ran from front porches and stores to the road to cheer their native son. Even schools let out as the Bunion Derby threaded across Oklahoma, with students taking impromptu field trips to see Payne and the other runners. "They were the biggest athletes in the world," Hugh Davis, then 18 or 19, told author Susan Croce Kelly of the day the derbyites ran through Catoosa. "We perched up on a wall for hours and watched the runners come along."[14]

Maintaining his lead, Andy Payne became Oklahoma's favorite native son — and C.C.'s "athlete of the moment," every bit as important to his running venture as Red Grange was to football and Susan Lenglen to tennis. With Andy focused on the race and saying little, reporters flocked to old Doc Payne, his father, for comments as the state's most famous celebrity, Will Rogers, reminisced that Doc had once worked at his son's farm. Known as the "Cherokee Kid," Rogers in his syndicated newspaper column humorously conceded that Andy had replaced him as the state's favorite son, and even swiped his nickname. For members of the Cherokee tribe, Payne's success became a particular point of pride; he was the most celebrated Native-American sportsman since Jim Thorpe.[15]

Passing through the town of El Reno, just west of Oklahoma City, Payne slowed down to walk for a spell to drink a cup of water, and was cheered on by thick clumps of men, women and children, with some watching from rooftops. Nearing Oklahoma City in the center of the state, Payne had triggered a full-blown traffic jam of cars. There were so many hundreds of cars filled with people driving to Route 66 to see him run by that Andy got worried that in an all the excitement, he could turn an ankle.[16]

Lucky for Payne, he didn't turn his ankle. Even luckier, he trotted into Oklahoma City on Friday the thirteenth of April with the promise of a $5,000 gift from grateful members of the state's chamber of commerce. Facing a similar windfall — a whopping $5,000 appearance fee from Oklahoma City officials — was Pyle, or so he thought. Waiting for the runners as they finished the 33.5-mile leg from El Reno as they entered the Oklahoma City Fairgrounds was Governor Henry S. Johnston. But waiting for Pyle downtown at the courthouse was a piece of unfinished business — a writ from Ralph Scott, the New York Yankees football coach who was looking for *his* $5,000, the amount he claimed that C.C. owed him in back wages. Apparently, the judge agreed and made Pyle fork over his fee to Scott. The incident resulted in newspaper headlines, and by the next day, Pyle's mounting financial troubles was national news.[17]

Payne clung to the lead as he headed into eastern Oklahoma, running even or behind the other leaders to preserve his strength for the six weeks of running ahead. Crowds swelled as the runners headed toward Tulsa, the derby's halfway point, and to Payne's hometown of Foyil, giving rise to a new challenge of keeping runners clear of the almost constant traffic tie-ups. Heading into Chandler, the inevitable happened when a car struck runner Mike Baze of Huntington Park, California, fracturing his leg. Dodging cars had become an occupational hazard for the runners; by the end of the great race, 12 runners would drop out after being struck by cars, motorcycles, and in one case, a bicycle.[18]

The grind was getting to Payne. Some spectators thought nothing of wandering out to shake hands and congratulate their new hero, which impeded his stride and gobbled up valuable minutes. Payne's lead dropped. By the time they hit Tulsa, Payne was second, 66 minutes behind Peter Gavuzzi, and clearly rattled. "I'm just one of the bunch," he said at the finish line in Tulsa. "I wish they would let me rest a bit."[19]

Then just like that, Payne was back in front, having charged back into

Derbyites passing through El Reno, Oklahoma (courtesy the El Reno [OK] Library).

the lead in a long 52-mile stretch northeast of Tulsa, between Chelsea and Miami, clearly reinvigorated by a night at home and a visit with his girl-friend, Vivian. Continuing to run strongly, Payne increased his lead to 13 minutes as the derby neared Missouri. Leaving the hoopla behind, Payne crossed into Missouri intent on adding to his lead over Gavuzzi and third-place John Salo, nearly 2½ hours behind.[20]

Andy Payne and Peter Gavuzzi had turned the Bunion Derby into an intriguing two-man race. They were runners, but in another sense, they were soldiers, united by the sweat, sacrifice and the sheer magnitude of their intimidating task. In doing so, these two very different men had become friends.

Newspapermen, looking for an angle, any angle, in the daily drudgery of reporting race results, called them "The Sister Act," for their tendency to run together. Payne liked the sound of that and took to calling Gavuzzi his "sister," joking to a radio reporter that he had "three more just like them back in Oklahoma," a reference to his real sisters. "Not one of them has a beard though (and) can't run as good as he can either," Andy said. "But they're a whole lot prettier."

That much was true. At 22, just two years older than Payne, Gavuzzi,

Halfway through the Bunion Derby, the race had become an intriguing two-man competition between Andy Payne (left) and Peter Gavuzzi (right), pictured here in Missouri. Newspapermen, looking for an angle, had taken to calling them "The Sister Act" for their tendency to run together. Payne liked the sound of that, joking that he had "three more just like them back in Oklahoma," a reference to his real sisters. "None of them has a beard though (and) can't run as good as he can either," Payne said. "But they're a whole lot prettier" (courtesy the El Reno [OK] Library).

with his beard now grown to biblical proportions, looked far older, like a cross between a nomad and a prophet. And despite the "sister" tag, he and Payne were about as different as two people could be. Born in Liverpool to an Italian father, a former chef to King Umberto, and a French mother who was a former hotel chambermaid, Gavuzzi was an intriguing blend of cultures with a personality to match. He "spoke with a Liverpool accent, moved with Italian gestures, and lived with French passions," said an admirer. With reporters, he was funny and quotable, and punctured his conversation with infectious Cockney-speak like "bloomin'" and "blimey." And unlike Payne, Gavuzzi lived life off the road as hard as he could by smoking and indulging his fondness for whiskey. In the years before anyone much understood the benefits of packing carbohydrates, Gavuzzi wolfed down the calories by helping himself to heaping breakfasts of spaghetti.

Reporters took to the heart and the eccentricity of this short, slender runner, calling him the "Iron Man." The name caught on, and spectators in the small towns of Missouri cheered Gavuzzi on with cheers of "Run, Iron Man, Run!" The excitement had particular resonance in the Italian parts of towns, where residents considered Gavuzzi one of their own.[21]

The drama of this two-man race energized the Bunion Derby, which needed every jolt of excitement it received. Leaving Joplin, an old-fashioned egg hurling greeted the caravan's lead car in Carthage, which Pyle described as a protest because he had passed the town as a potential rest stop. Meantime, the number of runners continued to drop. Patrick De Marr of Los Angeles was banished when Pyle grew wary of his surprising third-place finish on the leg to Springfield, Missouri, and found De Marr had caught a lift part of the way. Just a few south miles in Waynesville, Missouri, a more unfortunate fate awaited Blisters, the dog who had accompanied John Salo all the way from Arizona. When a race official noticed that the pads on the bottom of Blisters' paws had become raw and infected, he took the dog to a clinic for care. Nine days later, the little dog rejoined the race on the road to Joliet, Illinois, before disappearing forever, presumably to the home of a sympathetic pet lover. He is remembered forever as the gutsy little mascot of C.C. Pyle's great transcontinental journey.[22]

Grinding toward Rolla, Payne and Gavuzzi ran mostly together before Payne gradually began to pull away, picking up a minute up here and there, and expanding his lead to 36 minutes. Gavuzzi grabbed back a chunk of time during a 45.6-mile chug into Hillside View outside St. Louis and retook the lead, which he soon expanded to a more comfortable 1-hour, 49-minute advantage.

When the caravan crossed the Mississippi River into southern Illinois, the field was down to 71. Citing exhaustion, 18-year-old Nick Persick of Long Beach, California dropped out. So did Harry Rea, also of Long Beach, California, after an attack of acute indigestion near Staunton, Illinois. Lucian Frost, the bearded Hollywood actor, was tossed from the derby for the same reason as De Marr: he had snuck a car ride. "I just couldn't stand the gaff," Frost said.[23]

Heading into Springfield, the Illinois state capital, Gavuzzi increased his lead to nearly five hours. But then Payne trounced him in a 34.6-mile jaunt to Normal that ripped 35 minutes from this lead, and the eccentric Englishman decided the culprit was his beard, which he said was weighing him down. Gavuzzi sheared off his whiskers, and with renewed vigor pronounced himself fit to continue, vowing to not cut another hair until he reached New York.

But things for C.C. Pyle were steadily unraveling. With the runners heading toward Chicago and the end of the trail along Route 66, the promoter's money troubles multiplied. His problems were not just from an occasional bad check, but from misdeeds of past years that would plague him the rest of his life. When C.C. defaulted on a three-year-old $21,500 debt due to a Champaign bank, deputy sheriffs found him in Elwood, near Joliet, and seized his luxury motor home as payment. C.C. got his vehicle back when a company in Joliet claimed it was merely renting the vehicle to him.[24]

In Joliet, another chapter in Pyle's randy past pushed unexpectedly to the forefront. Some years before, Pyle had agreed to manage the financial affairs of a former silent film star named Valeska Suratt, whose career as a "vamp" in the Theda Bara "femme-fatale" mode had rocketed her to stardom in the World War I era. A native of Terre Haute, Indiana, Suratt made her name in the 1915 silent classic, *The Immigrant*, and starred in a dozen popular films before turning to the lucrative New York vaudeville scene through much of the 1920s.

Suratt was an entertainer of unusual fortitude and depth. More than an actress, a singer and a dancer, she was a stylish dresser, a successful screenwriter and a Biblical scholar. Valeska also possessed solid business sense, and used her earnings to buy a house in Terre Haute as a clothing boutique for her sister. A pillar of the community back home, she quietly donated $500 a week during World War I to the Red Cross.

With her film and stage career nearing an end, Suratt was preparing for retirement from acting by getting what she figured was rightfully hers. Also in 1928, she sued Cecil B. DeMille, alleging he had plagiarized her screenplay in his production, *The Kind of Kings*; the suit would be settled three years later. So it went with Pyle, who received word from Suratt that he had bilked her out of $2,000 that she entrusted to his care.

Talking to reporters, Pyle brushed off the lawsuit as frivolous. "It's just another of those things," he said. "I guess I am the most attached man in the world. Ever since we started on this race from Los Angeles last March, I have been sued and threatened. But all have come to naught, and the race goes on, and will go on."

Writing to Suratt, C.C. took a paternalistic tone, insisting that the shares of stock he had chosen for her "will make you money." Rattling on, C.C. insisted that Suratt could have her investment back anytime she wanted. "Cant [sic] write much but honey I am thinking of you," he wrote. "Your [sic] a sweet girl. I love you very much."

The judge, however, wasn't buying the love. He ordered Pyle to pay up.[25]

On Sunday, May 6, 1928, the great transcontinental foot race derby
arrived at the foot of Route 66 in Chicago. How fitting it would have been
for C.C. Pyle to have enjoyed a triumphant day back in his hometown. At
least things started out that way, when the lead runner, John Salo, steamed
toward the finish of the day's 43.2-mile jaunt through the heart of the big
city. Down Michigan Avenue, the city's spacious thoroughfare, and past
cheering spectators flew the hard-charging Salo to the finish at the First Regiment Armory. Adding to the festive atmosphere was the music emanating
from a spot in front of the city hall, where a band known as the City Machine
Gun Corps, a tongue-in-cheek reference to Chicago's reputation as a mafia
haven, entertained the crowd with a series of tunes, including one called "The
Bunion Bearer."

But things soon began falling apart. A car grazed Olli Wantinnen, fracturing his rib. Wantinnen would somehow finish the day's run, taking third,
and then dropped out, ending the journey of one of gutsiest runners. In addition to his rib injury, the 98-pound Finnish star had persevered nearly 2,300
miles from Los Angeles with a painful case of shin splits, a sore foot and a
bruised toe.[26]

Later that day came Pyle's most crushing blow. Meeting with the Route
66 officials in Chicago, association officials briskly informed the derby impre-
sario that they wouldn't be paying him the $60,000 fee he had been prom-
ised. For starters, the adverse publicity about Pyle's money troubles had
embarrassed association officials. And not only had Pyle hogged most the
publicity — he had named the race after *himself* for goodness sakes — but he
had also done next to nothing to drum up attention on the wonders of traveling Route 66. Hadn't one of the major goals been to extol the joys of motor
camping in the wilds of Arizona and Oklahoma?[27]

It was as if C.C. Pyle's dubious behavior and questionable business
ethics were starting to catch up to him all at once. Around the same time,
C.C. Pyle was being sued by a Detroit architect, claiming that C.C. owed
him more than $1,000 for a theater he had designed back in 1921. And in a
minor inconvenience, referee Arthur Duffy left the caravan, stating he needed
to get back to Boston to resume his job as a sportswriter. At least he wasn't
mad; Pyle replaced Duffy with Red Grange.[28]

C.C.'s troubles were growing more complicated by the day. Creditors
hounded him for money that he didn't have. With so many legal issues, Pyle
needed help in the daily challenge of running the derby. Thank goodness
then for Freeman Fremont "Dick" Gunn, the wealthy Utah executive who
was determined to see his son, Harry, finish the race, and offered his services.

Gunn was Pyle's guardian angel, paying off Pyle's debts and loaning him $50,000 to ensure the runners get to New York. For his troubles, Gunn was handed the day-to-day coordination of the race, but he wanted no publicity for the agreement, most likely so the folks back home wouldn't think he had lost his sanity. Exactly why Gunn stepped in has never been adequately explained; chances are he just wanted to see his son finish. But *TIME* reported another possibility; Gunn, described as a "sportsman," which was another world for a gambler, was said to have bet $75,000 that Harry would finish. Gunn, a father of six, was a legitimate big shot as the owner of the Gunn Supply Company, which supplied workers to western railroad lines. He had successfully built his business by offering laborers free meals at his restaurant in return for doing railroad work.[29]

Gunn made an immediate impression with the runners by raising the daily food and lodging allotment 30 cents to $1.50—in cash, not coupons. But he soon discovered just how difficult the Bunion Derby could be to operate on a day-to-day basis. As the runners headed due east—across Indiana, Ohio and a slither of northwest Pennsylvania and into New York—towns seemed to have lost all interest in hosting the running caravan. Finding it more difficult to find towns willing to house his runners, Gunn created longer and longer routes, sending runners on their first full day in Indiana on an almost inhumane 66.2-mile route, from Gary to Mishawaka, outside South Bend. Adding to the oppressive daily mileage were more unwelcome articles that detailed Pyle's financial woes.

Nobody blamed Gunn. They blamed Pyle. Reporters had little trouble finding sources of discontent, particularly the derby's back-of-the-pack runners, many of whom were bitter about how they were being treated, and about the length of the daily runs. One runner, Mike Smith of Cleveland, said he was staying in the race just to run up his expenses and stick it to Pyle.[30]

The overall mood spiraled ever downward when some runners began raising questions about the legality of the contracts they had signed back in Los Angeles. Pressed by reporters, whose ranks were growing now that the derby was reaching more populated eastern areas of the U.S., the runners discovered that Pyle had pulled a fast one and was, in fact, not obligated to pay them so much as a single cent of the promised prize money. The contract certainly sounded legitimate, but in reality was a muddle of mumbo-jumbo and tongue-twisting legalese, which had given a Pyle an out. Whereas the runners had signed their contracts under a litany of rules back in Los Angeles, Pyle affixed his swirling signature to one section only, the all-revealing

line that "this entry is hereby accepted" and getting him off the hook on a
technicality. Another part of the contract stipulated that runners were due
to receive half the appearance money received from towns and cities along
the way — with Pyle pocketing the rest.[31]

On May 11 came more drama, this time on the roads when midway
through a brutal 64.5-mile stretch south of Toledo, Ohio, Peter Gavuzzi
dropped out. For days, the Englishman had been suffering from an infected
tooth that sapped his appetite, strength and consequently his lead, making
it impossible to continue. Rescued by a patrol car with his once-command-
ing five-hour lead cut to 44 minutes, Gavuzzi said he had not eaten solid
food for two weeks. "I was so weak that I could not make any progress." he
said, conceding the lead to Andy Payne. "So there was nothing to do but
drop out."[32]

But amidst the drumbeat of news about sore joints and impending
financial doom, C.C. Pyle was still making an impression as a big shot, able
to impress the rural folk in the small towns with his convincing pitch and
suave ways. Typical is the hubbub he raised on the afternoon of Wednesday,
May 10, in Elyria, Ohio, about 20 miles southeast of Cleveland, where he
hoped to rally local businesses to support his plan to have his runners camp
there that Saturday evening. Pulling up unannounced at 4:30 P.M. in front
of the Elyria Board of Trade, he was promptly informed that most of the
businessmen who worked in the building were absent on a golf outing at
nearby Spring Valley Country Club.

No problem at all, announced Pyle. Inviting what few businessmen
were in the office aboard his land yacht, he set out for the country club just
in time to catch the Rotarian-Kiwanis banquet program and announce the
proceedings to the surrounding countryside via his broadcasting station,
KGGM. What fortune for Pyle! And how fortunate for one U.S. Representative James T. Begg, who was attending the banquet in hopes of securing
votes for the Republican nomination to become governor of Ohio. Meeting
Begg on the porch of the country club, Pyle rigged up the radio equipment,
introduced the congressman as "the next governor of Ohio," and broadcast
his speech. (For the record, Begg never did become governor. He retired
from Congress and became a banker and a dairy farmer.)

Well, *that* caught the interest of James T. Begg, who then asked Pyle
about his real purpose of having Elyria host his runners.

C.C. smiled. "Well, of course, I'm not a man who likes to commer-
cialize sport," he joked. "But I had thought that at the start that I might
make a little profit of the affair. Right now, I'm $150,000 in the red." And

where he'd make his real profit, Pyle told Begg, was at the end of the derby in a 10-lap race around Yankee Stadium in New York.

For a moment at least, Pyle had won the day. On Thursday, May 11, he was the featured attraction at the Elyria Kiwanis Club luncheon where he spun tales of making it big in sports — how it wasn't the main attraction that made the big money, but rather the "by-products," such as candy, tennis racquets and perfumes that were named for stars and paid royalties with every purchase. Sure enough, on Saturday, May 13, the caravan rolled into Elyria, and the runners were given the star treatment, the top five anyway. Along with Red Grange, they joined the Elks Club for a free meal.[33]

Peter Gavuzzi's misfortunes seemed to invigorate John Salo, the new second-place runner. Salo took all three legs in Ohio, and would go on to win 14 of the last 27 daily stages. The 34-year-old American emigrant, was like Payne, an unheralded runner who had endured in a race of attrition to outlast the big names. A veteran of the U.S. Merchant Marine, Salo had made 10 perilous Atlantic crossings in The Great War through submarine-infested waters and risen to the rank of ensign. After the war, he settled in Passaic, across the Hudson River from New York City, and captained riverboats. Salo, who was married with two children, had been running for all of two years, and did much of his by running laps on the decks of boats.

But Salo and the other 53 remaining runners were simply too far back to catch Andy Payne. Reaching the 3,000-mile mark in the rugged Catskill Mountains of western New York, with slightly more than 420 miles to go, Payne had built up a commanding lead of nearly 22 hours. He had done so by continuing to conserve his strength — hanging back, seldom winning a leg, and maintaining his health — thanks in part to daily massages from Tom Young. Salo continued to take the daily legs and chip away at Payne's lead, but managed to pick up only a few minutes here and there, but little more. Jogging into Wellsville, New York, in sixth place for the 49.8-mile stretch — the 66th day out — Payne still led by 19 hours, and exuded a quiet, unflappable confidence.[34]

"(I'm) setting my own pace and running my own race and not a bit worried," he told reporters. To emphasize his point, Payne on May 20 ran side-by-side with Salo on a particularly brutal stretch from Bath to Waverly — some 58.3 miles. But that distance was short compared to the next day, May 21, when runners headed from Waverly to Deposit — an almost-inhumane 74.6 miles, the derby's longest distance. "Did you know those footracers ran 76 miles yesterday?" Will Rogers wrote in his weekly syndicated column. "That's three marathons in one day. Try to ride a horse 76 miles in one day and you'll truck him back home." No wonder that three days later on the way to Middletown, Salo lagged because of a chaffed foot. As a result, Payne regained nearly two hours of his lead, now at 17½ hours.[35]

But just as Payne's home state of Oklahoma had enthusiastically welcomed him, Salo was looking forward at reaching his hometown of Passaic, New Jersey, only a day or so and a handful of miles short of Madison Square Garden, where Pyle had announced the runners would finish with a 20-mile run around the indoor track. Just as Oklahomans had done for Payne, Passaic was ready to let loose with a thunderous welcome for Salo, one of its own, who had even carried the name of his hometown across the front of his shirt for more than 3,000 miles. "I'll come in leading the pack," Salo promised before pushing off from Suffern, 20 miles north of Passaic. He kept his word, running well ahead of everyone upon reaching his hometown, where Mayor William Jordan and an escort of motorcycle policemen met John at the city limits and accompanied him downtown as banners and flags draped the streets. Like Andy, Salo had left his hometown as an unknown and returned a celebrity; for now anyway, he was the most famous man in Northern New Jersey. This "feel good" story was welcome respite for Pyle, whose honesty and integrity was becoming daily grist for newspaper columnists in New York.[36]

If only Pyle could have replicated this feeling across the country! As Salo and the other runners reached town, Passaic let loose like it was New Year's Eve. Children ran alongside the runners, shouting encouragement. Girls rushed into the road trying to shake their hands. Car horns tooted, whistles blew and people tore up newspapers and hurled the remnants out the window as confetti. Placards stuck on car windows read "Welcome Johnny," and police cars carried stickers that read "Welcome to John Salo." Passaic's reception for Salo, wrote Frank Wallace in the *New York American*, "was a regular Lindbergh affair."

Salo's wife, Amelia, and the couple's two children gathered at Passaic High School — the day's finish line — as did about 10,000 others, including Salo's friends from the Jones Point, Staten Island shipyard, most of whom paid 25 cents apiece to watch the runners role in and be introduced individually by Red Grange through a megaphone. Later, after all the dignitaries realized that the day before had been Salo's 35th birthday, they got together and offered him a job as a patrolman, backdating the appointment one day to squeeze him in under the town's maximum age limit. That evening, Passaic threw a parade and a celebratory dinner at the Ritz Restaurant, after which most of the runners enjoyed a fitful night's sleep at the American Legion post — Salo was a member — or on the third floor of the police station.[37]

For C.C. Pyle, the upbeat coverage was a one-day respite from his troubles. The next day, his public relations nightmare resumed in the New York papers as reporters hammered him about the contracts and his dirty little secret that he owed nothing to his runners. And they wondered just how Pyle would ever be able to fork over the $48,500 in prize money he had promised the top 10 finishers at the finish line in Madison Square Garden. Pyle swore he would have the money. Meantime, his back-of-the-pack runners said he wouldn't, and Grange said he didn't know. Nonsense, assured Bill Pickens, dispatched to the area to perform damage control on the Bunion Derby's new "big" story. Of course Pyle had the money, Pickens had said in Suffern, New York, with the grumbling growing louder. And not only that, but C.C., or the "Commodore," as Pickens affectionately called him, had always treated his athletes with nothing but fairness and fatherly concern, he said.[38]

"The going has been tougher since leaving Chicago because there is no highway, and the Commodore has found it necessary to get out and raffle off a box of chocolates now and then," Pickens said. "But the financial situation is this: The Commodore (is collecting) 50 percent of earnings, and there will be plenty.... You see, it is a new racket altogether. It is a freak show and good old Jerome Publique is falling for it."

In hindsight, Pickens' grating, patronizing attitude underscored just why some of the back-of-the-packers runners had developed such a loathing of Pyle. "The Commodore rides along the road with his little ones," Pickens said, "and when one of them complains or looks tired, or anything like that, the Commodore says: 'Give the lad a drink of water.'

"It is things like that which make Mr. Pyle so popular with his little ones. He will buy them another pair of shoes any time their old ones wear out."

But those "little ones" — the 45 or so runners not likely to win a prize — were far from satisfied. Egged on by reporters who asked a lot of questions and wrote that they were being treated shabbily, the runners had thought about striking while in Suffern. But what were their options? "This race was absolutely fair," said Pickens, deftly changing the subject to a debate on cheating. "We disqualified three men for cheating. It was impossible to cheat without discovery. Every runner was a detective, as his own chance to win would be lessened if a rival stole a ride."

Backing up Pickens was C.C. himself—back to his old silver-tongued, double-talking best in explaining in several different ways that he indeed had the prize money to pay the runners. "I'll pay the runners off in real money, not buttons," he had assured everyone in Suffern. It was as if Pyle hadn't a care in the world, as long as he was the star attraction and reporters sought him out. "Why certainly I have (the prize money)," C.C. told Paul Gallico of the *New York Daily News.* "I had it before the race started. Certainly I may have lost $100,000 before they hit New York, but I hope to get it back. This race is an investment. I will start getting it back with our 26-hour race.... But in the meantime, they'll get their money."[39]

To recover a fraction of his losses, Pyle announced he was tacking on a 26-hour race at Madison Square Garden on the weekend following their 20-mile run there to close out the trek across America. For the runners, most of whom were sore and tired and just wanted to wrap things up, the news was an unwelcome surprise. But Pickens was talking big, predicting that the Garden would be packed for the event. Besides, all the grumbling wasn't going to work, added C.C., who said he would only pay the prize money once his runners completed that last race.

Runners well back of the pace considered their options. Far from finishing in the money, they wondered if it was really worthwhile to hang in there to the end. It certainly wasn't part of the original contract, but if Pyle withheld the $100 deposit for getting home, many runners might be left broke and destitute on the streets of New York and unable to get home. One runner, sixth-place Bill Kerr of Minneapolis, had already consulted a lawyer and was said to be having Pyle's finances investigated, not believing for a moment Pickens' prediction that the Garden would be filled for the 26-hour finale. "The bearded runners got religion as they neared the end," wrote Frank Wallace of the *New York American.* "It is a religion of skepticism, chiefly skepticism about the prize money." Even Pyle's patron saint, Dick Gunn, questioned C.C.'s business methods; "a bit loose," he called them.[40]

Pyle agreed to honor the $100 deposits. It was the least he could do for his 50-some remaining runners for whom the derby had taken a fearful toll, both physically and emotionally. Having covered vast distances day in and day out for nearly 12 weeks, the runners were a collection of broken-down men, bone-skinny and ravaged by aches, blisters, swollen ankles and shin splits. Pain was constant. They had been struck by cars, bitten by dogs, and run across deserts, over mountains, and through searing heat, sandstorms, rainstorms and blizzards. "I was in the war," bunionite Stanley Stevens of Calgary told reporters in Passaic. "The only difference between this and the war is there are no bombs dropping here." Most just wanted to finish and head home — "keep(ing) faith," the *American* wrote, only "with the people who had been sending them money and telegrams of encouragement."[41]

Eying the ravaged condition of the runners, the big-city newspapermen hurled scorn at Pyle. They nicknamed C.C. derisive names for his shoddy treatment of the runners, from "Massa Charley" and "Simon Legree" to "Corns and Calluses" and "Cached Cash." Nor did they spare the runners, calling them a "lumbering herd of Uncle Toms" for putting up with Pyle's blarney and exploitation. The derby itself, reporters wrote, had became "the Continental Corn Conflict" and "the Pacific-to-Atlantic chiropodists' steeplechase."[42]

"Charles C. Pyle is a character out of a book," penned Paul Gallico of the *Daily News*. "He is today the most interesting man in sports. A news person could keep his notebook, and for that matter his entire paper, pretty well filled up merely by assigning himself to follow Charles about the country, and observe the birth, the incubation and the hatching of the various schemes that enable him to make page one of the Metropolitan dailies, free for nothing, most any time he cares to do so."

Gallico was right on target. "Pyle, himself, has a circus personality," he wrote. "He seems to exude the atmosphere of the big top. ... He wears quiet clothing and a little scrubby, toothbrush mustache, but he is cheating himself, because he belongs in a frock coat, gold-plated chain across his front, brilliant in his bosom and a fine silk topper. ... Thus, when Charley looks me right square in the pan and purrs in his silky-soft voice that he has the money to pay off his marathoners, I believe him implicitly. I believe him whether he has it or not."[43]

So *did* Pyle have the money? A few days earlier, he said he had it. Now, C.C. said he didn't have it — not exactly anyway — but would have it soon, so everybody could receive their shares and go home. Nor did Pyle seem to mind all the abuse hurled his way by the runners. "I have grown to love my actors," he said, sounding more like a theater director than a man with a veritable target on his chest. "I even love the newspapers. Didn't you fellows put me on the front page?"[44]

For the 55 runners who had made it this far, the finish loomed just ahead. At 4:00 P.M., Saturday, May 26, the derbyites left Passaic and headed down Paterson Plank Road some 10.5 miles to the West Shore Terminal at Weehawken, New Jersey, across the Hudson River from New York City. After all the small, dusty towns and seemingly never-ending stretches through deserts, mountain passes and the plains, the runners thought of the soaring

Manhattan skyline, which "seemed to give them new courage and strength for a final sprint," the *New York Times* wrote. Some even prepared by shaving for the first time in weeks to look spiffy for the big finish.[45]

At the ferry in Weehawken, a group of teenage girls besieged the runners for autographs. Then the runners ate dinner and crossed the Hudson at 8:00 P.M., their movements now tracked by a battery of movie cameras. But the meal break hadn't done the runners much good; many tightened up during the meal, which fortified by existing sprains, strains and aches, made their plodding especially painful. Arriving in Manhattan at the foot of Forty-second Street, the runners headed their last mile or so on the road to Madison Square Garden at Fiftieth and Eighth.

Trotting, limping, half-walking around the track at the Garden as if they were on eggshells in their final 20 miles — 200 laps total, 10 to the mile — they looked like a stream of battered, beaten down unfortunates headed to the shelter. Anxious to look lively before the whirring movie cameras, Pyle went into a rage. "Come on, you fellows," he exhorted, having run down to trackside. "Streak it, boys, streak it. Show 'em what I've brought to New York."[46]

This was supposed to be the apex of Pyle's triumphant finish in New York, with his athletes charging magnificently toward the finish line of their epic race across America, cheered by thousands. Pickens had assured everyone that the Garden would be rocking — packed to the rafters with admirers — but few showed up. Newspapers estimated that 4,000 were there, but that was generous. What did Pyle and Pickens expect? It was Memorial Day Saturday in New York City, and anyone intent on seeing a sporting event had a lot to choose from, ranging from baseball at the Polo Grounds and Ebbets Field to racing at Belmont and Aqueduct. Nor was the Bunion Derby the most spectator friendly of events, with attendees having to work hard just to keep track of the clutter and confusion of watching 55 emaciated men slog 200 laps.

Albert Rogers of New York generated moderate interest by winning the Garden's $100 prize for the fastest mile. But this was unlike any of the big track meets for which the arena was famous; under the glaring lights of the big arena, the runners were so spent that few mustered little beyond the slow, steady trot shuffle they had used to get across the country. Garden owner Tex Rickard had put out sandwiches and water for the runners, who eagerly devoured the snacks as they ran, giving the proceedings the feel of a frantic vaudeville show. "New Yorkers who missed the lunatic gathering at the Garden ... will never see anything like it again until Mr. Cached Cash Pyle chooses to run another of these whirligigs," Paul Gallico wrote. "Broadway should have been there. The things that the strange characters were doing around that stone track were not one bit stranger than those many of us on the satyrs' street do. ... Saturday night at the Garden was a gathering place for the nuts."

How fitting that Wildfire Thompson of Bear Hollow, Arkansas, a man noted for his distinctive name and walrus-shaped mustache, chose for no apparent reason to run around the track backwards. Watching the back-peddling Wildfire and the other runners, Gallico couldn't resist one more dig: "I was waiting for them to all break out into a gibberish and go leaping and dancing around the track," he wrote. "There was something so infectious in the idiocy of the whole thing and I wanted to get out onto the track myself and run around and wave my arms."[47]

John Salo won the 20-mile stretch, becoming the first to complete the 3,422-mile run, timed in 588 hours, 40 minutes, good for second place overall. Then came Andy Payne, the Bunion Derby's overall winner at 573 hours, four minutes, some 14 hours and 36 minutes in front. Philip Granville of Hamilton, Ontario, the walker who had been persuaded to run, and had been since Chicago, took third overall. Mike Joyce of Cleveland was fourth, Guisto Umek of Italy, fifth, and Bill Kerr, sixth. Payne was due $25,000; Salo, $10,000; Granville, $5,000; and Joyce, $2,500; with the sixth-to-10th-place finishers, $1,000 each.[48]

So Pyle's great transcontinental run was done, all except for the matter of collecting $48,500 for prize money to be awarded at the 26-hour finale the following weekend at the Garden. The runners would get a break. They were housed in the basement of the Garden, where some said the stench of the elephants from the circus was overpowering. But Pyle, camped at a spacious suite at the Vanderbilt Hotel, had anything but an easy week ahead; he needed a lot of money fast, and people were busy suing him.[49]

8

"Everyone Will
Be Satisfied"

"Ceremony?" asked Pyle. "Cash or check? Well, we have not decided on these details as yet, but everyone will be satisfied."

C.C. was holding court with reporters on the Sunday morning after at his suite at the Vanderbilt, as if his Transcontinental Footrace had been a rip-roaring success. As usual, he brimmed with hearty cheer, an air of confidence and a lot on his mind, starting with the reason he hadn't as yet paid off the top 10 runners. Was he broke? "There was nothing in the contract to say when I had to pay it, and I want to wait until I get the official time of my checkers," C.C. explained. "I am reasonably sure that the finishes were correct, but suppose there was a difference and I had paid off."[1]

There were announcements, starting with details of the 26-hour race, which would start at 9:00 P.M. Friday, June 1 at the Garden and end the following evening. To be contested with two-man teams, this final competition would include the top finishers who had to stick around in order to be paid — and feature the return of Arthur Newton, Peter Gavuzzi and Willie Kolehmainen, all of them big names who had dropped out. There was Pyle's new "miraculous foot fixer" to promote. "C.C. Pyle's Patent Foot Box" contained remedies "for every one of the 3,000 maladies of the human foot" from toe, heel, instep and ankle trouble to shin splints. Included, Pyle said, would be his treatise on chiropody to be given away with every purchase of the box.[2]

So why hadn't New Yorkers filled Madison Square Garden to the rafters for Saturday's 20-mile race? "There was no contest," C.C. said, "but in the 26-hour race, there *will* be a contest." Assuming everything went well, Pyle said he would stage more races — a six-day event at the Garden "before the hot weather comes" and then a series of track meets in Boston, Detroit,

Montreal and other big cities. Like most things involving Pyle, the really big event, the one that would make everybody rich and famous, was just around the corner.

After all, C.C. said in turning to his latest idea of selling foot medication, "we are just entering the golden age of the foot."

"We are going to have hundreds of thousands of distance runners in this country, and every one of them will naturally buy C.C. Pyle's Patent Foot Box," he continued. So the transcontinental footrace was only a start of something greater — a nationwide craze and a movement of which Pyle was its guru. "This business has just begun," C.C. said. "We were pioneering in this race, which has just ended. We lost money — we expected to — but we will make it back."[3]

Pyle was rolling now, his mind bursting with new impractical get-rich schemes, few of which stood much of a chance to ever happen or earn him a penny. A series of races? "Andy Payne will be worth $100,000 to me around the country fairs of Oklahoma," C.C. gushed. "There will be plenty of money from the by-products of this race. We ought to know how to take care of feet, shouldn't we?" Well, yes, but the Bunion Derby hadn't exactly been a financial windfall. Nor had the grim procession of a bunch of runners traipsing endlessly around a track compared to the genuine thrills of Pyle's other ventures, like seeing Red Grange break a tackle or Suzanne Lenglen rocket a serve.[4]

But C.C. Pyle's triumphs in football and tennis seemed like ages ago. For now, Pyle was busily comprising new schemes for a windfall, having badly extended himself. As if to put an exclamation mark on his continuing parade of legal troubles, officials of the Continental Illinois National Band and Trust Company, to whom Pyle owed more than $16,000, had again served notice, this time filing a complaint in the Manhattan Supreme Court the previous Friday to make their previous suit in Illinois effective in New York. Then, the bank announced it was pushing to take additional action — this time against Grange — for another $20,278 it claimed to be owed. That same day, deputy sheriffs served C.C. with yet another suit — this one for $3,183, the amount he owed his radio crew of three, who said they had arrived in New York virtually penniless and unable to afford the railroad fare home. On top of that, Pyle's radio man claimed that C.C. still owned nearly $2,500 for equipment rental.[5]

Meantime, Pyle's derbyites coped with something they hadn't known since early March: blissful free time. On Monday, Andy Payne flew to Washington, D.C., where he sat in the gallery at the U.S. Capitol and was lauded by Oklahoma Representative Everette Howard of Tulsa as "America's greatest" runner. More good news for Payne arrived later in the week when the Oklahoma City Chamber of Commerce voted to award him some $4,099 of the $5,000 it had refused to fork over to Pyle back at the fairgrounds in Oklahoma City. Meanwhile, a group of 20 middle-of-the-pack bunion runners journeyed to Jefferson Hospital in Philadelphia, where Dr. John Baker made them men of science, studying the effects of the long run on their feet, legs, hearts and respiratory systems. From Philadelphia, most of the 20, who had no chance of receiving prize money and had collected their $100 deposits, headed home.[6]

In New York, the remaining 35 or so runners comprised a mass of aching humanity. Rousted from their quarters at the Garden, they spread among low-budget hotels of the Hell's Kitchen area of the West Side of Manhattan and tended to their considerable pains. One hobbling runner, wanting to see nearby Times Square, had to drape his arms around the shoulders of two friends for help just to get there. Sympathetic New Yorkers befriended other runners and took to driving them around town because walking for many was too difficult. Wildfire Thompson fared better, staying loose by playing catch with a group of boys on a West Side street, and presumably getting about by himself.[7]

Pyle waved off complaints that most of the remaining athletes were sore, tired and nearly destitute by declaring that the real issue is that they had stopped running — and missed it. "I believe in tapering off," C.C. said. "When all the misery's gone, you feel kind of lonesome and lost. A lot of the boys are feeling terrible and don't know what is the matter with them. I'll tell what's the matter with them: The thing they are suffering from is lack of pain."

Oh, so that was it. Challenged by reporters that the contracts left the runners with next to nothing for their considerable labors, Pyle agreed, saying, "Sure, my contract was one-sided" because "I'm building these fellows up." Asked to comment about the runners, like Kerr and Stevens, who had complained publicly about their treatment, Pyle grew hostile. "Those fellows who kicked are just Bolsheviks," he told the *New York Daily News*, finally sounding frustrated at the flogging he was taking from some of the runners. "This fellow Kerr is a plain Red.... They tell you of the few tough spots we were forced to stop at, but they never tell you of the swell chicken dinners we bought for them."[8]

Just then, the telephone in C.C.'s hotel suite rang. On the other end was a back-of-the-pack runner, Sidney Morris, looking for train fare to get home to Los Angeles.

"Is $100 all I get?" Morris protested. "Think what I suffered in this race, Mr. Pyle! Shouldn't I get a little something extra for my suffering?"

Hearing that, Pyle got steamed. "What do I get for *my* suffering?" he thundered. "I've suffered too, Morris! I have wrinkles in my trouser pockets from digging, and writer's cramp from signing checks to bring you from Los Angeles to New York. See me in the morning and get your $100."

After hanging up, C.C. calmed down and grew philosophical. "This pioneering a sport is a tough racket," he said. "You know you have to have a sense of humor in this promotion business and you must keep it working overtime."[9]

On Thursday, May 31, New York newspaper reporters and photographers were summoned to be at Madison Square Garden at 4:30 P.M. sharp. That's when C.C. Pyle would hand over the $48,500 in prize money to Tex Rickard, the boxing promoter and Garden owner, as payment to the top runners at Friday evening's finale. Yes, he *was* a guy who kept his word, C.C. insisted. But what he did not acknowledge was that Rickard, embarrassed by the adverse publicity the Bunion Derby was bringing to Madison Square Garden, was actually giving Pyle the money. It was the price to pay for saving face, Rickard figured.

Reporters and photographers were at the Garden at 4:30 P.M., but Pyle wasn't in attendance. Nor was he there at 5:00 P.M. or 5:30 P.M. Finally, at 5:35 P.M., a man in Pyle's headquarters called to say that C.C. had just left the Vanderbilt, a five-minute cab ride away, and would be there soon with $48,500 in prize money that he would then present to Rickard.

Then, at 5:45 P.M., it was announced that Pyle was still at the Vanderbilt, and was about to leave, finally.

But 10 minutes later — 5:55 P.M. — it was found that Pyle hadn't been at the hotel since 4:00 P.M. There is no accounting of his whereabouts.

Now *here* was a story, and reporters sat back to record the evolving details:

- 6:05 P.M.: Pyle's headquarters announces that C.C., in fact, had left the Vanderbilt 20 minutes before with a suitcase full of cash to give to Rickard.
- 6:15 P.M.: Word arrives from Pyle's headquarters that C.C. hadn't been there since the early morning, and nobody knows where he had gone.
- 6:25 P.M.: A flash! Pyle has just arrived at the Vanderbilt, armed with the cash. He will be leaving for the Garden at once.

- 6:40 P.M.: Actually, Pyle left for the Garden two hours ago, though nobody can still say what became of him. "Are there any hold-up men still operating in New York?" the *Times* wonders.
- 7:00 P.M.: It is announced that a California bank made an error and sent the money to the wrong New York bank. Everyone can go home. The error will be rectified Friday when the prize money is awarded.[10]

So at 9:00 P.M. Friday at the Garden, there was Pyle dressed in a conservative dark suit and described by the *Chicago Tribune* as "debonair and smiling," as he stood next to Tex Rickard, also looking particularly dapper in a new, green hat. Then the two men took off to stride purposely across the Madison Square Garden floor toward a microphone to make what looked like an important announcement. With both men looking at ease and confident, it certainly appeared they had the prize money, the runners figured.[11]

To the side of the spiffy Millrose Athletic Association track, the runners limbered up for the final race of the derby. Inside the track was a rubbing table manned by a masseuse, along with two rows of iron beds, each equipped with blue mattresses, sheets, pillow cases and two chairs, thanks to Pyle's deposit of $1.10 for each bed sent from a nearby hotel. Nearby, a brass band entertained what seemed to be about an equal number of spectators — estimated at 500 and so sparse that the voice of the public address announcer bounced off all the empty seats.

That didn't bother the announcer, who flung about superlatives for posterity amidst the popping of flashbulbs and whirring of motion-picture cameras. Pyle was described as "the greatest" and the race as "most extraordinary." Used a half-dozen times or more was the phrase, "in the history of the world" as a way of putting the derby in context. And with that, Pyle stepped to the microphone to perform what many had thought would never happen — hand over certified checks in full to the top 10 runners. And just like that, much of the bitterness and accusations of the last several weeks vanished. "Well, I made good," said Andy Payne, suddenly $25,000 richer and smiling broadly. "Some time folks are going to wake up to the fact that when C.C. Pyle says he'll do a thing, that thing is as good as done." Then, the 20 two-man teams took off in one last spasm of running; already running was Harry Gunn, Dick's son, who had actually started out at 8:00 P.M. in an effort to set the world's 100-mile non-stop record.[12]

Gunn gave up after nearly seven hours, having covered 25 miles, his long run across America finally done. Four of the two-man teams, spent from their long run from Los Angeles, quit as well. An accumulation of problems ranging from fatigue to indigestion nagged at many of the others. Resting runners lay on cots, wiggling their toes and rinsing their throats from water bottles by spitting water on the floor. Crumpled newspapers lay by their beds, with limp, damp clothes dangling over the back of the chairs.[13]

It all had the look of a giant sleepover of emaciated men as they circled the track of the nearly deserted arena — hardly the heroic finale that Pyle had pictured. The band did its best to keep up everyone's flagging spirits by periodically bursting into lively, three-minute pieces. That drew an occasional yell from the tiny crowd, few of whom had paid their way into the Garden. For Westbrook Pegler, the scene on the floor was "a depressing spectacle."

On the track, the relay team of Philip Granville and Frank Von Flue covered more than 183 miles to withstand a late challenge from Arthur Newton and Peter Gavuzzi and earn the evening's top prize of $1,000. By 11:00 P.M. Saturday when the derby finally ended, perhaps 150 spectators, fewer than most of the crowds that had greeted them in the smallest towns, were there. "For 26 hours, the almost empty temple had resounded with the dull thud-thud-thud of plodding feet," Pegler wrote, "but never once had it resounded with the shrill cry of excited customers, the only music that a promoter recognizes." And just like that, C.C. Pyle's 3,422-mile transcontinental footrace was done.[14]

Close to midnight Saturday at a speakeasy across the street from the Garden, Pyle sucked the foam off the top of a cold beer — and came as close as he ever would to admitting he was whipped. "I seem to have made a mistake," he told Westbrook Pegler. "I felt certain that after those 55 fellows of mine had run all the way across the continent, the customers would come out to see them finish indoors. But they didn't ... I was expecting more.... So, I will just have to admit that C.C. Pyle has taken one on his chin this time."

But Pyle's mind was already buzzing with new ideas. He wanted to take Payne — "that boy Stanley Payne or Andy Payne or whatever his name is" — on an exhibition tour through Oklahoma. There was the foot-cure product. And then, incredibly, Pyle talked of plans for another transcontinental race to be staged in 1929; that is, after C.C. had vacationed over the summer in Europe and scouted for new talent at the 1928 Olympic Games in Amsterdam.[15]

Who cared that that Bunion Derby has cost Pyle $100,000? Everything C.C. said or did still attracted attention. He was still interesting, very much a big shot, a man who commanded headlines, a one of a kind. The next big thing might be around the corner, C.C. preached, and sometimes believed. Another Bunion Derby would be a hit, provided he did a few things differently the next time, he added. Pyle knew it, felt it in his bones, provided he made adjustments. And, oh yes, he still had a football team to run.[16]

On a drizzly, overcast autumnal Sunday afternoon on the last day of September 1928, C.C. Pyle was in Providence, roaming the sideline of his New York Yankees' opening game of the season against the Steam Roller. Only 5,000 had journeyed to watch the contest in what was probably the NFL's oddest stadium ever.

The Cycledrome was a 10,000-seat oval that had been built for bicycle races, not football. Spectators sat on a wooden oval that banked steeply around the turns and flattened on the straight-aways, leaving barely the space to squeeze in a football field. The track, equipped with seats and a bench for the players on each side, hugged the sidelines so closely that players tackled near the boundary line frequently careened into the front row. One end zone extended a regulation 10 yards, but the other end zone went only five yards, cut off by the banked track.

The Cycledrome had only one locker room with two showers, built with a couple of bicycle racers in mind, and wholly inadequate for two football team of 18 men each. No wonder the Yankees, as did all visitors to the Cycledrome, dress at their hotel and take a bus to the stadium.[17]

They needn't have bothered. Red Grange was gone, having dissolved his three-year partnership with Pyle at the close of the Bunion Derby. Grange's knee had yet to heal properly, and rather than play sparingly, football's greatest gate attraction decided to walk away. But Red's decision was based in part by finances. Concerned that the football Yankees had continued to hemorrhage money, Grange said he "could no longer afford to continue pouring money into the property." The two men parted as friends, so with his football livelihood seemingly finished, Red needed a new way to make a living. Adding to his troubles was that nasty business of the suit by the Continental Illinois National Bank and Trust Company, which would take another three years to settle.

Weighing heavily on Grange's decision to retire were the opinions of doctors, several of whom told him that he risked the possibility of never walking again if he kept playing. Unable to suit up for the first time since he was a boy growing up in Wheaton, Red admitted as the 1928 football season started that he felt "like a duck out of water." Unsure of what to do next, Grange talked of starting a ranch in California, and in the meantime, jumped on an opportunity to head west on a six-month vaudeville tour.[18]

To replace the great Galloping Ghost in the Yankee backfield, Pyle had recruited Gilbert "Gibby" Welch, an All-American all-purpose runner from Jock Sutherland's powerful Pitt Panthers. But on this day in Providence, Welch and the Yankees ran into a smothering Steam Roller defense that lived up to its nickname by limiting the Yankees to a measly 54 total yards. Providence, behind Grange's old rival, Wildcat Wilson, romped, 20–7. The only Yankee score was on Welch's interception return for a touchdown.[19]

Pyle had fought tooth and nail for a NFL franchise — and for this? Welch continued to excel, but the Yankees went nowhere in 1928, finishing 4–8–1 to take seventh in the 10-team league. All in all, it was another wacky NFL season, one in which teams drew up their own schedules, which meant that some teams played a lot of games —16 for the Frankford Yellow Jackets — while others played just six or seven. With the Yankees' baseball namesakes playing another World Series, Pyle's team was forced to the road for its first three games, while the Chicago Bears were at home for 10 of their 13 games.

At least Pyle's Yankees managed to take two of their three games against the cross-town Giants, including the season-ender, a December 7–6 squeaker before 15,000 at the Polo Grounds. That was one of the better crowds, for as the Yankees played out the string, home gates sagged to a little more than 3,000 a game, hardly enough to keep a team solvent. At 9–1–1, Providence took the NFL title, bringing joy to the brethren at the cramped Cycledrome, where two years later, the Steam Roller would host the league's first night game. At least Pyle could take small comfort that the Giants had an equally dismal slog of it in 1928; playing before microscopic crowds at the Polo Grounds, Mara's team won only four of 13 games, finishing sixth.[20]

With New York City clearly incapable of supporting two NFL franchises, the Yankees faced a bleak future. With crushing debts and still facing the animosity of several NFL owners, Pyle got the message, and a few days after the close of the season, sold the team and its few assets to Mara. And so ended C.C. Pyle's roller-coaster ride in professional football, the sport he had used to muscle his way from small-town theater owner to the top of big-time sports promotion. It was all for the best, said C.C. in a rare moment of genuine reflection. In fact, Pyle, who seldom traveled anymore without a lawyer, was relieved to be out of football, where he couldn't run things himself, the weather was unpredictable, and the odds for success were long — too long.[21]

By early 1929, C.C. had turned his attention to Bunion Derby II, which with big, new names, a new route and a new direction, would be the latest and "greatest" sporting event in history, or so he said. Spending his time in New York watching the Yankees, C.C. became convinced that the troubles of the first derby stemmed by starting on the West Coast, and not the East, where the power of the New York press corps would get behind him this time around. So he flip-flopped the direction and decided to start on the East Coast and head west: New York to St. Louis on the old U.S. Highway 40, then hopping on Route 66 to Chelsea, Oklahoma, southwest to Dallas and due west on Highway 1 to Los Angeles. "I was a sap to brings the boy on from Los Angeles last year; that's why it flopped," Pyle said. "Everything that's a success must come from New York. If I had started in New York and run to Los Angeles, I would have cleaned up out there."[22]

Things would be different in Bunion Derby II, C.C. insisted. He had already sewed up contracts in hand with chambers of commerce of towns clear across the U.S., which were eager to have his caravan visit — or so he said. "They are paying me various sums to travel by way of their towns," he said. And this time, C.C. planned to send his runners through bigger towns than in the first derby, meaning bigger daily payoffs. "I can't lose," he predicted.

There was $60,000 in prize money this time, he said, and the promise of a new group of young athletes getting fit. "The race affords them an opportunity to improve their health," C.C. said, conveniently overlooking the image of the previous year's broken down and discouraged runners trudging around Madison Square Garden like bedraggled refugees. "It will keep them out in the open air. Physicians who examined the runners who completed last year's race found them splendid specimens of physical manhood."[23]

Pyle's new emcee — in place of Grange — was the great Jim Thorpe, a bona fide magnet to build excitement along the way, C.C. assured everyone. Andy Payne would be there as well, though as an official, not a runner. The reserved Oklahoman had done what he said in going back to Foyil and using his prize winnings from Bunion Derby I to build a house for his parents. In late 1929, he would teach running to football players at the Oklahoma Military Academy, and marry Vivian.[24]

Brimming with renewed cheer and optimism, Pyle said he had learned to contain costs. Gone in Bunion Derby II was the pricy land yacht, replaced by a new form of transport for race officials in the form of practical roadsters, all of them painted red with Pyle's name plastered on the doors. And because things with Pyle's radio crew had ended badly the previous year, C.C. decided to save the cost and forgo a crew this time. No need, he assured everyone: In the press-saturated East, the newspapers would provide plenty of upbeat coverage.[25]

The papers already had, thanks to a story in the early part of 1929 that C.C. had bagged a famous name for Bunion Derby II—the great Boughèra El Ouafi, the 1928 Olympic marathon champion who had recently competed indoors at the Garden. Born in Algeria, El Ouafi had won the gold with considerable drama by snatching the lead with about three miles left in the race. Pyle had first spotted El Ouafi at the Olympic Games in Amsterdam and became convinced that the runner, who competed for France, was the key to making Bunion Derby a big success.[26]

A former member of the French Colonial Army who earned his living as an auto mechanic in Paris, El Ouafi recognized the potential financial windfall and seemed anxious to give the derby a shot. Pyle announced the news that he had snared the great champion in the late winter, just after he had gone to Chicago to give away his step-daughter, Florence Arnold, in marriage. A few weeks later, C.C. said that El Ouafi would sail from Algiers on March 12, to provide plenty of time to rest in New York and get ready for the start of the race. But just like that, El Oaufi decided the better of it and said he would not be running. (Some 28 years later, in 1956 after another French-Arab runner, Alain Mimoun O'Kacha, won that year's Olympic marathon, journalists discovered El Oaufi still living in Paris, but unemployed and destitute. French sportsmen put together a fund to aid the forgotten hero of Amsterdam. In 1959, the 60-year-old former champion was sitting in a Parisian café, and senselessly shot to death by members of the Algerian Liberation Movement after he had refused to support them.)[27]

At least Bunion Derby II shoved off as scheduled, at 3:00 P.M., March 31, 1929, at the command of Will Rogers from Columbus Circle on the Upper West Side of Manhattan. On one hand, Pyle had chosen an ideal time for the send-off—Easter Sunday, with some 500,000 brought outside by the balmy 55-degree temperatures and a chance to show off their holiday finery.

But despite the festive atmosphere and the throngs, Pyle had little apparent way to profit. As had happened more than a few times the previous summer, many thousands attended, but few paid. C.C. still hadn't quite figured out a sure-fire method of dipping into the pockets of those who chose to watch without opening their wallets. Happily adorned in their Easter hats, the festive crowds heartily cheered the runners and then went their way, unlike a football game, where fans had to buy a ticket. That tore at Pyle. "Isn't this hell?" he muttered. "All these people here, and I can't collect a dime out of any of them. Wish I could have enclosed this Circle."[28]

Meantime, Pyle had incorporated Bunion Derby II with other embellishments. Runners paid a $300 entry fee this time, triple the previous
amount. Also, C.C. had overhauled the sideshow, creating what he called a
more highbrow brand of entertainment to match the more sophisticated
tastes of eastern audiences. There were no snake charmers, three-headed ani-
mals or dead bodies this time, though Pyle's entertainment gang still had a
decidedly carny feel. Named "C.C. Pyle's Cross Country Follies," the show
was billed as "a high speed thriller ... brilliantly conceived, gorgeously produced (and) the most captivating beauty chorus ever coaxed away from dear
old Broadway." Not only could derby spectators cheer on the runners, they
could enjoy the dancers, according to the ads, "amid the most refined sur-
roundings for the delectation of the public."[29]

Performing in Bunion Derby II for the public's delectation were 21
female dancers, between the ages of 17 and 21, though it wasn't clear if any
of them had ever set foot on a Broadway stage. Looking after them would
a caretaker, a surrogate mother of sorts, the exotic-sounding Madame Duvall,
an Englishwoman who had managed to charm even the cynical Pegler.
"Remarkable fortitude and the strange capacity for domesticity under
difficulties," the newspaperman wrote of the Madame. Also along for Bunion
Derby II was Chicago's La Belle Irene, the self-proclaimed female champion
slap-tongue baritone saxophonist. "Cut to the quick by the criticism of his
side show last year," wrote Paul Gallico in the *Daily News,* "Charley has
insisted that only the most elevating and stimulating entertainment will be
offered the susceptible peasants each day at control points across the country."[30]

Pyle was raring to go, saying he had learned from Bunion Derby I. "It
is different now," he told reporters in a near-whisper since he had lost his
voice. "We are on a firm business basis, and that cannot fail to be a big success. The tent show will be a big feature. It will be a high-class performance
throughout: 21 women and six men playing matinees, nights, every day but
a few Sundays where the local laws will not permit these performances on
Sunday." C.C. went on to say the dancers — and the runners — would be
stopping at 250 towns and cities between New York and Los Angeles. As
with most things Pyle, that was wishful thinking.

But on the roads, things were looking up since several of Pyle's big-
name runners from 1928 were back, including John Salo, Philip Granville
and Arthur Newton, as was Peter Gavuzzi, still clean-shaven and engaging
as ever. This time, they would be competing for the $60,000 in prize money
to be split 15 ways instead of 10. Left intact was the $25,000 winner's share.[31]

So down Eleventh Avenue on the West Side of Manhattan thundered the pack of runners in launching another 3,400-mile jaunt across America, this time accompanied by their eclectic entourage of the dancers, Madame Duvall and La Belle Irene, along with Jim Thorpe, the Bunion Derby's master of ceremonies. Hopping on the 23rd Street Ferry to cross the Hudson River into New Jersey, the caravan planned to make Elizabeth its first stop, and head on to Trenton, Philadelphia, Wilmington, Delaware, and into West Virginia.[32]

But the rousing send-off was about the last upbeat thing to happen in Bunion Derby II. The race was mired with problems, starting Sunday afternoon in Elizabeth, where the town's chief of police, not a man with an appreciation for the finer things, forbade Pyle's dancers from performing. Nor was C.C. permitted to sell any programs in Elizabeth.

On Monday, things got worse. During the 46 miles to Trenton, a derby baggage wagon rolled into a field and landed on its side. About the same time, C.C. received news that the Trenton City Council had refused to let the caravan perform that evening or even stay in town.

It soon became clear what had everyone so riled up. Pyle was so broke that he couldn't pay any of his contractors, and they were complaining. One of them, a New Jersey man from whom C.C. had agreed to pay $800 to rent circus seats for his dancers, went to court to receive his fee, prompting police to find Pyle to serve him the first of many writs of attachment. They caught up with C.C. just after he had sidestepped Trenton and was about to cross the Delaware River into Pennsylvania.

"But officer," C.C. said, "the seats were no good and I sent them back."

As he chatted amicably, C.C. casually told his driver to move on ahead, across the river into Pennsylvania, and he would catch up in a second.

"Nevertheless," the officer said, "I must serve the attachment on your property."

"Well, ha ha, officer," C.C. replied with a devilish laugh. "That will be perfectly all right with me as I have no property in New Jersey now."

But along came Andy Payne, not running in part because of a lingering and painful case of shin splints, and serving as a patrol judge from the driver's seat of one of Pyle's snappy roadsters. What a case of bad timing. Police officers quickly impounded both Payne's car and another of C.C.'s vehicles that happened by a few minutes later.[33]

Pyle suddenly had a heap of trouble on his hands. Prohibited from stopping in Trenton, C.C. changed course and set up the caravan for the evening in Morrisville, north of Philadelphia, where the city fathers were more welcoming. Meantime, Pyle and his organizers struggled to deal with another headache: the mystery of how the derby had actually *grown* by 16 runners, all of whom required shelter and meal money. Asked by Pat Robinson of the *New York American* how that could happen, Pyle was stumped. "Damned reporter," he muttered.

But runners were the last thing on C.C.'s mind for the moment. To get his cars returned, Pyle disappeared with the police officers, giving both runners and dancers a day off while he sorted things out. He got the cars back, but the ordeal got several of the young dancers wondering if they would ever get a chance to perform. Enter the sensible Madame Duvall, who spent the day assuring them that everything would work out.[34]

But without a radio crew, there were few wire reports about the progress of the race. As a consequence, newspaper coverage was spotty, just the opposite of what Pyle had predicted. As in the first race, things held together in Bunion Derby II, more or less, before falling apart for good in the Midwest. In Oklahoma, C.C. broke his arm in an accident. In Texas, Pyle ran of out cash and stopped paying several employees, despite owing them considerable back pay. Then he fired them.

Florence Carr of Los Angeles, an actress with Pyle's vaudeville show, was discharged in El Paso without cause, she claimed. Scotty Findel and Ernie Mack, a couple of Los Angeles–based actors with the caravan, were fired in Amarillo, but labored on to the end — assured by Pyle that they would be paid from a $10,000 bonus he said the City of Los Angeles had promised him to finish the race there. Neither man ever saw another dime from Pyle, nor is there a record that the City of Los Angeles had ever promised a bonus. Mack said later he had spent large amounts from his own pocket just so several of the dancers and crew had something to eat.[35]

In Fort Worth, Pyle's secretary, Jeannette Richards of New York, was fired. About the same time, New York City patrolman Leon Spencer, who was working as Pyle's security guard, was let go. All said they had at least seven weeks' wages due them.

In Stanfield, Arizona, Pyle's advanceman, Charles Thompson was fired. With all of 20 cents in his pocket and a flat tire on his truck, Thompson had no way of getting home, but was reassured by a smooth-talking Pyle that he would be paid just as soon as the caravan made it another 20 miles to Phoenix. The caravan arrived, but Thompson's promised funds never did.[36]

With erratic newspaper coverage, few people took notice of Bunion Derby II. On the few occasions when big-city reporters ventured to the race, the reports came back soundly negative, most of it of the "Simon Legree" spin of the previous year. "There is a lot of laughter as C.C. Pyle's mad caravan moves on," wrote Ralph McGill of the *Atlanta Constitution*. "It is a ridiculous and bizarre bit with it all, there are men running about 40 miles per day, rain or shine, warm or cold...Of course, it is very hard on Mr. Pyle: He has to ride on an automobile all day and that does get so tiresome. And then there are the small hotels and their beds. It is very hard on Mr. Pyle. His mad runners have nice smooth concrete to run on."[37]

The turmoil obscured what had become a terrific two-man race in Bunion Derby II as Peter Gavuzzi and John Salo chased one another across America. Whereas Payne had stretched his lead in 1928 to hours, mere *minutes* separated these two, both of whom knew how to pace themselves over the long haul. On June 17, when 31 remaining runners filed across the finish line at Wrigley Field in Los Angeles, Salo won by all of 2 minutes, 47 seconds. A reporter called it "the most exciting finish in the history of foot racing" and wasn't kidding. But few noticed.

Financial turmoil awaited Pyle in Los Angeles. For starters, he was penniless, having dropped $50,000 in the Bunion Derby II with nothing to pay the top 15 finishers, who included the 1928 veterans, Guisto Umek in third place, and Philip Granville in sixth. Nonsense, C.C. countered. "The boys will get their money," he promised, before actually having the chutzpah to announce his plans for *another* race, Bunion Derby III, in 1930. "The race was a great improvement over my initial effort, and expect my third ... to be even better."[38]

Pyle's promises sounded distressingly familiar. Several disbelieving Los Angeles businessmen jumped to the runners' defense in an effort to secure the prize money. Concerned that the constant negative headlines would soil the reputation of Los Angeles with the 1932 summer Olympic Games headed to the city, the California businessmen worked earnestly on behalf of the runners, but found they could do little. Pyle was bankrupt, and the effort died at the end of June after most runners had gone home. Salo, a hero all over again, went home to Passaic, but he and the others would never receive payment for the heroic efforts in Bunion Derby II.[39]

Several of the dismissed performers lodged complaints with the California State Labor Commission. Pyle, with his arm still in a sling from his mishap in Oklahoma, ignored three summons, and was served with a subpoena. When C.C. finally made it to court, his auditor didn't, which was unfortunate, Pyle said, because he had the books and could have cleared things up right away. But when C.C.'s old friend Jim Thorpe, the emcee for

Bunion Derby II, sued him for $259 in back wages, Pyle finally came clean, admitting to reporters that he was "dead broke." C.C. said he would do his best to pay off the employees with the help of his brother, Ira.[40]

Financial and health troubles would plague C.C. Pyle the rest of his life. But his legend was only starting to build.

9

"More Ideas Than Most Men Came Up With in a Lifetime"

On a sweltering Chicago evening in June 1928, a promoter named Harry Caplan gathered 274 young men and women for a unusual trial of stamina — an endurance dancing contest for what he called the world championship title and a purse of $3,500. When asked his inspiration, he said, "C.C. Pyle."[1]

Two years later, W.C. Fields opened a Broadway comedy, *Ballyhoo*, in which he played a flamboyant con artist named Q.Q. Quale, the promoter of a cross-country footrace complete with emaciated runners and dancing girls. There was no mistaking who the drool, wise-cracking Fields was mimicking: Pyle. "Funnyman Fields exhibits a rich form of comedy which appeals freshly because his foibles and frustrations are the sort that take place in life, never in the theatre," wrote a *Time* magazine reviewer. "As may be expected, Mr. Fields' marathon is not a happy one financially and his troubles are many." Fields had some difficulties of his own with the play. As the Great Depression took its toll, theater-goers stayed away and the play closed in two weeks. It was Fields' only flop in nearly two decades on Broadway.[2]

Indeed, the Great Depression, which had hit the U.S. in October 1929 like a freight train, seemed to drain all the fun from American culture. With banks, businesses and farms failing, millions of Americans by the early 1930s were scraping to get by, having neither the funds nor any mood for frivolity. The flag-pole sitters, marathon dancers and Bunion Derby runners of the Age of Ballyhoo had lost their appeal. In May 1938, a trio of singing cowboys called the "Ranch Boys" announced they would ride their horses from the San Fernando Valley north of Los Angeles to Chicago, accompanied on their 2,875-mile jaunt by a specially built trailer carrying extra horses and camping equipment. "Shades of C.C. Pyle," wrote a *Los Angeles Times* reporter.[3]

But for all the enduring interest in Pyle, there would no third Bunion
Derby — its promise slammed shut by the Great Depression and C.C.'s sudden health problems. In 1930, Pyle suffered a devastating stroke that paralyzed most of his right side, leaving him unable to speak, walk or use his
right arm. Most men would have packed it in, resolving to live the rest of
their lives in seclusion. But Pyle wasn't like most men.[4]

C.C.'s fall had been long and hard. Press conferences, entourages and
big pronouncements were suddenly all in the past. Newspapers that only two
years before had granted Pyle big headlines wrote little about C.C. now, saying only that he was suffering from "health problems." Doctors were more
blunt, telling Pyle that he would never walk again.[5]

Only 50, Pyle threw himself into rehabilitation with the same energy
he had given his various schemes and promotions. C.C. rented a cottage in
northern Wisconsin, where he rigged a pulley to a big tree in the yard in an
effort to work himself back to health. Hooking a rope to his arm and running it through the pulley, Pyle hired a group of neighborhood children to
pull the rope and give motion to his arm. Over and over the boys pulled,
every day for months, and after thousands upon thousands of repetitions,
C.C. regained the use of his right arm. Then Pyle had the boys pull his legs
up and down in the same way — thousands of times, day after day — and several months later, C.C. was walking. Regaining his ability to talk was easier: Pyle just talked to anyone within range — something he never had any
trouble doing — and got his voice back too.

C.C.'s remarkable recovery may have been his finest, most determined
performance to date, all of it done in near-anonymity. He stayed at the cabin
in Wisconsin for 10 months and then went home to Chicago, where he ran
into Grange, his old friend who he hadn't seen in two years. "It seemed
impossible," Grange said of Pyle's recovery. "What a dogmatic fellow Charley
was ... How many people would have done (what he did)?"[6]

By 1933, Pyle was healthy enough to work and itching for a new challenge. He found it that May in a position that thrust him back into the public eye by managing Robert Ripley's Believe It or Not Odditorium at the
"Century of Progress" at the World's Fair in Chicago, held on Lake Michigan landfill just south of downtown. Billed as a celebration of American
modernity and industry, the fair was a giant fairgrounds topped off by a
wonder of the age — Paul Philippe Cret's Art Deco Hall of Science, featuring a 175-foot carillon tower that tolled with electrically triggered chimes.
There was the popular Sky-Ride that crossed the lagoon between the Hall
of Science and Raymond Hood's Electrical Group, from which red, white

and blue lights soared into the sky from 70-foot towers. There was the General Motors complex, with a full-scale Chevrolet assembly line, and the Chrysler building that housed a test track. And then there was C.C. Pyle, whose contribution to the fair was about as far as one could get from its slogan "Science Shoots Upward."

Ripley's Believe It or Not! Odditorium was a show filled with attractions like shrunken heads, medieval chastity belts and instruments of torture, the kind that had made Ripley famous. Among the assortment was a man who could talk without vocal chords, the girl with the world's longest red hair, the couple with the weightlifting eyelids, and the scholar who wrote 2,871 legal letters on a single grain of rice. They were C.C. Pyle's new flock, a group the old promoter had no trouble working into one of the biggest, most popular fair attractions of all.[7]

Pyle and Ripley were peas of a pod. They were entrepreneurs of the eccentric, curators of the weird. A 39-year-old native of Santa Rosa, where Pyle's family lived, Ripley was the better businessman, having turned a modest career as a sports cartoonist into a syndicated Hearst strip and a best-selling book chronicling the world's oddities under the moniker, *Ripley's Believe It or Not!* It seemed just about everyone had a cross-eyed cat or an uncle who could remove nails with his teeth and wanted to tell Ripley about it. Hooking up with newspaper baron William Randolph Hearst, Ripley took on a team of assistants just to sort and edit the thousands of letters he received daily. To supplement his findings, Ripley became a world traveler, often pictured wearing desert garb and a pith helmet. Known as "the Modern Marco Polo," he wended his way through exotic locations via luxury steamers and airplanes, but also by donkey, camel and gufa boat. Ripley's association with Hearst was lucrative, giving him a $500,000 annual income and an unlimited travel budget.[8]

Pyle was overjoyed to be back in the public eye. At his carny best, he viewed himself as a father figure and trusted elder to the assortment of contortionists, razor-blade eaters and sword swallowers that worked the Odditorium. C.C.'s old friend and admirer, Westbrook Pegler, came calling to sample what he called "Prof. C.C. Pyle's astounding and amazing aggregation of unique educational oddities." Pegler marveled at the unusual collection of eccentrics, like Arjan Desur Dangar, the Bombay policeman with a 78-inch mustache, and Estelle, the woman with rubber skin. At each show, C.C. proudly and loudly introduced his collection of new friends as if he were back in the Sacramento Valley pitching *Deadwood Dick*.

"This is Eddie, the Ossified Man!" Pyle would belt out, hoping to lure visitors to see Eddie's skin, said to be solid as concrete. "Eddie is a little stiff from La Crosse (Wisconsin)!"

"Scranton," Eddie would shoot back, correcting C.C., with a dash of hometown pride.

"Oh yes, Scranton," Pyle would answer. "Well, anyway, Eddie *is* a little stiff."[9]

Fainting visitors were a pesky problem, and Pyle hired a nurse, ready with smelling salts to revive the faint-hearted. The show was a smash, and by the end of 1933, more than two million people had filed through the Odditorium doors. So successful was the Odditorium that Ripley would open shows in Cleveland, San Francisco, San Diego, Dallas and New York. When the Chicago Fair ended, Pyle took over for a year as manager of the San Diego Odditorium.[10]

More at home in California anyway, and with his third marriage, to Effie Arnold, in trouble, C.C left her in November 1934 and moved to Santa Rosa, where his mother, brother and sister lived. In December 1936, the Pyles divorced, with C.C. arguing, as he had successfully in the past, that he should not pay support. But this time, the judge disagreed; Effie received a $5,000 lump sum and $300 a month in alimony.[11]

Dogged by fragile health and beleaguered by persistent financial troubles, C.C. lived quietly, stepping out occasionally to attend football games, and popping up from time to time on the social pages after attending a party. On July 2, 1937, Pyle married for a fourth time, to Elvia Allman, at the First Methodist Episcopal Church in Hollywood. A native of Enochville, North Carolina, the 32-year-old Allman was reminiscent of Pyle's first two marriages; she was in show business. A radio comedienne billed as the "Old Fashioned Girl," Elvia had been a Los Angeles radio fixture for years as a voice performer for cartoons, most prominently as Clarabelle the Cow in Disney cartoons. The couple lived in North Hollywood.[12]

By then, the old gang was steadily fading away. Bill Pickens died in 1934 at the age of 60, a victim of blood poisoning after stepping on a rusty nail while touring the grounds at Mines Field outside Los Angeles while preparing for a stock-car race. That the old sportsman died while in the midst of promoting something fast and a little risqué was appropriate; the *Los Angeles Times* remembered him as a man "who blazed a colorful trail in sports promotion that probably will never be equaled."[13]

In 1938 came sad news from Paris that Suzanne Lenglen had died at 38 from pernicious anemia. The great French tennis star had spent her last years as one of the world's best-known designers of sports dresses, so driven in her new profession that she had a tennis court built in the gardens of her Paris shop, where she could model her latest designs. The temperamental Lenglen never did marry Baldwin M. Baldwin or anyone else, although she was said to have been engaged to several men, from the Duke of Westminster to her occasional tennis partner, the exquisitely named Count Ludwig Salm von-Hoogstraeten. Sadly, she did not survive a series of blood transfusions in her last hours in a desperate attempt to save her life.[14]

Also passing away far too young was John Salo, the Bunion Derby hero from Passaic, New Jersey. Working as a patrolman in his hometown in 1931, he was struck in the head by a baseball during a game at Newark Park and badly injured. The 38-year-old runner died that night, leaving his wife, Amelia, and two children.[15]

Some of Pyle's other associates passed away as well. After dropping his weight a good hundred pounds to a healthier 200 or so in his later days, Big Bill Edwards died in 1943, at 66. Grange made it all the way to 1991 when he died at the age of 87 in Lake Wales, Florida. For the most part, good fortune had continued to fall on the Galloping Ghost. After ending his business relationship with Pyle, he returned to the NFL, where he played five more years on a damaged knee with the Bears, but he was hardly the darting, elusive runner he had been. The Depression wiped out most of Grange's fortune, but he recovered on the strength of a long and successful second career as a radio and television analyst for the Bears and for college games.

Grange and his wife, Margaret — they never had children — retired to Indian Lake Estates, Florida, where Red owned an orange grove and an insurance agency and sold real estate. Among the 17 charter members elected in 1963 to the Pro Football Hall of Fame, Grange was humble to the end, always taking time to sign an autograph, insistent on flying coach, and never interested in exploring the source of his talent. "Hell, I'm not that great," Grange told a gathering of old friends in 1978 in Wheaton. "I'm an ordinary guy." Asked late in life for his fondest college football memory, Red overlooked his five-touchdown performance against Michigan and chose a game at Iowa that teammate Earl Britton had won with a 55-yard field goal. "I held the ball for him," he explained. After the death of Old Number 77, Margaret insisted that he be cremated. "He specifically didn't want any viewing," she explained.[16]

Bunion Derby I winner Andy Payne would enjoy a similar long and fruitful life. Despite periodic reports that Payne was ready to resume training, he would never again run competitively after 1928. In 1934, Payne took up a different kind of race. Jobless and with the country wallowed in the

Depression, he ran for clerk of the Oklahoma State Supreme Court, and won. Payne was re-elected for decades, leaving only for two years of army service during World War II. Along the way, he earned a law degree and bought land where the discovery of coal, oil and gas made him wealthy. Payne served as clerk for 38 years and retired in 1972. Five years later, in 1977, he died, "leaving his family a small fortune and a large legend," wrote Dan Bigbee and Lily Shangreaux, creators of the 2002 documentary *The Great American Foot Race*. Today, statues of Payne in his hometown of Foyil and in front of the Cherokee Heritage Center in Tahlequah, Oklahoma, commemorate his great victory in the first Bunion Derby; the Andy Payne Marathon and 10- and 5-kilometer road races are held every year in Oklahoma City.[17]

As the 1930s rolled on, C.C. Pyle maintained an increasingly low profile while going to work again, this time in more sedentary form as head of a new and low-key company that produced audio tapes of radio shows. Some said C.C. was well on his way to another fortune by heading the Radio Transcription Company of America when, on February 3, 1939, at the age of 57, Pyle died at home of a cerebral thrombosis or a blood clot. Besides his wife, Elvia, who was at his side when he died, Pyle was survived by his daughter, Kathy, who in 1935 had married Clarence Malan of San Francisco, their son and Pyle's grandson, Charles, age three; along with his brother, Ira, and sister, Anna Ronk. Funeral services were two days later at Pierce Brothers Funeral Home; Pyle's body was cremated.[18]

It was a quiet end to a hard-charging life. Predictably, Pyle left a heap of debt. There was $14,500 he owed to Val Reis, a St. Louis-based music company. There was more than $5,500 claimed by Continental Illinois National Bank and Trust Company, a dispute on Pyle's famous bus that dated all the way back to Bunion Derby I. Even the U.S. Government had been after C.C. for not paying his income taxes from 1935 to 1938. And Pyle had been bickering with Robert Ripley for what he claimed was back salary due his way; Ripley eventually came through with $1,500 and the case was settled. To pay off what she could after C.C.'s death, Elvia sold Pyle's gym equipment and several hundred dollars in stock. But the total value of C.C.'s estate at the time of his death was all of $2,113 — a far cry from the hundreds of thousands of dollars the promoter had earned in his heyday.[19]

After his Pyle's death, Westbrook Pegler called him "the most interesting man I met in 15 years in the sport business." It was high praise indeed from the Chicago-based columnist, who by then had left sports to become one of America's most read — and acerbic — political columnists. Pegler would write periodically about Pyle for years.[20]

An admirer to the end, Red Grange was heartbroken at the passing of his old friend. "He was pictured as a notorious money-hungry promoter who ruthlessly exploited and used me to further his own ambitions," Red said of Pyle. "Nothing could be further from the truth. Pyle was always more than fair to me and one of the finest men I have ever known. ... He was suave, brilliant and perhaps the great super-salesman of his day. Pyle came up with more ideas in one day than most men come up with in a lifetime."[21]

Epilogue: "Everything He Touched Turned to Gold"

For the most part, the obituaries were kind. C.C. Pyle was saluted for his colorful ways and lauded for helping to make the Golden Age of American sports in the 1920s, well, golden. Back home in Ohio, the *Delaware Gazette* went further, and in a spasm of hometown pride, called him a one-time grocery clerk-turned "international figure who turned everything he touched to gold."[1]

Not exactly. But in the 1920s, C.C. Pyle's sudden rise to success and sharp fall was unique. He was a dreamer and a schemer, an American original with a flair for the dramatic, a gift for the gab, and a belief that the next big thing really was right around the corner. And if it really wasn't, he would talk his way out of a jam. C.C. Pyle fit the times as the little guy who became a big shot and never forgot his roots — always more comfortable with people in the small towns and the blue highways of Montana, New Mexico or Ohio than with the honchos of Chicago or New York.

No question Pyle got a lot of things wrong. He tried being a businessman, but failed, as Red Grange aptly put it, squandering hundreds of thousands of dollars and rifling the pocketbooks and the patience of investors in the process. For someone who revolutionized the sports world, Pyle often mistreated his athletes, overworking them in the extreme and arrogantly ignoring their concerns. No question that Grange was injured with overwork as were all those Bunion Derbyists limping around New York City. The only possible excuse is that Pyle had a lot, maybe too much, on his mind.

But C.C. Pyle's influence on sports was enduring. Representing Red Grange and Suzanne Lenglen, he became the first agent in the modern sense — decades ahead of what today is a well-known, high-profile and lucrative profession. He showed Madison Avenue that athletes, if positioned the

199

right way, could help sell their products. Although Pyle had no long-term involvement with the NFL, he demonstrated to Tim Mara of the Giants and the rest of the team owners that there were big opportunities in professional football, though it would take decades to find out. In promoting pro tennis, he beat the stuffy amateur officials at their own game, and showed that there was a future in the professional game — the kind of game where the world's best players could be paid at a rate worthy of their talents. The legacy of the Bunion Derbies are harder to assess; yes, they were financial flops, but the Route 66 bigwigs got at least some of the publicity they had desired, fueling the legend of traveling the great "Mother Road." We'll never know how many people said to themselves as a result of the derbies, "If people can run across the country, I can drive it."

As it happened, the year of Pyle's death, 1939, was a devastating one for his family. Just five days before C.C. died, his mother, Sidney, passed away at the age of 82 at the family home on Humboldt Street in Santa Rosa. Mrs. Pyle, who in 1927 had suffered a paralytic stroke, died on Sunday, January 31 at 6:10 A.M. — the same day of the week and the exact time, down to the minute, that her late husband, William, had died. Then, on November 13, 1939, C.C.'s brother, Ira, passed away at the age of 59 after an attack of indigestion. While Ira Pyle's death was sudden, he had been in ill health for many of his final years, possibly from the same family heart troubles that afflicted C.C.[2]

After C.C.'s death, his immediate family members remained for the most part in California. Pyle's daughter, Kathy Malin, lived mostly in San Francisco and San Mateo County, and after her Charles, who had been born in 1936 (and would die at age 14 in 1950), had a daughter, Margarita, who, in turn would have four children, all daughters. For the record, Kathy died in 1986. Meantime, C.C.'s sister, Anna Ronk, died in 1961 in Santa Rosa on the same day Ernest Hemingway killed himself in Idaho. Anna had spent her final years as a widow, renting out rooms in the house on Humboldt Street to working women and female students from Santa Rosa Junior College.[3]

After C.C.'s death, Elvia Allman went on to enjoy considerable success in Hollywood as an actress and a comedienne, typically playing homely, shrewish women. Her most prominent role came in the 1940 film *Road to Singapore* as the pursuer of Bob Hope, and one of her steadier radio roles was on the Blondie series in the part of Cora Dithers, the dominating wife of Dagwood Bumstead's boss, J.C. Dithers. In the 1950s and 1960s, Allman achieved lasting fame as a television regular as a local busy-body named Elverna Bradshaw on *The Beverly Hillbillies* and as a near-duplicate character, Selma Plout, on *Petticoat Junction*. She even has a pivotal scene in the famous *I Love Lucy* scene at the chocolate-factory; Allman is the husky-voiced forewoman who yells "Let 'er roll" before Lucy and Ethel are devoured by the assembly line.

Allman's career slowed down in the 1970s and 1980s when she sold real estate, including a house to Mary Tyler Moore. Still, Elvia continued to appear on television and in films, including *The Adventures of Huckleberry Finn* (1981) in which she played Aunt Sally. In her final appearance, in 1991, Allman revived a role that took her full-circle, playing the voice of Clarabelle the Cow in the Mickey Mouse cartoon feature version of *The Prince and the Pauper*. In 1992, Elvira Allman died at 87, perhaps the last direct link to the colorful times of C.C. Pyle.[4]

As nostalgia for the 1920s has intensified in recent years, so has the occasional mention of Pyle's name. In 1978, a play about Pyle and the Bunion Derby, written by Michael Cristofer, was directed by Paul Newman and inaugurated the theater at Kenyon College in Gambier, Ohio. Cristofer, whose play *The Shadow Box* earned a Tony Award, a Pulitzer Prize, and the Drama Desk Award for outstanding new American play, had hoped to take the play to Broadway, but it never got there.[5]

Pyle's influence on professional sports would take decades to take hold, mainly because professional teams refused to deal with agents. In 1964, a contract dispute with the Green Bay Packers led Jim Ringo to bring an agent with him to negotiate a new contract — and according to legend, was traded on the spot.

Reportedly, Ringo entered the Packer offices with the agent and Head Coach Vince Lombardi excused himself. A few minutes later, Lombardi reentered the room and told Ringo, "You are now a member of the Philadelphia Eagles." In a 2007 article in *USA Today,* Ringo's former teammate Willie Davis said the story is true. "Jim was probably not out of place," Davis said. "But at that point, Lombardi was not prepared to have an intermediary."[6]

In 1965, Sandy Koufax and Don Drysdale, star pitchers of the Los Angeles Dodgers, hired a Hollywood agent named Bill Hayes to represent them in negotiating contracts. Hayes orchestrated a joint holdout for the two players in which each pitcher demanded a three-year $1 million contract, a considerable increase from the $85,000 and $80,000 the Dodgers had paid them the year before. When the Dodgers balked, Hayes lined up an exhibition tour for the two players and threatened to sign Drysdale to a movie contract.

Though the two players were major stars, they had little bargaining power because Major League Baseball rules didn't allow them to negotiate with other teams. As a result, Koufax settled for $125,000 and Drysdale for

$115,000. It was a great deal less than the two players had sought, but more than they would have received without an agent.

By then however, other athletes were catching on to the advantage of using an agent. In 1967, Bob Woolf counseled Detroit Tigers' pitcher Earl Wilson on a new contract, but from a distance. Wilson went to the team's front office alone, while Woolf stayed in Wilson's apartment. Whenever Wilson had a question, he removed himself from the room and called Woolf for advice.

Around the same time, Bobby Orr shook up the National Hockey League by bringing an agent with him to negotiate his first contract with the Boston Bruins. His agent, Toronto attorney Alan Eagleson, stunned the Bruins by declaring Orr wouldn't play unless he received a contract worthy of his immense talent. The Bruins gave in and Orr signed a two-year, $150,000 deal. It was worth the expense. Orr became one of hockey's greatest players, "the only player capable of filling every rink in the NHL," according to Eagleson.

In 1970, the MLB Players Association negotiated for a player's right to be represented by an agent. And in 1977, free agency took off when an arbitration ruling involving two other pitchers, Andy Messersmith and Dave McNally, essentially freed players to play out their contracts and negotiate with other teams. Sports agents were now in demand.

Today, a lot of people use agents though the exact number is hard to pinpoint. The most recent estimate was in 2004, when there were 4,200 athletes in the four major U.S. sports leagues and 1,978 agents registered or certified with the respective players associations.[7]

In recent years, Pyle's life has earned more attention with the release of several books on the Bunion Derby and the history of Route 66. In 2003, an informative, entertaining documentary on the Bunion Derby produced by Dan Bigbee and Lily Shangreaux that focused on the story and legacy of Andy Payne, aired on PBS, and features a brief audio clip of Pyle at a press conference. And in 2007, Rodale Press published the informative and lively *C.C. Pyle's Amazing Foot Race: The True Story of the 1928 Coast-to-Coast Run Across America* by Geoff Williams.[8]

But the Bunion Derbies tell just part of the tale of C.C. Pyle. Today, every sports agent in the business owes a tip of the hat to the sweet-talking sports promoter from Delaware, Ohio, by way of a thousand small towns across America. Sure, he went bankrupt and backed some failures. But in his time, no one was better or more visionary in the sports world than Charles Cassius Pyle, a man born too soon. There will never be another like him.

Chapter Notes

Introduction

1. *New York Times*, May 28, 1928; *Decatur* (IL) *Herald*, May 28, 1928.
2. *Los Angeles Times*, Feb. 4, 1939.
3. *New York Daily News*, May 24, 25, 28, 1928.
4. *New York Times*, May 28, 1928; *Decatur* (IL) *Herald*, May, 28, 1928.
5. *New York Herald Tribune*, Feb. 4, 1939; *New York Times*, Feb. 4, 1939; Grange, Red, and Ira Morton, *The Red Grange Story: An Autobiography* (Champaign, IL: University of Illinois Press, 1993), p. 94.
6. Bigbee, Dan, and Lily Shangreaux. "The 'America' Traveling Coach" (online article), www.itvs.org/footrace/progress/cycle.htm. Prohibition story: Cope, Myron, *The Game That Was* (Tulsa, OK: World Publishing Co., 1970), pp. 48, 49.
7. *Chicago Tribune*, Feb. 4, 1939; *New York Times*, Feb. 4, 1939, Jan. 29 ,1991.
8. *New York Herald Tribune*, Feb. 12, 1939; *New York Times*, Feb. 12, 1939; Engelmann, Larry, *The Goddess and the American Girl: The Story of Suzanne Lenglen and Helen Wills* (New York: Oxford University Press, 1988), pp. 242, 243.
9. *New York Times*, May 28, 1928; *Decatur* (IL) *Herald*, May 28, 1928.
10. Engelmann, *The Goddess*, p. 241.

Chapter 1

1. *New York Daily News*, Dec. 8, 1925; *New York Times*, Dec. 8, 1925.
2. Lowry, Phillip J., *Green Cathedrals: The Ultimate Celebration of Major League and Negro League Ballparks* (New York: Walker & Company, 2006), pp. 153 ,154; (football game) Frederic D. Schwarz, "Time Machine: Seventy-five Years Ago, The Galloping Ghost and the Four Horsemen," *American Heritage* (October 1999).
3. *New York Herald Tribune*, Oct. 19, 1924.
4. Carroll, John M., *Red Grange and the Rise of Modern Football* (Champaign, IL: University of Illinois Press, 1999), p. 8.
5. Peterson, Robert W., *Pigskin: The Early Days of Pro Football* (New York: Oxford University Press, 1997), pp. 88, 89.
6. *New York Daily News*, Nov. 2, 1925; *New York Times*, Dec. 26, 2000.
7. "Cover" statistic: http://www.time.com/time/covers; quote: *TIME* magazine, Oct. 5, 1925.
8. Peterson, *Pigskin*, p. 88.
9. *New York Daily News*, Dec. 7, 1925; *New York Times*, Dec. 7, 1925.
10. *New York Times*, Dec. 8, 1925.
11. *New York Times*, Feb. 17, 1959.
12. Izenberg, Jerry, *New York Giants: Seventy-Five Years* (San Diego: Tehabi Books and The New York Football Giants, Inc., 1999), pp. 23, 24, 25, 26; *New York Times*, Feb. 17, 1959.
13. *New York Times*, Nov. 26, 2000.
14. *New York Times*, Nov. 26, 2000; "Gravy train" quote; Carroll, *Red Grange*, p. 112.
15. *New York Times*, Nov. 26, 2000.
16. Carroll, *Red Grange*, pp. 111, 112.
17. *New York Times*, Nov. 26, 2000.
18. Carroll, *Red Grange*, pp. 98, 99.
19. *New York Daily News*, Dec. 8, 1925; *New York Times*, Dec. 8, 1925.
20. *Chicago Tribune*, Dec. 29, 1929.
21. Halas, George S., Gwen Morgan and Arthur Veysey, *Halas: An Autobiography* (Santa Monica, CA: Bonus Books, 1986), p. 109; *New York Daily News*, Dec. 8, 9, 1925; *Chicago Tribune*, Dec. 29, 1929.
22. *Chicago Tribune*, Dec. 29, 1929.
23. Carroll, *Red Grange*, p. 113.
24. Cope, *The Game That Was*, p. 46.
25. Cope, *The Game That Was*, p. 53.
26. Peterson, *Pigskin*, p. 90.
27. *New York American*, Dec. 8, 1925.
28. *New York Times*, Dec. 7, 1925.

29. Peterson, *Pigskin*, p. 86.
30. Grange, *Red Grange Story*, p. 91.
31. Carroll, *Red Grange*, p. 82.
32. Carroll, *Red Grange*, p. 85.
33. *Sheboygan* (WI) *Press*, Jan. 7, 1926.
34. Peterson, *Pigskin*, pp. 87, 88; Halas, *Halas*, p. 103.
35. *Chicago Tribune*, Jan. 26, 1967; ("seen the 'Galloping Ghost'" quote) Halas, *Halas*, p. 102; ("true rarity" quote) Halas, *Halas*, p. 99.
36. background: Hickock Sports, Chicago & *Chicago Tribune*, Jan. 26, 1967; quote: Halas, *Halas*, p. 104.
37. background: Hickok Sports, Chicago & Peterson, *Pigskin*, p. 86; Halas quote: *Chicago Tribune*, Jan. 26, 1967.
38. Peterson, *Pigskin*, p. 86.
39. Halas, *Halas*, p. 103, 104.
40. Peterson, *Pigskin*, p. 87.
41. *Chicago Tribune*, Jan. 26, 1997; Halas, 105, 106.
42. Halas, *Halas*, p. 105.
43. Heinz, W.C., *What a Time It Was: The Best of W.C. Heinz on Sports* (Cambridge, MA: Da Capo Press, 2002), pp. 33, 34, 35, 36.
44. Carroll, *Red Grange*, pp. 12, 13.
45. Carroll, *Red Grange*, p. 12; quote: *Chicago Tribune*, Jan. 29, 1991.
46. Grange, *Red Grange Story*, p. 9.
47. Carroll, *Red Grange*, pp. 37, 38; "I was a pro" quote: *Chicago Tribune*, Jan. 29, 1991.
48. Grange, *Red Grange Story*, p. 20; *New York Times*, Dec. 23, 1957.
49. Heinz, *What a Time*, p. 37.
50. Heinz, *What a Time*, p. 38; Carroll, *Red Grange*, p. 53.
51. Heinz, *What a Time*, pp. 35, 36.
52. Grange, *Red Grange Story*, pp. 39, 40; Carroll, *Red Grange*, p. 54.
53. Carroll, *Red Grange*, p. 55; *New York Times*, Oct. 28. 1923.
54. Carroll, *Red Grange*, p. 56; "great runner" quote: Grange, *Red Grange Story*, p. 50.
55. Peterson, *Pigskin*, pp. 85, 86; "You knew something was happening" quote: *Chicago Tribune*, Jan. 29, 1991.
56. Grange, *Red Grange Story*, p. 56.
57. Grange, *Red Grange Story*, pp. 56, 57; Carroll, *Red Grange*, pp. 7,8.
58. Stagg quote: Heinz, *What a Time*, p. 39; "Given his place" quote: Carroll, *Red Grange*, p. 71; Dempsey background: Kahn, Roger, *A Flame of Pure Fire: Jack Dempsey and the Roaring '20s* (Orlando, FL: Harcourt Brace, 1999), pp. 19, 20, 24, 122, 126, 127.
59. Thorn, John, Pete Palmer, Michael Gershman and David Pietrusza, *Total Baseball: The Official Encyclopedia of Major League Baseball — Fifth Edition* (New York: Viking, 1997),p p. 295, 1976 & 1977.

Chapter 2

1. Carroll, *Red Grange*, p. 76.
2. Rice quote: *Chicago Tribune*, January 29, 1991; Carroll, *Red Grange*, p. 76.
3. Carroll, *Red Grange*, pp. 77, 78.
4. Reisler, Jim, *Babe Ruth: Launching the Legend* (New York: McGraw-Hill, 2004), p. 5
5. Reisler, *Babe Ruth*, introduction; *New York Times*, May 28, 1920; "Ruth has become the most alarming presence" quote: *New York Times*, May 27, 1920.
6. Lieb, Fred, *Baseball as I Have Known It* (Lincoln, NE: University of Nebraska Press, 1977), p. 158.
7. Wagenheim, Kal, *Babe Ruth: His Life and Legend* (Baltimore: Olmstead Press, 2001), p. 69.
8. Reisler, *Babe Ruth*, pp. 8, 9.
9. Kahn, *A Flame*, p. 229.
10. Pegler quote: Woods, Henry F., *American Sayings: Famous Phrases, Slogans and Aphorisms* (New York: Duell, Sloan and Pearce, 2007), p. 249; Runyon quote: *New York American*, March 18, 1920.
11. Reisler, *Babe Ruth*, pp. 27, 28.
12. First Grange quote: *Chicago Tribune*, Jan. 29, 1991; second Grange quote: Grange, *Red Grange Story*, p. 57.
13. Carroll, *Red Grange*, p. 79, 80; "Graduation" background: Heinz, *What a Time*, pp. 39, 40.
14. Carroll, *Red Grange*, p. 81.
15. *New York American*, Nov. 1, 1925.
16. *New York Daily News*, Nov. 2, 1925.
17. Carroll, *Red Grange*, p. 71; "Hype" and Zuppke quote: Grange, *Red Grange Story*, p. 76.
18. Train background and quote: Heinz, *What a Time*, p. 40; Carroll, *Red Grange*, pp. 91, 92.
19. Carroll, *Red Grange*, p. 93.
20. Carroll, *Red Grange*, pp. 92, 93.
21. Heinz, *What a Time*, p. 40.
22. Carroll, *Red Grange*, pp. 95, 96; Cubs Park background: Lowry, *Green Cathedrals*, p. 54.
23. Carroll, *Red Grange*, pp. 95, 96.
24. Carroll, *Red Grange*, p. 97; *Chicago Tribune*, Nov. 27, 1925; *Milwaukee Sentinel*, Nov. 23, 1925.
25. Carroll, *Red Grange*, p. 99; *New York Times*, Dec. 6, 1925.
26. Robinson, Ray, *Rockne of Notre Dame: The Making of a Football Legend* (New York: Oxford University Press, 1999), p. 53.
27. Boxing background: Kahn, *A Flame*, pp. 231, 234.
28. Reisler, *Babe Ruth*, pp. 167, 255, 256.
29. *The New Yorker*, Dec. 8, 1928.

30. *Van Wert County Chapter of the Ohio Genealogical Society, Van Wert County, Ohio Cemetery, FHL Book,* 1990; 1870 U.S. Census, Van Wert County, Ohio.

31. Williams, Geoff, *C.C. Pyle's Amazing Foot Race: The True Story of the 1928 Coast-to-Coast Run Across America* (Emmaus, PA: Rodale Inc., 2007), p. 131.

32. Pyle background: Williams, *Foot Race,* p. 131; Delaware, Ohio, background: www.ohiohistorycentroal.org (*Ohio History Central: AmericaOnline Encyclopedia of Ohio History*), article, "Delaware."

33. Williams, *Foot Race,* p. 131; background on William Pyle's career: Archives of Ohio Methodism.

34. 1900 U.S. Census, 1900, Delaware Township, Ohio; background on train butchers: Williams, *Foot Race,* p. 131; background on family jobs: *Delaware Gazette,* Feb. 4, 1939.

35. www.bishops.owu.edu (Ohio Wesleyan University Battling Bishops Athletics: "Ohio Wesleyan Football History"); Williams, *Foot Race,* p. 86, Yost background: *New York Times,* Aug. 21, 1946.

36. Williams, *Foot Race,* pp. 86, 87.

37. *The New Yorker,* Dec. 8, 1928; Oldfield background: http://en.wikipedia.org/wiki/Barney_Oldfield.

38. Ward, Geoffrey C., *Unforgivable Blackness: The Rise and Fall of Jack Johnson* (New York: Knopf, 2004), pp. 240, 242, 243.

39. *The New Yorker,* Dec. 8, 1928.

40. Williams, *Foot Race,* pp. 67, 68; *New York Herald Tribune,* Feb. 4, 1939.

41. *The New Yorker,* Dec. 8, 1928.

42. *The New Yorker,* Dec. 8, 1928; background on Dorothy Fischer: Margarita Fischer Papers, MS 81-04, Wichita State University Libraries, Department of Special Collections; background on location of marriage: Williams, *Foot Race,* p. 69.

43. http://en.wikipedia.org/wiki/Margarita_Fischer.

44. *The New Yorker,* Dec. 8, 1928; Carroll, *Red Grange,* p. 83; *New York Herald Tribune,* Feb. 4, 1939.

45. Carroll, *Red Grange,* p. 83; *The New Yorker,* Dec. 8, 1928.

46. Williams, *Foot Race,* p. 82, 83; background on Sidney Pyle, Ira Pyle & Anna Pyle Ronk, *Santa Rosa Press Democrat,* Jan. 31, 1939, Nov. 14, 1939, July 3, 1961.

47. Williams, *Foot Race,* pp. 70, 71, 128.

48. Williams, *Foot Race,* p. 93; *The New Yorker,* Dec. 8, 1928.

49. *The New Yorker,* Dec. 8, 1928; Williams, *Foot Race,* p. 94.

50. *The New Yorker,* Dec. 8, 1928.

51. Williams, *Foot Race,* p. 95.

52. Margarita Fischer Papers, MS 81-04, Wichita State University Libraries, Department of Special Collections; http://en.wikipedia.org/wiki/Margarita_Fischer.

53. http://en.wikipedia.org/wiki/Essanay_Studios.

54. Williams, *Foot Race,* pp. 210, 211; background on Satex: tsha.utexas.edu/handbook/online (*Handbook of Texas Online*), article, "Wesley Hope Tilley."

55. Williams, *Foot Race,* p. 211.

56. U.S. Census, 1920 (Chicago); Williams, *Foot Race,* pp. 211, 212.

57. Williams, *Foot Race,* p. 129; http://en.wikipedia.org/wiki/Barton_Organ_Company.

(58) "Publicity" quote: *The New Yorker,* Dec. 8, 1928; Staff quote and football background: Carroll, *Red Grange,* p. 102.

59. "Gipp" background: Robinson, *Rockne,* pp. 80, 81; Marx Brothers' background: Anobile, Richard J., ed., *Why a Duck? Visual and Verbal Gems from the Marx Brothers Movies* (New York: Avon Books, 1972), p. 128.

60. Watterson, John Sayle, *College Football: History, Spectacle, Controversy* (Baltimore: Johns Hopkins University Press, 2000), p. 66.

61. Watterson, *College Football,* pp. 66, 67, 68; quotes from *Washington Post* & university presidents: Carroll, *Red Grange,* pp. 29, 30.

62. New rules: Carroll, *Red Grange,* p. 31; Thorpe background: Wallechinsky, David, *The Complete Book of the Olympics* (London: Little, Brown and Co., 1991), pp. 12, 13, 14, 15; Peterson, *Pigskin,* p. 57.

63. sports.espn.go.com/espn/classic (*ESPN Sports Classic: Signature Game*—Jim Thorpe); Peterson, *Pigskin,* pp. 58, 59.

64. http://en.wikipedia.org/wiki/Jim_Thorpe; Koehler, Michael D., *Journal of American Indian Education: Jim Thorpe, Legend and Legacy* (Volume 15, Number 3, May 1976).

65. Baseball background: Wallechinsky, *Olympics,* p. 125; basketball background: *New York Times,* March 29, 2005.

66. Peterson, *Pigskin,* pp. 25, 26, 60, 61, 62.

67. Peterson, *Pigskin,* pp. 64, 65; Daly, Dan and Bob O'Donnell, "Chicago Bears," Hickok Sports.com: Sports History.

68. Williams, *Foot Race,* p. 129; background on buildings: National Register of Historic Places (Champaign, Ill.), www.nationalregisterofhistoricplaces.com/IL/Champaign/state.

69. http://www.thevirginia.org (Virginia Theatre web site, "history of the theatre").

70. Jenkins, Sally, *The Real All Americans: The Team That Changed a Game, a People, a Nation* (New York: Doubleday, 2007), pp. 272, 273.

Chapter 3

1. Peterson, *Pigskin*, pp. 67, 68, 69; Daly, "Chicago Bears"; Halas quote: Halas, *Halas*, pp. 60, 61.

2. Peterson, *Pigskin*, p. 48; Halas, *Halas*, pp. 39, 40, 41, 48, 49.

3. Daly, "Chicago Bears."

4. Peterson, *Pigskin*, pp. 70, 71; Carroll, *Red Grange*, p. 47; *New York Times*, Dec. 23, 1957.

5. Peterson, *Pigskin*, pp. 73, 74, 75.

6. Daly, "Chicago Bears"; Pollard background: *Washington Post*, August 7, 2005; Peterson, *Pigskin*, pp. 77, 78.

7. Daly, "Chicago Bears"; Peterson, *Pigskin*, pp. 81, 82; Underwood quote: *Sports Illustrated*, Sept. 4, 1985.

8. *New York Daily News*, Dec. 8, 1925.

9. Cope, *The Game That Was*, p. 44.

10. *Chicago Tribune*, Dec. 29, 1929.

11. Cope, *The Game That Was*, pp. 48, 50.

12. Carroll, *Red Grange*, p. 110.

13. Halas, *Halas*, pp. 107, 108; Peterson, *Pigskin*, p. 88.

14. Both game summary & quote: *Chicago Tribune*, Nov. 27, 1925.

15. Halas quote: Carroll, *Red Grange*, p. 108; Mary Driscoll quote: Halas, *Halas*, p. 108.

16. *Chicago Tribune*, Nov. 30, 1925.

17. *New York Daily News*, Dec. 3, Dec. 6, Dec 7, 1925.

18. *New York Times*, Dec. 8, 1925; Pyle quote: Carroll, *Red Grange*, p. 111.

19. Carroll, *Red Grange*, p. 114.

20. *Chicago Tribune*, Dec. 29, 1929.

21. Carroll, *Red Grange*, p. 115; quote: *Providence Journal*, Dec. 10, 1925.

22. Carroll, *Red Grange*, p. 115.

23. www.footballhistorian.com, article, "American Heroes: The Way It Was — 1925."

24. *New York American*, Dec. 9, 1925.

25. *Lincoln* (NE) *Sunday Star*, Dec. 13, 1925.

26. Carroll, *Red Grange*, pp. 118, 119.

27. *Chicago Tribune*, Dec. 22, 1925.

28. Hotel background: http://www.nyc-architecture.com, article, "Gone but not forgotten" and *New York Times*, July 23, 1989; Grange quote: *Chicago Tribune*, Dec. 29, 1929

29. Grange, *Red Grange Story*, p. 109.

30. *Chicago Tribune*, Dec. 29, 1929; Grange, *Red Grange Story*, p. 109; quote: Cope, *The Game That Was*, p. 45.

31. *New York Times*, Jan. 1, 1926; real estate & hurricane background: Carroll, *Red Grange*, p. 121.

32. *New York Times*, Jan. 2, 1926; Grange, *Red Grange Story*, p. 109; Carroll, *Red Grange*, p. 122.

33. *New York Times*, Jan. 3, 1926; Grange, *Red Grange Story*, p. 110; Carroll, *Red Grange*, p. 122.

34. *Los Angeles Times*, Jan. 21, Jan. 22, 1926

35. Reisler, Jim, *Guys Dolls and Curveballs: Damon Runyon on Baseball* (New York: Carroll & Graf, 2005), Introduction.

36. *New York American*, Jan. 16, 1926.

37. *New York Times*, Jan. 18, 1926; *New York American*, Jan. 18, 1926.

38. *New York American*, Jan. 17, Jan. 18, 1926.

39. Halas, *Halas*, p. 115, 116; Halas quote: Carroll, *Red Grange*, p. 125, 126; Grange, *Red Grange Story*, p. 121; Carroll, *Red Grange*, p. 126.

41. *Los Angeles Times*, Feb. 1, 1937; Carroll, *Red Grange*, p. 129.

42. *Los Angeles Times*, Feb. 1, 1937; Grange, *Red Grange Story*, p. 124.

43. Cope, *The Game That Was*, p. 49; Grange quote: Carroll, *Red Grange*, p. 130.

44. Grange, *Red Grange Story*, p. 123; Carroll, *Red Grange*, p. 130.

45. Grange, *Red Grange Story*, p. 126.

46. Grange, *Red Grange Story*, p. 127; *New York Times*, Sept. 6, 1926.

47. *Chicago Tribune*, Sept. 6, 1926; *New York Times*, Sept. 6, 1926; Grange quote: Grange, *Red Grange Story*, p. 127.

48. Kahn, *A Flame*, p. 414; Ward, *Unforgivable*, pp. 399, 400.

49. Kahn, *A Flame*, pp. 161, 131 & 132 (draft); 214, 431 (restaurant).

50. http://en.wikipedia.org/wiki/Gertrude_Ederle.

51. http://en.wikipedia.org/wiki/Gertrude_Ederle; Pyle background & quotes: *Chicago Tribune*, Aug. 25, 1926.

52. http://en.wikipedia.org/wiki/Charles_Lindbergh; Pyle comments: *Edwardsville* (IN) *Intelligencer*, June 7, 1927.

53. http://en.wikipedia.org/wiki/RMS_Lusitania; http://en.wikipedia.org/World_War_I.

54. Kolata, Gina, *The Story of the Great Influenza Pandemic of 1918 and the Search for the Virus That Caused It* (New York: Farrar, Straus and Giroux, 1999), pp. 6, 7, 8, 9

55. Reisler, *Babe Ruth*, pp. 90, 91, 92.

56. Kahn, *A Flame*, p. 298, 299; Allen, Frederick Lewis, *Only Yesterday: An Informal History of the 1920s* (New York: Harper Perennial Modern Classics; Perennial Classics Edition, 2000;), p. 112; Reisler, *Babe Ruth*, pp. 93, 94.

57. http://www.whitehouse.gov/history/presidents/w(arren)h(arding)29.html.

58. http//www.whitehousegov/history/presidents/c(alvin)c(oolidge)30.html.

Chapter 4

1. Cope, *The Game That Was*, pp. 47, 48.

2. Runyon, Mason background: *New York American*, Feb. 22, 1926; Grange quote: Cope, *The Game That Was*, p. 48.

3. Izenberg, *New York Giants*, p. 26.

4. Bob Carroll, "The Grange Wars: 1926: Footballresearch.com/articles (Professional Football Research Association); Halas, *Halas*, p. 121.

5. Halas, *Halas*, p. 121; *New York Herald Tribune*, Feb. 8, 1926.

6. *New York Herald Tribune*, Feb. 9, 1926.

7. Carroll, Footballresearch.com article.

8. *New York Times*, Feb. 6, 7, 9, 1926; Carroll, *Red Grange*, p. 127.

9. *New York Herald Tribune*, Feb. 8, 1926; *New York Daily News*, Feb. 8, March 8, 1926; Carroll, *Red Grange*, p. 127.

10. *New York Herald Tribune*, March 8, 1926; *New York Daily News*, March 8, 1926.

11. *New York Times*, March 8, 1926, Jan. 5, 1943.

12. Quote: *New York Times*, March 8, 1926; Carroll, *Red Grange*, p. 127.

13. *New York Times*, March 8, 1926; *New York Herald Tribune*, March 8, 1926.

14. *New York Times*, July 17, 1926; background & quote: *New York Herald Tribune*, July 17, 1926; Peterson, *Pigskin*, p. 101.

15. Peterson, *Pigskin*, p. 101; Carroll, *Red Grange*, pp. 132, 133; Rice quote: http://www.answers.com/topic/ernie-nevers.

16. Cope, *The Game That Was*, pp. 29, 30.

17. Cope, *The Game That Was*, p. 31.

18. Grange, *Red Grange Story*, p. 113; *New York Daily News*, Sept. 27, 1926, Oct. 4, 1926.

19. *New York Daily News*, Oct. 4, 1926; Grange quote: Robert S. Gallagher, "The Galloping Ghost: An Interview with Red Grange," *American Heritage* (January 1974).

20. *New York Times*, Oct. 25, 1926; *New York Daily News*, Oct. 26, 1926.

21. *New York Daily News*, Nov. 1, Nov. 8, 1926.

22. Carroll, *Red Grange*, p. 136; Grange & Pegler quotes: Cope, *The Game That Was*, p. 49.

23. *New York Daily News*, Nov. 15, 1926; Carroll, *Red Grange*, p. 137; *New York Times*, Nov. 28, 1926.

24. *New York Times*, Nov. 29, 1926; background on final game and Grange quote: Carroll, *Red Grange*, p. 138.

25. Carroll, Footballresearch.com; financial figure: Carroll, *Red Grange*, p. 138.

26. answers.com, article on Ernie Nevers; Carroll, *Red Grange*, p. 140; hockey background: *Los Angeles Times*, March 28, 1927.

27. *Los Angeles Times*, March 28, 29, 1927.

28. *Los Angeles Times*, April 3, 9, 11, 1927, Feb. 16, 1928, Nov. 8, 1937.

29. Grange, *Red Grange Story*, pp. 128, 129.

30. http://en.wikipedia.org/wiki/Jobyna_Ralston; Grange, *Red Grange Story*, pp. 130, 131, 132.

31. *New York Times*, Feb. 6, 7, 1927.

32. Grange, *Red Grange Story*, p. 133.

33. Grange quote: Grange, *Red Grange Story*, p. 134; Injury story: Carroll, *Red Grange*, p. 145.

34. Carroll, *Red Grange*, p. 145; Grange quotes: Grange, *Red Grange Story*, p. 135.

35. Carroll, *Red Grange*, p. 145; *New York Times*, Nov. 9, 1927.

36. First quote: Carroll, *Red Grange*, p. 147; Grange quote: Cope, *The Game That Was*, p. 56.

37. *New York Daily News*, Nov. 25, 1927; Grange, *Red Grange Story*, p. 137.

38. http://www.professionalfootballhof.com/history/team (New York Giants); Carroll, *Red Grange*, p. 149.

39. Carroll, *Red Grange*, p. 139.

40. Engelmann, *The Goddess*, p. 239.

Chapter 5

1. Englemann, *The Goddess*, p. 239.

2. Engelmann, *The Goddess*, pp. 17, 18, 21, 86, 87.

3. Deford, Frank, *Big Bill Tilden: The Triumphs and the Tragedy* (Toronto: Sport Classic Books, 2004), pp. 13, 86, 87.

4. Quote: Deford, *Big Bill*, p. 56; Deford, *Big Bill*, p. 36, 135, 136.

5. Englemann, *The Goddess*, p. 50.

6. Tennisfame.com/fame (International Tennis Hall of Fame web site section, "Enshrinees"— Suzanne Lenglen ... http://www.tennisfame.com/famer, article, "Suzanne Lenglen"); http://www.wimbledon.org/en_GB/about/history/suzanne_lenglen, article, "The Goddess of Tennis; "My method" quote: *New York Times*, July 4, 1938.

7. *New York Times*, July 4, 1938; Englemann, *The Goddess*, pp. 27, 28, 248, 249, 250.

8. Engelmann, *The Goddess*, pp. 239, 240.

9. *Los Angeles Times*, July 21, 1934; *New York Times*, July 21, 1934; Washington, D.C. "air show" background: *Saturday Evening Post*, Nov. 12, 26, 1927.

10. *Los Angeles Times*, July 21, 1934.

11. Engelmann, *The Goddess*, p. 240.

12. Engelmann, *The Goddess*, pp. 240, 241.

13. Tennisfame.com/fame (International Tennis Hall of Fame web site section, "Enshrinees"— Suzanne Lenglen; Engelmann, *The Goddess*, p. 242, 243; *Los Angeles Times*, July 21, 1924.

14. Engelmann, *The Goddess*, p. 243; *New York Times*, July 21, 1934.

15. Tennisfame.com/fame (International Tennis Hall of Fame web site section, "Enshrinees"—Suzanne Lenglen; Pickens quote: Engelmann, *The Goddess*, p. 244.

16. *New York Times*, July 21, 1934; quote: Engelmann, *The Goddess*, p. 244.

17. http://en.wikipedia.org/wiki/Suzanne_ Lenglen; quote: Engelmann, *The Goddess*, pp. 244, 245.

18. Engelmann, *The Goddess*, p. 245.

19. *Los Angeles Times*, July 21, 1934; quote: Engelmann, *The Goddess*, pp. 244, 245.

20. *Chicago Tribune*, July 19, 1926.

21. Engelmann, *The Goddess*, p. 246.

22. *Los Angeles Times*, July 21, 1934; *New York Times*, July 4, 1938.

23. http://en.wikipedia.org/wiki/Suzanne_ Lenglen; "Artistic celebrity" quote: Engelmann, *The Goddess*, pp. 246, 247.

24. *New York Times*, July 4, 1938; http://en. wikipedia.org/wiki/Suzanne_Lenglen; Engelmann, *The Goddess*, pp. 247, 248.

25. Engelmann, *The Goddess*, pp. 248.

26. *New York Times*, Nov. 29, 1918; The National Archives (http://www.archives.gov/education/lessons/369th Infantry), article, "369th Infantry" of World War I.

27. Engelmann, *The Goddess*, pp. 251, 252.

28. http://en.wikipedia.org/wiki/Suzanne_ Lenglen; *New York Times*, July 21, 1934; Pyle quote: Engelmann, *The Goddess*, p. 254; *New York Times*, Aug. 3, 1926; *New York Herald Tribune*, Aug. 3, 1926.

29. *New York Times*, July 4, 1938; Pyle quote on finances: *New York Times*, Aug. 17, 1926, and *New York Daily News*, Aug. 17, 1926; Pyle quotes on Lenglen: Engelmann, *The Goddess*, p. 254.

30. Both quotes: Engelmann, *The Goddess*, p. 254.

31. http://en.wikipedia.org/wiki/Suzanne_ Lenglen; quote: Engelmann, *The Goddess*, p. 255.

32. Engelmann, *The Goddess*, p. 260; http:// en.wikipedia.org/wiki/Helen_Wills; Wills quote: *New York Times*, Aug. 19, 1926; Mallory quote: *Philadelphia Bulletin*, Sept. 9, 1926; Lacoste quote: *New York Times*.

33. *Chicago Tribune*, Nov. 1, 1926; Deford, *Big Bill*, pp. 94, 95.

34. *New York Times*, Sept. 7, 1926; *New York Daily News*, Sept. 7, 1926; http://en.wikipedia. org/wiki/Mary_Browne.

35. http://en.wikipedia.org/wiki/Mary_ Browne; Browne quotes: *New York Times*, Sept. 7, 1926 and *New York Herald Tribune*; Lenglen quotes: Engelmann, *The Goddess*, pp. 263, 264.

36. *New York Times*, Sept. 30, 1926; *New York Herald Tribune*, Sept. 30, 1926.

37. *New York Daily News*, Sept. 30, 1926.

38. *New York Herald Tribune*, Sept. 30, 1926; *New York Times*, Sept. 30, 1926.

39. *New York Daily News*, Sept. 30, 1926.

40. *New York Herald Tribune*, Sept. 30, 1926.

41. *New York Times*, Oct. 4, 1926; Engelmann, *The Goddess*, pp. 266, 267.

42. *New York Herald Tribune*, Sept. 30 and Oct. 1, 1926; *New York Times*, Oct. 1, 1926.

43. *New York Herald Tribune*, Oct. 1, 1926; *New York Times*, Sept. 29, 1926 and Oct. 3, 1926; Tennisfame.com/fame (International Tennis Hall of Fame web site section, "Enshrinees"—Vince Richards ... http//www.tennis fame.com/famer, article, "Vince Richards").

44. *New York Herald Tribune*, Oct. 1, 1926; *New York Times*, Oct. 1, 1926.

45. *Chicago Tribune*, Dec. 29, 1929.

46. *New York Times*, Oct. 1, 1926; *New York Herald Tribune*, Oct. 3, 1926.

47. http://www.tennissever.com/lines/lines _99_10-31.html, article in the "Between the Lines" section, "Suzanne Lenglen and the First Pro Tour" by Ray Bowers, Oct. 31, 1999.

48. *New York Herald Tribune*, Oct. 3, 1926.

49. *New York Times*, Sept. 5, 1926; *Washington Post*, Sept. 8, 1926; http://hickoksports. com/biograph/PadddockCharlie.html.

50. *New York Times*, Aug. 17, 1926, *New York Herald Tribune*, Aug. 17, 1926.

51. *New York Herald Tribune*, Oct. 3, 1926, "Sport magnates" quote & game background: *New York Times*, Oct. 3, 1926.

52. Baseball game background: *New York Times*, Oct. 3, 1926 and Thorn, *Total Baseball*, p. 297; quotes: *New York Herald Tribune*, Oct. 3, 1926.

53. *New York Herald Tribune*, Oct. 6, 7, 1926; *New York Daily News*, Oct. 7, 1926; *New York Times*, Oct. 7, 1926.

54. *New York Herald Tribune*, Oct. 9, 10, 1926; *New York Daily News*, Oct. 10, 1926; *New York Times*, Oct. 10, 1926.

55. *New York Herald Tribune*, Oct. 10, 1926; Lardner quote: Engelmann, *The Goddess*, p. 269; Engelmann, *The Goddess*, p. 270; *New York Times*, Oct. 10, 1926.

56. *New York Herald Tribune*, Oct. 10, 1926; Engelmann, *The Goddess*, p. 270; *New York Times*, Oct. 10, 1926.

57. *New York Herald Tribune*, Oct. 11, 1926; Engelmann, *The Goddess*, p. 272; "Baltimore" information: *New York Times*, Oct. 15, 1926.

58. "Toronto" background: *New York Times*, Oct. 13, 1926 and *New York Daily News*, Oct. 13, 1926; "Philadelphia" background: *New York Times*, Oct. 20, 1926; financial figures: *New York Times*, Oct. 21, 1926.

59. *Los Angeles Times*, Feb. 16, 1927; *New*

York Times, Feb. 16, 1927 and July 4, 1938; Snodgrass quote: Engelmann, The Goddess, pp. 273, 274.

60. Los Angeles Times, Feb. 17, 1927; New York Times, Feb. 16, 1927 and Feb. 18, 1927; Pyle and Snodgrass quotes: Engelmann, The Goddess, pp. 273, 274, 275.

61. San Francisco Chronicle, Dec. 7, 8, 9, 1926.

62. "Phone call" & Fuller quote: Engelmann, The Goddess, pp. 277, 278; Los Angeles Times, Dec. 15, 16, 1926.

63. Los Angeles Times, Dec. 16, 1926.

64. Los Angeles Times, Oct. 24, 1926.

65. Los Angeles Times, Dec. 16, 1926.

66. Los Angeles Times, Dec. 18, 1926.

67. Engelmann, The Goddess, p. 279; Los Angeles Times, Dec. 19, 1926.

68. Engelmann, The Goddess, p. 280, Los Angeles Times, Jan. 15, 1927.

69. Los Angeles Times, Jan. 15, 1927 and January 27, 1927; Engelmann, The Goddess, p. 281.

70. Engelmann, The Goddess, p. 282; New York Times, Feb. 16, 1927; Los Angeles Times, Feb. 17, 1927.

71. Los Angeles Times, Feb. 17, 1927.

72. Financial background: Engelmann, The Goddess, p. 283; http://en.wikipedia.org/wiki/Mary_Browne.

73. Los Angeles Times, Jan. 17, 1927 and Feb. 20, 1927; Lenglen quotes: New York Times, Feb. 20, 1927.

74. Los Angeles Times, Feb. 20, 1927.

Chapter 6

1. Pyle background & quotes: Chicago Tribune, June 21, 1927; marathon background: Wallechinsky, Olympics, pp. 51, 54.

2. Richard White, "Born Modern: An Overview of the West," History Now Issue 9 (September 2006) http://www.historynow.org/09_2006/historian5.html; Linda Lawrence Hunt, Bold Spirit: Helga Estby's Forgotten Walk Across America (Moscow, ID: University of Idaho Press, 2003), Introduction.

3. http://en.wikipedia.org/wiki/Edward_Payson_Weston.

4. http://www.thegreatautorace.com, Centennial Celebration 1908–2008: The Great Auto Race of 1908.

5. Michael Korda, Ike: An American Hero (New York: HarperCollins, 2007), pp. 145, 146.

6. Atlanta Constitution, July 31, 1927.

7. Atlanta Constitution, July 31, 1927; Molly Levite Griffis, The Great American Bunion Derby (Austin, TX: Eakin Press, 2003), pp. 6, 8, 9; Chicago Tribune, June 21, 1927.

8. Susan Croce Kelly and Quinta Scott, Route 66: The Highway and Its People (Norman,

OK: University of Oklahoma Press, 1988), pp. 33, 34.

9. Wallis, Route 66, pp. 1, 2.

10. Wallis, Route 66, pp. 1, 2, 3; Karen Fetter, "Honoring America's First Transcontinental Highway," Drive Magazine: The Magazine from Subaru (Summer 2005).

11. Wallis, Route 66, p. 7; Kelly, Route 66, pp. 10, 11, 12.

12. Kelly, Route 66, p. 33; Wallis, Route 66, pp. 5, 6, 7.

13. Kelly, Route 66, p. 33; quote: Wallis, Route 66, p. 12.

14. Atlanta Constitution, July 31, 1927.

15. New York Times, March 6, 1928.

16. Wallis, Route 66, p. 13.

17. Atlanta Constitution, July 31, 1927.

18. Dan Bigbee and Lily Shangreaux, "The 'America' Traveling Coach," The Great American Foot Race, 2002; Williams, Pyle's Amazing Foot Race, p. 135, 136.

19. Kelly, Route 66, p. 33.

20. New York Times, March 6, 1928.

21. Chicago Tribune, Dec. 29, 1929; Pyle quote: Wallis, Route 66, p. 13.

22. Griffis, Bunion Derby, p. 16; Bigbee and Shangreaux, article, "Training Camp."

23. Bigbee and Shangreaux article, "The 'America' Traveling Coach"; Grange, The Red Grange Story, p. 140; Williams, Pyle's Amazing Foot Race, p. 54.

24. Williams, Pyle's Amazing Foot Race, p. 54; Grange quote: Cope, The Game That Was, p. 47.

25. Los Angeles Times, Feb. 25, 1928.

26. Los Angeles Times, March 1, 2, 3, 5, 1928.

27. Los Angeles Times, March 4, 1928; New York American, March 4, 1928; Granville background: Williams, Pyle's Amazing Foot Race, p. 99.

28. Bigbee and Shangreaux article, "About the Runners: Tobie 'Cotton' Joseph"; Frost background: Williams, Pyle's Amazing Foot Race, pp. 44, 45; Joseph background: Griffis, Bunion Derby, pp. 30, 31.

29. Bigbee and Shangreaux articles, "About the Runners" and "Time Keeping."

30. New York Times, March 5, 7, 8, 1928.

31. Los Angeles Times, March 8, 1928; New York Times, March 8, 10, 1928.

32. Bigbee and Shangreaux article, "Time Keeping."

33. New York Times, March 10, 11, 20, 1928.

34. Bigbee and Shangreaux article, "About the Runners; Andy Payne"; http://www.cherokee.org, Cherokee Nation, Fall 2000 Newsletter article, "Payne Remembered as 'World's Greatest Distance Runner.'"

35. Background on Native Americans in marathons: New York Times, June 15, 23, 24,

1927; Griffis, *Bunion Derby*, pp. 1, 3; Bigbee and Shangreaux article, "About the Runners: Andy Payne."
36. Griffis, *Bunion Derby*, pp. 5, 6, 7, 8, 9; Williams, *Pyle's Amazing Foot Race*, pp. 14, 15, 16.
37. *Atlanta Constitution*, April 24, 1929; *Washington Post*, Feb. 22, 1927; *New York Times*, April 29, 1927.
38. *Washington Post*, Feb. 22, 1927; Griffis, *Bunion Derby*, pp. 53, 54; Bigbee and Shangreaux article, The Carnival."
39. Bigbee and Shangreaux article, The Carnival."

Chapter 7

1. *New York Times*, March 19, 20, 21, 22, 28, 29, 31, 1928.
2. *Los Angeles Times*, May 18, 1928; http://www.trackandfieldnews/general/back_track/5.html (1959 *Track and Field News* article, "Fabulous Bunion Derby"); Albuquerque background: *New York Daily News*, May 28, 1928.
3. Bigbee and Shangreaux article, "Points of Interest"
4. *Los Angeles Times*, May 18, 1928; Pegler quote: *Washington Post*, Feb. 22, 1927; Bigbee and Shangreaux article, "The Carnival."
5. http://www.trackandfieldnews/general/back_track/5.html (1959 *Track and Field News* article, "Fabulous Bunion Derby"); Kelly quote: *New York Times*, April 3, 1928.
6. Johnson background and wife's quote: *New York Times*, March 30; Frank Johnson quote: *New York Times*, April 7, 1928.
7. Griffis, *Bunion Derby*, pp. 19, 20, 21.
8. http://www.copacabanarunners.net article, "History of Running Shoes."
9. Griffis, *Bunion Derby*, pp. 43, 44, 45.
10. *New York Times*, April 6, 1928; Griffis, *Bunion Derby*, pp. 46, 47.
11. Background on meal money: Griffis, *Bunion Derby*, p. 48; *New York Daily News*, May 25, 1928; Gunn background: *TIME*, June 4, 1928.
12. *New York Daily News*, May 25, 1928.
13. *New York Times*, April 9, 1928.
14. Griffis, *Bunion Derby*, pp. 55, 56; Davis quote: Kelly and Scott, pp. 34, 35.
15. Bigbee and Shangreaux article, "Featured Runners (Andy Payne)"; Griffis, *Bunion Derby*, p. 53.
16. Griffis, *Bunion Derby*, pp. 58, 59, 60; *New York Times*, April 13, 1928.
17. *New York Times*, April 14, 1928; *Chicago Tribune*, April 19, 1928.
18. *New York Times*, April 15, 16, 17, 18, 1928; *Washington Post*, Feb. 22, 1937.
19. *New York Times*, April 17, 1928.

20. Griffis, *Bunion Derby*, pp. 58, 59 & 60; *New York Times*, April 19, 20, 1928.
21. Bigbee and Shangreaux article, "Featured Runners (Peter Gavuzzi)"; *New York Times*, May 4, 1928; http://www.david blaike.com/david_blaike/boston_baa_1940.html.
22. *New York Times*, April 21, 22, 1928; dog background: Bigbee and Shangreaux article, "Progress of the Race"; Mara Bovsun, "American Icons," *AKC Gazette: The Official Journal for the Sport of Purebred Dogs*, (July 2006).
23. *New York Times*, April 26, 27, 28, 29, 1928 (quote on April 27).
24. *New York Times*, May 3, 5, 1928.
25. *Chicago Tribune*, May 5, 1928; *New York Times*, May 5, 1928; background on Suratt: http://en.wikipedia.org/wiki/Valeska_Suratt; www.nytimes.com; movies/filmography: Valeska Suratt: www.hoosierswoodindiana.com; Williams, *Pyle's Amazing Foot Race*, p. 221.
26. *Chicago Tribune*, May 6, 1928; *New York Times*, May 6, 1928.
27. Bigbee and Shangreaux article, "Progress of the Race."
28. Williams, *Pyle's Amazing Foot Race*, p. 218; Bigbee and Shangreaux article, "Progress of the Race."
29. *TIME*, June 4, 1928; Williams, *Pyle's Amazing Foot Race*, p. 218.
30. *New York Times*, May 5, 1928; *New York Daily News*, May 25, 1928.
31. *New York Daily News*, May 24, 25, 1928.
32. *New York Times*, May 12, 1928.
33. *Elyria* (OH) *Chronicle-Telegram*, May 10, 1928; *New York Times*, May 14, 1928; Bigbee and Shangreaux article, "Progress of the Race."
(34) *New York American*, May 26, 27, 1928; *New York Times*, May 11, 17, 19, 20, 22, 26, 1928.
35. Background on "Tall Feather" and "Mad Bull": June 14, 15, 1927 and June 23, 24, 1927; Payne quotes: *New York Times*, May 21, 24, 1928.
36. *New York American*, May 26, 28, 1928; *New York Times*, May 25, 1928.
37. *New York American*, May 26, 1928; *New York Daily News*, May 26, 1928.
38. *New York Daily News*, May 22, 25, 1928.
39. *New York American*, May 22, 24, 1928; *New York American*, May 22, 1928; "Real money" quote: *Syracuse Herald*, May 25, 1928; "Why certainly" quote: *New York Daily News*, May 24, 1928.
40. *New York Daily News*, May 27, 1928; "Gunn" quote: Williams, *Pyle's Amazing Foot Race*, p. 218.
41. *New York Daily News*, May 25, 1928; *New York American*, May 25, 1928.
42. *New York Daily News*, May 24, 25, 26, 27, 28 and June 2, 1928; *New York American*, May 25, 28, 1928.

43. *New York Daily News*, May 29, 1928.
44. *New York Daily News*, May 27, 1928.
45. *New York Times*, May 26 (quote), 27, 1928.
46. *New York American*, May 27, 1928; quote: Pyle quote: *New York Times*, May 27, 1928.
47. *New York Times*, May 27, 1928; Gallico quotes and Thompson background: *New York Daily News*, May 27, 1928.
48. *New York American*, May 27, 1928; *New York Times*, May 27, 1928.
49. *New York Daily News*, May 27, 28, 1928.

Chapter 8

1. *New York Daily News*, May 28, 1928.
2. *New York Times*, May 28, 1928.
3. *New York Daily News*, May 27, 28, 1928; *New York Times*, May 28, 1928; *Decatur* (IL) *Herald*, May 28, 1928.
4. *Atlanta Constitution*, May 29, 1928.
5. *New York Times*, May 27, 30, 1928; *New York American*, May 27, 1928.
6. *New York American*, May 30, 1928; *New York Daily News*, June 1, 1928; *New York Times*, June 1, 1928.
7. *Chicago Tribune*, June 2, 3, 1928.
8. *New York Times*, May 28, 1928; "Bolsheviks" quote: *New York Daily News*, May 28, 1928.
9. *Decatur* (IL) *Herald*, May 28, 1928.
10. *New York Times*, June 1, 1928.
11. *Chicago Tribune*, June 2, 1928.
12. *New York Daily News*, June 2, 3, 1928; *New York Times*, June 3, 1928.
13. *New York Daily News*, June 3, 1928.
14. Pegler quotes: *Chicago Tribune*, June 3, 1928; *New York Times*, June 3, 1928.
15. *Chicago Tribune*, June 3, 1928.
16. http://www.runacrossamerica2002.com/bunion.htm.
17. Peterson, *Pigskin*, p. 103.
18. Grange "could no longer afford" quote: Grange, *The Red Grange Story*, p. 142; Grange "duck" quote: Carroll, *Red Grange*, p. 153.
19. Grange, *The Red Grange Story*, p. 142.
20. *New York Times*, Aug. 3, Dec. 10, 1928; http://www.databasefootball/leagues /leagues year. html; http://www.en.wikipedia.org/wiki /NewYorkYankees (NFL).
21. *New York Times*, Feb. 22, 1929; "Lawyer" comment: *Chicago Tribune*, Feb. 4, 1939 and *Los Angeles Times*, Feb. 4, 1939.
22. *New York Daily News*, April 2, 1929.
23. *Decatur* (IL) *Herald*, March 25, 1929.
24. *Ada* (OK) *Evening News*, Sept. 9, 1928.
25. *Decatur* (IL) *Herald*, March 25, 1929; *Davenport* (IA) *Democrat and Leader*, March 31, 1929.

26. *Atlanta Constitution*, Oct. 8, 1928; *New York Times*, Feb. 22. 1929.
27. "Wedding" background: *Chicago Tribune*, Jan. 17, 1929; El Oaufi out of race: March, 31, 1929; El Oaufi background & biography: Wallechinsky, *Olympics*, p. 56.
28. *New York Times*, April 1, 1929; Pyle quote: *New York Daily News*, April 1, 1929.
29. *New York Times*, March 31, 1929; "Follies" background and ad: *Frederick* (MD) *Daily News*, April 6, 1929.
30. *New York Daily News*, April 2, 1929..
31. Pyle quote: *Davenport* (IA) *Democrat and Leader*, March 31, 1929; *New York Daily News*, March 31, 1929; *New York Times*, March 31, 1929.
32. *New York Daily News*, March 31, 1929; Thorpe background: *New York Times*, March 31, 1929; *Washington Post*, Aug. 27, 1929; *New York Times*, March 29, 1953.
33. *New York American*, April 2, 1929; *New York Daily News*, April 2, 1929; *Atlanta Constitution*, April 24, 1929.
34. *New York American*, April 1, 2, 1929; *New York Daily News*, April 2, 1929.
35. *Los Angeles Times*, July 3, 9, 1929.
36. *Los Angeles Times*, Aug. 4, 30, 1929.
37. *Atlanta Constitution*, April 24, 1929.
38. *Los Angeles Times*, June 15, 16, 19 and July 3, 1929.
39. *Los Angeles Times*, Aug. 4, 1929; *New York Times*, Aug. 4, 1929.
40. *Washington Post*, Aug. 27, 1929; *Los Angeles Times*, Aug. 30, 1929; *New York Times*, March 29, 1953.

Chapter 9

1. *Chicago Tribune*, June 3, 1928.
2. *TIME*, Jan. 5, 1931.
3. *Los Angeles Times*, May 10, 1938.
4. *Los Angeles Times*, Feb. 4, 1939.
5. *New York Herald Tribune*, Feb. 4, 1939.
6. Cope, *The Game That Was*, pp. 49, 50.
7. *Chicago Tribune*, Nov. 7, 1933; *Washington Post*, Feb. 22, 1937; World's Fair background: Stephen Biel, *American Gothic: A Life of America's Most Famous Painting* (New York: W.W. Norton, 2005), pp. 83, 84.
8. Mark Sloan, Roger Manley, Roger and Michelle Van Parys, *Dear Mr. Ripley: A Compendium of Curioddities from the Believe It or Not! Archives* (London: Little, Brown & Co., 1993), pp. 21, 22.
9. *Chicago Tribune*, Nov. 7, 1933; "Eddie" background & quotes: *Washington Post*, Feb. 22, 1937.
10. Sloan, *Dear Mr. Ripley*, p. 25; *Los Angeles Times*, Feb. 4, 1939.
11. *Los Angeles Times*, Dec. 16, 1936.

12. Los Angeles Times, Feb. 4, 1939; Elvia Allman background & biography: http://en.wikipedia.org/wiki/Elvia_Allman; http://movies.nytimes.com/person/1121/Elvia-Allman/ filmography; Marriage background: County of Los Angeles: Registrar-Recorder/County Clerk (Standard Certificate of Marriage).

13. Los Angeles Times, July 21, 1934.

14. New York Herald Tribune, July 4, 1938; New York Times, July 4, 1938.

15. New York Times, Oct. 5, 1931.

16. Edwards: New York Times, Jan. 3, 1943; Grange: New York Times, Jan. 29, 1981.

17. Bigbee, "Featured Runners (Andy Payne)"; Background on Andy Payne Marathon: http://www.marathonguide.com/races/racedetails.

18. Los Angeles Times, Feb. 4, 1939; New York Herald Tribune, Feb. 4, 1939; Delaware (OH) Gazette, Feb. 4, 1939; Cause of death: State of California Department of Public Health and Vital Statistics, Charles C. Pyle, Death Certificate No, 1893 (Feb. 3, 1939, North Hollywood, Los Angeles County, California); Background on Kathy Malin and Charles Lee Malin, Pyle's grandson: State of California Department of Public Health and Vital Statistics, Charles Lee Malan Birth Index (Jan. 9, 1926), Los Angeles County, California; Background on Pyle's cremation: Sacramento Bee, Feb. 4, 1939.

19. Superior Court of the State of California In and For the County of Los Angeles: Copy of (C.C. Pyle's) Inventory and Appraisement & Probate of Will, Letters of Testamentary: March 15, 1939; Nov. 14, 1939; July 3, 1941; Dec. 12, 1941; Aug. 21, 1944; Sept. 20, 1944.

20. Washington Post, Feb. 22, 1937.

21. Grange, The Red Grange Story, p. 94.

Epilogue

1. Delaware (OH) Gazette, Feb. 4, 1939.

2. Background on Sidney Pyle: Santa Rosa Press Democrat, Jan. 31, 1939; Background on Ira Pyle: San Rosa Press Democrat, Nov. 14, 1939.

3. Background on Pyle's descendents: Research compiled by My.Genealogist.com and written correspondence with Gina Laitinen, Pyle's great-granddaughter; Anna Ronk background: Santa Rosa Press Democrat, July 3, 1961.

4. http://en.wikipedia.org/wiki/Elvia_Allman; http://movies.nytimes.com/person/1121/Elvia-Allman/filmography.

5. http://www.Kenyon.edu/x6918.xml (article, "History of the College" in the Kenyon College 2007–2008 Student Handbook).

6. USA Today, Nov. 19, 2007; article is "Hall of Fame Center Jim Ringo Dead at 75."

7. Baseball stories and agent numbers: Principles and Practice of Sport Management by Lisa Pike Masteralexis, Carol A. Barr and Mary A. Hums, Jones & Bartlett Publishers, 2004, p. 222; Orr story and Eagleson quote: Hockey Chronicles: Year-by-Year History of the National Hockey League by Morgan Hughes, Stan and Shirley Fischler, Joseph Romain and James Duplacey, Publications International, Ltd., 2003, p. 292.

Bibliography

Books

Allen, Frederick Lewis. *Only Yesterday: An Informal History of the 1920's*. New York: Harper Perennial Modern Classics; Perennial Classics Edition, 2000.

Anobile, Richard J., ed. *Why a Duck? Visual and Verbal Gems from the Marx Brothers Movies*. New York: Avon Books, 1972.

Biel, Stephen. *American Gothic: A Life of America's Most Famous Painting*. New York: W.W. Norton, 2005.

Carroll, John M. *Red Grange and the Rise of Modern Football*. Champaign, IL: University of Illinois Press, 1999.

Cope, Myron. *The Game That Was*. Tulsa, OK: World Publishing, 1970.

Danzig, Alison. *Oh, How They Played the Game: The Early Days of Football and the Heroes Who Made It*. New York: Macmillan, 1971.

Deford, Frank. *Big Bill Tilden: The Triumphs and the Tragedy*. Toronto: Sport Classic Books, 2004.

Engelmann, Larry. *The Goddess and the American Girl: The Story of Suzanne Lenglen and Helen Wills*. New York: Oxford University Press, 1988.

Freidel, Frank. *The Presidents of the United States of America*. Washington, DC: White House Historical Association, 1995.

Grange, Red, and Ira Morton. *The Red Grange Story: An Autobiography*. Champaign, IL: University of Illinois Press, 1993.

Griffis, Molly Levite. *The Great American Bunion Derby*. Austin, TX: Eakin Press, 2003.

Halas, George S., Gwen Morgan, and Arthur Veysey. *Halas: An Autobiography*. Santa Monica, CA: Bonus Books, 1986.

Heinz, W.C. *What a Time It Was: The Best of W.C. Heinz on Sports*. Cambridge, MA: Da Capo Press, 2002.

Hughes, Morgan, Stanley Fischler, Shirley Fischler, Joseph Romain, and James Duplacey. *Hockey Chronicles: Year-to-Year History of the National Hockey League*: Publications International, Ltd., 2003.

Hunt, Linda Lawrence. *Bold Spirit: Helga Estby's Forgotten Walk Across America*. Moscow, ID: University of Idaho Press, 2003.

Izenberg, Jerry. *New York Giants: Seventy-Five Years*. San Diego: Tehabi Books and the New York Football Giants, Inc., 1999.

Jenkins, Sally. *The Real All Americans: The Team That Changed a Game, a People, a Nation*. New York: Doubleday, 2007.

Kahn Roger. *A Flame of Pure Fire: Jack Dempsey and the Roaring '20s*. Orlando, FL: Harcourt Brace, 1999.

Kelly, Susan Croce, and Quinta Scott. *Route 66: The Highway and Its People*. Norman, OK: University of Oklahoma Press, 1988.

Kolata, Gina. *The Story of the Great Influenza Pandemic of 1918 and the Search for the Virus That Caused It*. New York: Farrar, Straus and Giroux, 1999.

Korda, Michael. *Ike: An American Hero*. New York: HarperCollins, 2007.

Lieb, Fred. *Baseball As I Have Known It*. Lincoln, NE: University of Nebraska Press, 1977.

Lowry, Phillip J. *Green Cathedrals: The Ultimate Celebration of Major League and Negro League Ballparks*. New York: Walker & Company, 2006.

Masteralexis, Lisa Pike, Carol A. Barr, and Mary A. Hums. *Principles and Practice of Sport Management*. Jones & Bartlett Publishers, 2004.

Peterson, Robert W. *Pigskin: The Early Days of Pro Football*. New York: Oxford University Press, 1997.

Reisler, Jim. *Babe Ruth: Launching the Legend*. New York: McGraw-Hill, 2004.

_____. *Guys, Dolls and Curveballs: Damon Runyon on Baseball*. New York: Carroll & Graf, 2005.

Rittenhouse, Jack D. *A Guide Book to Highway 66*. Albuquerque, NM: The University of New Mexico Press, 2002.

Robinson, Ray. *Rockne of Notre Dame: The Making of a Football Legend*. New York: Oxford University Press, 1999.

Sloan, Mark, Roger Manley and Michelle Van Parys. *Dear Mr. Ripley: A Compendium of Curioddities from the Believe It or Not! Archives*. London: Little, Brown, 1993.

Thorn, John, Pete Palmer, Michael Gershman and David Pietrusza. *Total Baseball: The Official Encyclopedia of Major League Baseball—Fifth Edition*. New York: Viking, 1997.

Wagenheim, Kal. *Babe Ruth: His Life and Legend*. Baltimore, MD: Olmstead Press, 2001.

Van Wert County Chapter of the Ohio Genealogical Society, Van Wert County, Ohio Cemetery, FHL Book. LDS Family History Center, 1990.

Wallechinsky, David. *The Complete Book of the Olympics*. London: Little, Brown, 1991.

Wallis, Michael. *Route 66: The Mother Road*. New York: St. Martin's Press, 1990.

Ward, Geoffrey C. *Unforgivable Blackness: The Rise and Fall of Jack Johnson*. New York: Knopf, 2004.

Watterson, John Sayle. *College Football: History, Spectacle, Controversy*. Baltimore, MD: Johns Hopkins University Press, 2000.

Williams, Geoff. *C.C. Pyle's Amazing Foot Race: The True Story of the 1928 Coast-to-Coast Run Across America*. Emmaus, PA: Rodale Inc., 2007.

Woods, Henry F. *American Sayings: Famous Phrases, Slogans and Aphorisms*. New York: Duell, Sloan and Pearce, 2007.

Periodicals

Bovsun, Mara. "American Icons." *AKC Gazette: The Official Journal for the Sport of Purebred Dogs* (July 2006).

Fetter, Karen. "Honoring America's First Transcontinental Highway." *Drive Magazine: The Magazine from Subaru* (Summer 2005).

Gallagher, Richard S. "The Galloping Ghost: An Interview with Red Grange." *American Heritage* (January 1974).

Koehler, Michael D. "Jim Thorpe, Legend and Legacy." *Journal of American Indian Education*, Volume 15, Number 3 (May 1976).

Saturday Evening Post

Schwarz, Frederic D. "Time Machine: Seventy-five Years Ago, The Galloping Ghost and the Four Horsemen." *American Heritage* (October 1999).

The New Yorker
TIME Magazine

Newspapers

Ada (Oklahoma) *Evening News*
Atlanta Constitution
Chicago Tribune
Decatur (Illinois) *Herald*
Delaware (Ohio) *Gazette*
Edwardsville (Indiana) *Intelligencer*
Elyria (Ohio) *Chronicle-Telegram*
Frederick (Maryland) *Daily News*
Los Angeles Times
New York American

New York Daily News
New York Herald Tribune
New York Times
Sacramento Bee
San Francisco Chronicle
Santa Rosa (California) *Press Democrat*
Sheboygan (Wisconsin) *Press*
Syracuse Herald
USA Today
Washington Post

Documentaries/Reports

Bigbee, Dan, and Lily Shangreaux. *The Great American Foot Race*. BIG Productions, 2002.
County of Los Angeles: Registrar-Recorder/County Clerk. Standard Certificate of Marriage for Pyle/Allman Marriage; 1937.
State of California Department of Public Health and Vital Statistics. Charles Lee Malan Birth Index (Jan. 9, 1926), Los Angeles County, California.
State of California Department of Public Health and Vital Statistics, Charles C. Pyle, Death Certificate No. 1893. (Feb. 3, 1939), North Hollywood, Los Angeles County, California.
Superior Court of the State of California In and For the County of Los Angeles: Copy of C.C. Pyle's Inventory and Appraisement & Probate of Will, Letters of Testamentary: March 15, 1939; Nov. 14, 1939; July 3, 1941; Dec. 12, 1941; Aug. 21, 1944; Sept. 20, 1944.
U.S. Census figures. Ohio, 1880, 1890, 1900; California, 1910, 1920, 1930.

Archives and Special Collections

Archives of Ohio Methodism; Delaware, Ohio.
Delaware County (Ohio) Historical Society.
Methodist Archives and History Center of the United Methodist Church; Madison, NJ.
National Archives (http://www.archives.gov/education/lessons/369th Infantry), article, "369th Infantry" of World War I.
National Register of Historic Places (Champaign, Ill.) ... www.nationalregisterofhistoric places.com/IL/Champaign/state.
Wichita State University Libraries; Department of Special Collections: Margarita Fischer Papers (MS 81-4).

Internet Resources

Answers.com; article on Ernie Nevers.
Bishops.owu.edu; Battling Bishops Athletics: "Ohio Wesleyan Football History."
Cherokee.org; Cherokee Nation, Fall 2000 Newsletter article, "Payne Remembered as 'World's Greatest Distance Runner.'"
Copacabanarunners.net; Copacabana Runners; article, "History of Athletic Shoes."
David Blaike.com (david_blaike/boston_baa_1940.html).

Espn.go.com/espn/classic; ESPN Sports Classic: Signature Game — Jim Thorpe."
Databasefootball/leagues /leaguesyear; 1928 NFL Standings & Breakdown of Games.
Footballhistorian.com; "American Heroes: The Way It Was —1925."
Footballresearch.com/articles; Professional Football Research Association.
Hickok Sports.com: Sports History, articles: "Chicago Bears" by Dan Daly and Bob
    O'Donnell, Charlie Paddock biography.
Historynow.com; *History Now: American History Online*; Issue 9, September 2006, arti-
    cle, "Born Modern: An Overview of the West" by Richard White.
Hoosierwoodindiana.com (Valeska Suratt).
Kenyon.edu/x6918.xml; article, "History of the College" in the Kenyon College 2007–
    2008 *Student Handbook*.
Marathonguide.com/races.racedetails (Andy Payne Marathon).
MyGenealogist.com
Nyc-arhitecture.com; article, "Gone But Not Forgotten."
Nytimes.com (movies/filmography): Elvia Allman, Valeska Suratt.
Ohiohistorycentroal.org; *Ohio History Central: AmericaOnline Encyclopedia of Ohio His-
    tory*, article, "Delaware."
Professionalfootballhof.com/history/team; New York Giants.
Runacrossamerica2002.com.
Tennisfame.com/fame; International Tennis Hall of Fame web site section, "Enshrinees"—
    Suzanne Lenglen, Vince Richards.
Tennisserver.com article in the "Between the Lines" section, "Suzanne Lenglen and the
    First Pro Tour" by Ray Bowers, Oct. 31, 1999.
Theatreorgans.com.
Thegreatautorace.com; Centennial Celebration 1908–2008: The Great Auto Race of 1908.
Thevirginia.org; Virginia Theatre of Champaign, Ill.
Trackandfieldnews.com article, "Fabulous Bunion Derby" (1959).
Tsah.utexas.edu; *Handbook of Texas Online*.
Virginia.org/history; Virginia Theater in Champagne, Ill.
Whitehouse.gov/history/presidents.
Wikipedia.org (http://en.wikipedia.org), articles on Barney Oldfield, Barton Organ Com-
    pany, Charles Lindbergh, Elvia Allman, Essanay Studios, Gertrude Ederle, Jim
    Thorpe, Jobyna Ralston, Margarita Fischer, Mary Browne, Suzanne Lenglen, Valeska
    Suratt.
Wimbledon.org (wimbledon.org/en_GB/about/history/suzanne_lenglen), article, "The
    Goddess of Tennis."

Index

Aberdeen, WA 49
Abramowitz, Harry 149
The Adventures of Huckleberry Finn (film) 201
The Adventures of Huckleberry Finn (novel) 49
Akron Pros 62, 66, 67
Albany, OR 49
Albertsen, E.P. 23
Albuquerque, NM 156
Alexander, Joe 16
Algeria 185
Algerian Liberation Movement 185
Algiers, Algeria 185
All-England Lawn Tennis Club 108
Allen, Frederick Lewis 85
Allman, Elvia (C.C. Pyle's fourth wife) 194, 196, 200, 201
Altrock, Nick 128
Amarillo, Texas 159, 188
Amateur Athletic Union (AAU) 60
The America (Pyle's coach) 147, 148, 165, 184, 196
American Association 65
American Professional Football League (AFL) 92, 95, 96, 98, 99, 100, 101, 102
American Studios 54
Amsterdam, The Netherlands 185
Anderson, Bronco Billy 54
Anderson, Hunk 23
Andy Payne Marathon (Oklahoma City, OK) 196
Ansonia Hotel (New York City) 43
Aqueduct Racetrack (New York) 174
Arnold, Donald 55
Arnold, Eupehemia "Effie" B. (C.C. Pyle's third wife) 55, 97, 147, 194
Arnold, Florence (C.C. Pyle's step-daughter) 55, 185
Arrow Production Company 20, 78
Ascot Speedway (Santa Monica) 110, 146, 149
Ashtabula, OH 149
Asnières, France 137
Associated Highways Associations of America 142, 143

Associated Press 125
Athens, Greece 138
Atlanta, GA 134
Atlanta Constitution 189
Atlantic Ocean 83, 112
Aurora, IL 125
Avery, Cyrus 142
An Awful Skate 54

Badgro, Red 102
Baker, Dr. John 178
Baker, Ralph "Moon" 29
Baldwin, Baldwin M. 135, 136, 195
Baldwin, E.J. "Lucky" 135
Ball, Lucille 201
Ballyhoo 191
Baltimore, MD 35, 130
Baltimore News 130
Bara, Theda 165
Barnum, P.T. 8
Barrow, Ed 35, 78, 91
Barstow, CA 151
Barton Musical Instrument Company 56
The Bat 63
Batavia (IL) High School 28
Bath, NY 169
Baze, Mike 161
Beachey, Lincoln 110
Bear Hollow, AR 175
Beery, Wallace 54
Begg, U.S. Rep. James T. 168, 169
Begg, Dr. K.H. 150
Believe It or Not! Odditorium (formal name is *Ripley's Believe It or Not!* Odditorium) 192, 193, 194
Belmont Hotel (Chicago) 41
Belmont Park (New York) 14, 174
Bennett, Floyd 146
The Beverly Hillbillies 200
Bie, Ferdinand 60
Big Ten Athletic Conference 25, 29, 40
Bigbee, Dan 196, 202
Biltmore Hotel (Los Angeles) 75, 106, 109

Birmingham, AL 110, 134
Blisters the Dog 157, 164
Bloomington, CA 151
The Boat 63
Boise, ID 52, 53
Bombay, India 193
Boston, MA 60, 71, 84, 92, 99, 126, 130, 139, 149, 166, 176
Boston Braves 28, 61
Boston Bruins 202
Boston Bulldogs 96, 99
Boston Globe 34
Boston Marathon 149
Boston Red Sox 35
Braves Field (Boston) 71
Breslin, Jimmy 36
Breyer, Victor 112
Britton, Earl 29, 195
Britton, Nan 85
Bronx, New York 91, 93
Brooklyn, NY 92, 96, 135, 139, 149
Brooklyn Dodgers 92
Brooklyn Horse Lions 99
Brooklyn Horsemen 95, 96, 99
Brooklyn Lions 96, 99
Brown, Johnny Mack 38
Brown University 62, 72
Browne, Mary 108, 118, 119, 122, 123, 125, 128, 129, 130, 131, 133, 134, 136
Browne, Nat 128
Brownsville, OR 48
Brunswick-Balke Calendar Company 64
Buffalo, NY 126, 130, 139, 144
Buffalo Bisons 103
Bullock, Matt 31
Bunion Derby II 183, 184, 185, 186, 187, 188, 189, 190
Bunion Derby III 189
Busch, Bill 149
Butler University 38
Byrd, Richard 146

Cajon Pass, CA 151
Calac, Pete 62, 67
Calgary, Canada 172
California State Labor Commission 189
Camp, Walter 41
Camp Delaware (Delaware, OH) 44
Campbell-Hurd, Dorothy 119
Canada 117, 126
Cannes, France 132
Canton, OH 64
Canton Bulldogs 62, 66
Cap Gris Nez, France 82
Caplan, Harry 191
Carlisle (PA) Indian School 29, 39, 59, 62, 63
Carnegie Hero (award) 94
Carnegie Library (El Reno, OK) 2
Carpentier, Georges 111, 112, 127

Carr, Florence 188
Carr, Joe 14, 15, 66, 67, 92
Carroll, Bob 90, 91
Carroll, John M. 2, 34, 69, 104
Carthage, MO 164
Catoosa, OK 160
Catskill Mountains 169
C.C. Pyle's Amazing Foot Race: The Truly Story of the 1928 Coast-to-Coast Run Across America 202
C.C. Pyle's Cross Country Follies 186
C.C. Pyle's Greater Lewis & Clark International Exposition 52
C.C. Pyle's International Transcontinental Race 140, 153, 164, 166
Century of Progress (Chicago World's Fair) 192, 193, 194
Chamberlin, Guy 73
Chambers, Dorothea Douglass 108
Champaign, IL 22, 23, 26, 28, 30, 39, 42, 62, 77, 102, 165
Chandler, OK 161
Chaplin, Charlie 54, 63, 108, 134
Chariots of Fire 126
Chelsea, OK 162, 184
Cherokee Heritage Center (Tahlequah, OK) 196
Chicago, IL 12, 13, 23, 28, 30, 41, 53, 54, 56, 65, 67, 68, 69, 70, 72, 74, 88, 89, 92, 96, 97, 100, 103, 104, 111, 126, 130, 137, 141, 143, 144, 147, 149, 152, 165, 166, 175, 191, 192, 194, 195, 196, 199
Chicago Bears 11, 12, 15, 16, 19, 23, 24, 26, 29, 41, 67, 69, 70, 71, 72, 74, 75, 77, 78, 96, 97, 103
Chicago Black Hawks 101
Chicago Bulls (football) 96, 99, 100, 102
Chicago Cardinals (originally the Chicago-Racine Cardinals) 12, 41, 66, 69, 70, 104
Chicago Cubs 86
Chicago Journal 34
Chicago Stadium 56
Chicago Staleys (forerunners of Chicago Bears) 65, 67
Chicago Tribune 40, 70, 80, 99, 180
Chicago White Sox 43
Christopher, Dennis 126
Chrysler 193
Cincinnati, OH 92
Cincinnati Reds 61, 92
City Machine Gun Corps (Chicago band) 166
Civic Auditorium (San Francisco) 132
Civil War 44
Clark, William 138
Cleveland, OH 98, 99, 104, 130, 167, 168, 175, 194
Cleveland Bulldogs 103, 104
Cleveland Columbus & Cincinnati Rail Road 45
Cleveland Erin Brauts 62

Cleveland Panthers 96, 98, 99
Cobb, Ty 34, 80, 134
Cochet, Henri 118
Colgate University 38, 98
Coliseum (Chicago) 130
Coliseum (Los Angeles) 110
Collett, Glenna 127
Colony Theatre (New York City) 80
Columbus, OH 43, 44, 126, 130
Columbus Circle (New York City) 185
Columbus Panhandlers 62
Columbus Tigers 71
Combs, Earle 126
Comiskey, Charles 43
Comiskey Park (Chicago) 69
Commodore Hotel (New York City) 92
Conlin, Edward 128
Continental Illinois National Bank and Trust
  Company 177, 182, 196
Conway Building (Chicago) 97
Conzelman, Jimmy 72
Coogan's Bluff (New York City) 11, 14
Coolidge, Pres. Calvin 19, 21, 82, 86, 87
Coral Gables, FL 74
Cosmopolitan 37
Crane, C. Howard 63
Crete, Paul Philippe 192
Cristofer, Michael 1
Crowley, Jim 12, 72
Cuba 134
Cubs Park (Wrigley Field), Chicago 12, 41,
  67, 69, 103
Curtis, Tony 139
Custer, Gen. George 52
Cycledrome (Providence, RI) 182, 183

Dallas, TX 134, 184, 194
Daly, Dan 65
Danger, Arjan Desur 193
Danzig, Allison 20
Dartmouth College 23
Davies, David 159
Davis, Hugh 160
Davis, Willie 201
Davis Cup (Tennis Championship) 106, 107,
  118, 123, 124
Dayton, OH 102
Dayton Triangles 102
Deadwood Dick 52
Decatur, IL 65
Decatur Staleys 64
Delaware, OH 43, 44, 45, 46, 47, 83, 202
Delaware Gazette (Delaware, OH) 199
Delaware River 187
De Marr, Patrick 164
DeMille, Cecil B. 165
Dempsey, Jack 13, 14, 32, 33, 34, 39, 41, 42,
  80, 81, 82, 127
Denver, CO 126, 157
Detroit, MI 72, 78, 90, 141, 144, 152, 166, 176

Detroit Free-Press 31
Detroit Panthers 72
Detroit Tigers 202
The Devil's Assistant 54
DeWolf Lyman "Beans" 78, 101
Dieppe, France 115
Disco Security Company 56
Driscoll, Mary 70
Driscoll, Paddy 62, 66, 70
Drysdale, Don 202
Duarte, CA 151
Duffy, Arthur 149, 166
Duke of Westminster 195
Duluth, MN 96
Duluth Eskimos 96, 97, 101
Dunn, Red 69
Dyer, Braven 78

Eagleson, Alan 202
Eastern Carolina League 60
Ebbets Field (Brooklyn, NY) 92, 96, 174
L'Echo des Sports 112
Eddie, the Ossified Man 193, 194
Ederle, Gertrude 82, 83
Edison, Thomas 110
Edwards, "Big" Bill 92, 93, 94, 95, 96, 123,
  195
Eisenhower, Pres. Dwight 59, 139, 14
Elgin, IL 29
Elizabeth, NJ 187
Ellis, Thomas 145
Elmenhorst, Debbie 2
El Ouafi, Boughera 185
El Paso, TX 84, 188
El Reno, OK 145, 161, 162
Elwood, IL 165
Elyria, OH 168, 169
Elyria (OH) Board of Trade 168
Elyria (OH) Elks Club 169
Elyria (OH) Kiwanis Club 169
The End of the Feud 55
Engelmann, Larry 2, 8, 112, 128, 131
English Channel 82, 83
Enochville, NC 194
Erickson, Nestor 151, 156
Essanay Manufacturing Company 54
Estby, Clara 139
Estby, Helga 139
Estelle 193
Eureka, CA 50
Europe 84, 135

Fageol Motor Company 147
Fager, August 149
Fair Grounds Racetrack (New Orleans) 75
Fairbanks, Douglas, Jr. 79, 108, 134
Feret, Paul 122, 128
Fields, W.C. 63, 191
Findel, Scotty 188
Finland 152

First Methodist Episcopal Church (Holly-
    wood, CA) 194
First Regiment Armory (Chicago) 166
Fischer, Dorothy "Dot" (C.C. Pyle's first
    wife) 48, 49, 50, 51, 52, 53, 55
Fischer, John 48, 49, 50, 56
Fischer (a.k.a. Fisher), Margarita "Babe" 49,
    50, 51, 53, 54
Fitzgerald, F. Scott 83
Flagstaff, AZ 152
Flaherty, Ray 102, 104
Follett, Dwight 31
Forbes Field (Pittsburgh, PA) 72
Ford, Henry 110, 141
Fordham University 89
Forest Hills, New York 106, 114, 116, 121
Forksville, PA 27
Fort Worth, TX 188
Four Horsemen of Notre Dame 11, 12, 96
Foyil, OK 160, 161, 184
France 107, 111, 115, 118, 134, 135, 137
France (ship) 90, 119, 123, 136
Frankford (PA) Yellow Jackets 15, 71, 73, 89,
    92
Franklin Field (Philadelphia) 38, 98
Fremont, OH 89
French Open (tennis championship) 106
The Freshman 22, 63, 102
Friedman, Benny 103, 104
Frost, Lucian 150, 164
Fry, Harry 98
Fuller, Pop 133

Gallagher, James 94
Gallery, Tom 101
Gallico, Paul viii, 12, 13, 39, 68, 172, 173,
    175, 186
Gallup, NM 156
Gambier, OH 201
Garden, Mary 108
Gardner, Earle 157
Gary, IN 167
Gavuzzi, Peter 149, 156, 160, 161, 162, 163,
    164, 168, 169, 176, 181, 186, 189
Gaynor, William 94
Gehrig, Lou 126
General Motors 193
Georgetown University 58
Germany 82, 83, 84, 139
Getty, Frank 144
Gibney, Albert 128
Gibson, Billy 14
Gipp, George 57
The Golden Giant Mine 48
Gompers, Samuel 34
Gonzaga University 102
Gonzales, Seth 157
Goodwin, Ralph 149
Goshen, IN 158
Grange, Ernest 27

Grange, Garland 27, 38, 40, 74
Grange, Harold "Red" 3, 7, 12, 13, 15, 16, 17,
    18, 19, 20, 22, 23, 24, 26, 27, 28, 29, 30,
    31, 32, 33, 34, 37, 38, 39, 40, 41, 42, 56,
    57, 63, 67, 68, 69, 70, 71, 72, 73, 74, 75,
    76, 77, 78, 79, 80, 81, 87, 88, 89, 90, 91,
    92, 95, 97, 98, 99, 100, 101, 102, 104, 105,
    111, 112, 117, 121, 122, 124, 125, 146, 148,
    149, 157, 159, 160, 166, 169, 170, 177, 182,
    183, 184, 192, 195, 197, 199
Grange, Lyle 27, 40
Grange, Margaret 195
Granite City, IL 158
Grants Pass, OR 152
Granville, Phillip 149, 150, 175, 181, 186, 189
The Grapes of Wrath 141
The Great American Footrace 196
Great Depression 56, 191, 195, 196
Great Falls, MT 50
Great Lakes Naval Training Station 65
The Great Race 139
Great Race of 1908 139
Greb, Harry 88, 89
Greeley, Horace 47
Green Bay, WI 103
Green Bay Packers 41, 67, 103, 201
Griffin, Elmer 122
Griffith, Major John L. 25, 40
Griffs, Molly Levite 2
Gunn, F.F. "Dick" 159, 166, 167, 172, 180
Gunn, Harry 159, 166, 167, 180
Gunn Supply Company 167
Guthrie, Woody 141
Guthrie, OK 155
Guyon, Joe 62, 67

Hagen, Walter 127
Haggard, Merle 141
Halas, George 19, 23, 24, 25, 26, 62, 64, 65,
    69, 70, 71, 72, 74, 77, 97
The Halfback 78
Hall, Harry 38
Hall, Mordaunt 80
Hamilton, Canada 149, 175
Hammond All-Stars 62, 65
Hanny, Duke 23
Harding, Pres. Warren G. 37, 85, 86
Harlem River (New York City) 11, 91
Harrison, James 154
Hartford, CT 96, 135
Harvard University 39, 58, 59
Haskell, KS 59
Havana, Cuba 117
Hawthorne, Fred 123, 127
Hay, Ralph 64
Hayes, Bill 202
Hayes, Rutherford B. 44
Hayes, Will 94
Haynes Photo and Framing (El Reno, OK) 2
Hayward, Col. Bill 115, 116, 121, 123

Healy, Ed 23, 97
Hearst, William Randolph 36, 76, 193
Heinz, W.C. 29
Heisman Trophy 26
Hell's Kitchen (New York City) 178
Hemingway, Ernest 200
Her Hour of Triumph 55
Herald Square (New York City) 74
Herrmann, Garry 92
Hiers, Walter 102
Hillside View, MO 164
Hillyard, George 108
Hoboken, NJ 94
Hogan, J.J. 57
Holbrook, AZ 156
Hollywood, CA 101, 108, 114, 117, 134, 150, 151, 155, 164, 194, 200, 202
Hollywood Millionaires 101
Homestead Act 138
Hood, Raymond 192
Hope, Bob 200
Hornberger, Dub 2
Hornsby, Rogers 92
Horsefeathers 57
Hotel Astor (New York City) 16, 17, 20, 99
Hotel del Coronado (Coronado, CA) 133
Hotel McAlpin (New York City) 74, 82
Hotel Statler (Detroit) 90, 91
Hotel Vanderbilt (Los Angeles) 136
Houston, TX 134
Howard, U.S. Rep. Everette 178
Hubert, Pooley 98
Hudson River (New York) 120, 169, 173, 187
Huntington Park, CA 161

I Love Lucy 201
Igoe, John 43
The Immigrant 165
Indian Lake Estates, FL 195
Internal Revenue Service 94
International Lawn Tennis Foundation 106
International Olympic Committee 60, 61
Interstate Highway System 140
Irish Championships (tennis) 116
Italy 150, 175

Jack Dempsey's (New York City) 82
Jacksonville, FL 75
James, Jesse 52, 54
The James Boys of Missouri 52, 54
Japan 139
Jefferson Hospital (Philadelphia) 178
Jeffries, Jim 79, 80
Johnson, Christopher 3
Johnson, Frank 158
Johnson, Jack 47, 81
Johnson, Walter 1, 33, 34
Johnston, "Little" Bill 120, 122, 123
Johnston, Gov. Henry S. 161
Joliet, IL 164, 165

Jolson, Al 39
Jones, Bobby 13
Joplin, MO 164
Jordan, David Starr 58
Jordan, William 170
Joseph, Tobie "Cotton" 150, 151
Joyce, Mike 175

Kahn, Elizabeth 3
Kaiser Wilhelm der Gross 94
Kearns, Doc 42
Keaton, Buster 63
Kelly, Alvin "Shipwreck" 146
Kelly, "Wild" Bill 102
Kelly, Mike 158
Kelly, Susan Croce 146, 160
Kennedy, John F. 68
Kennedy, Joseph P. 68, 80
Kennedy, Joseph P, Jr. 68
Kenyon College 1, 201
Kerouac, Jack 141
Kerr, Bill 172, 175, 178
KGGM Radio 144, 168
Kiernan, John 144
The Kind of Kings 165
King, Don 8
King Gustav V (Sweden) 59, 60
King Umberto (Italy) 163
Kingdown, UK 82
Kinosolving, Anne 130
Kinsey, Howard 122, 135
Knop, Oscar 23
Kokomo, IN 23
Kolehmainen, Johan "Hannes" 149
Kolehmainen, Willie 149, 151, 176
Kosh, Harry 20
Koufax, Sandy 202

La Belle, Irene 186, 187
Lacoste, René 108, 118
La Crosse, WI 194
Laitnen, Gina (C.C. Pyle's great-grand-daughter) 2
Lake County (IN) 55
Lake Michigan 141
Lake Wales, FL 195
Landis, Judge Kenesaw Mountain 94
Lardner, Ring 36, 37, 127, 128
La Rue, OH 67
Lasker, Albert 86
Lassa, Nikolas 67
Latrobe, PA 62
Layden, Elmer 12, 95
Legion of Honor (France) 115
Lemmon, Jack 139
Lenglen, Anias "Mama" 113, 120, 136
Lenglen, Charles "Papa" 108, 109, 113, 135
Lenglen, Suzanne 7, 8, 90, 97, 106, 107, 108, 109, 110, 111, 112, 113, 114, 115, 116, 117, 118, 119, 120, 121, 122, 123, 124, 126, 127, 128,

129, 130, 131, 132, 133, 134, 135, 136, 137, 160, 176, 194, 195, 199
S.S. *Leviathan* 8
Lewis, Meriwether 138
Lewis and Clark 138
Lexington, KY 82
Lieb, Fred 35, 36
Lindbergh, Charles 83, 146, 170
Lindy's (New York City) 76
Lingo, Walter 67
Lippmann, Walter 86
Liverpool, U.K. 163
Lloyd, Harold 22, 75, 134
Lombardi, Vince 201
London, England 50, 106
Long Beach, CA 164
Long Island, New York 114
Los Angeles, CA 5, 73, 75, 76, 77, 78, 88, 98, 101, 106, 110, 124, 125, 135, 136, 140, 141, 143, 149, 150, 151, 153, 155, 157, 164, 166, 167, 178, 179, 181, 184, 186, 188, 189, 191, 194
Los Angeles Angels (Pacific Coast League) 80
Los Angeles Dodgers 202
Los Angeles Richfields 101
Los Angeles Times 78, 133, 134, 191, 194
Los Angeles Wildcats 96, 97, 98, 99, 102
Los Lunas, NM 156
Lossman, Juri 149
Lotshaw, George 72
Louisville Brecks 67
The Love Game 114
Loyola University 58
Luna Bowl (Cleveland) 98
Lupton, AZ 156
Lusitania 83

Mack, Ernie 188
Mad Bull 152
Madame Duvall 186, 187, 188
Madison Square Garden (New York City) 6, 42, 117, 126, 127, 170, 171, 172, 174, 175, 176, 178, 179, 180, 184
The Maine (ship) 144
The Majestic (ship) 149
Major League Baseball 202
Major League Baseball Players Association 202
Malan, Clarence 196
Malan, Margarita (C.C. Pyle's granddaughter) 200
Mallory, Molla 109, 118
Man o' War 39, 81, 82
Manhattan (New York, NY) Supreme Court 177
Manley, W.G. 42
Mara, Tim 2, 14, 15, 40, 89, 90, 91, 92, 100, 104, 183, 200
Mara, Wellington 15, 90
Marathon, Greece 138
March, Harry 14

Mare Island Marines 65
Margarita Fischer Company 49
Marine Grill (New York City) 74
Marion, OH 67
Marquette University 69
La Marseillaise 128
Marx, Groucho 57
Marx, Zeppo 57
Marx Brothers 57, 63
Mason, Red 89
MasterCard 51
Matoon, IL 62
Maxwell, Dan 70
Maxwell House Coffee 157, 159
McClure's 57
McCurdy, Elmer 154, 155, 157
McEnroe, John 123
McGeehan, Bill 91, 122, 124, 125, 130
McGill, Ralph 189
McGinnity, "Iron Man" Joe 65
McIlwain, Wally 31
McKinley, Pres. William 85
McLaughlin, Thomas 60
McNally, Dave 202
McNevin, H.E. 23
Memorial Coliseum (Los Angeles) 77
Memorial Stadium (Champaign, IL) 30
Merrihew, Stephen Wallis 125, 128
Messersmith, Andy 202
Miami, FL 74
Miami, OK 162
Mickey Mouse 201
Middletown, NY 170
Miller, Don 12, 72
Millrose Athletic Association (New York City) 180
Milwaukee Journal 23
Milwaukee Sentinel 41
Milwaukee, WI 23, 28, 92, 152
Mimoun O'Kacha, Alain 185
Mines Field (California) 194
Minneapolis, MN 139, 144, 172
Minneapolis Marines 67
The Miracle of Life 54
Mishawaka, IN 167
Mississippi River 164
Missouri Valley Conference 42
Mix, Tom 54
Mojave Desert (U.S.) 150, 151
Mojave Wells, CA 152
Monte Carlo 82, 112
Montreal, Canada 126, 130
Morgan, Byron 78
Morris, Sidney 178, 179
Morrison Hotel (Chicago) 23, 25, 88, 97
Morrisville, PA 187
Moscow, ID 52
Moss, Edward 111, 112
Muncie Flyers 66, 67
mygenealogist.com 3

National Football League (started as the American Professional Football Association) 12, 23, 24, 39, 62, 64, 67, 69, 77, 78, 91, 92, 96, 97, 102, 183, 195
National Hockey League 101, 202
National League (baseball) 15
National Register of Historic Places 62
Navajo, AZ 156
Navin Field, a.k.a. Tiger Stadium (Detroit) 72
NEA News Service 23
Neptune's Daughter 55
Nevers, Ernie 75, 96, 97, 101
New England 84
New Haven, CT 135
New Orleans, LA 75, 134, 135
New York, NY 5, 6, 11, 12, 13, 16, 17, 19, 36, 59, 71, 73, 74, 76, 78, 80, 82, 83, 89, 91, 93, 94, 95, 97, 99, 100, 101, 102, 104, 111, 115, 117, 120, 121, 123, 124, 126, 137, 139, 140, 143, 144, 149, 151, 164, 167, 169, 171, 172, 173, 174, 176, 178, 179, 180, 183, 184, 185, 186, 188, 194, 199
New York American 72, 75, 170, 172, 173, 188
New York Daily News (a.k.a. *Illustrated Daily News*) viii, 13, 36, 39, 68, 172, 173, 178, 186
New York Giants (baseball) 11, 15, 61, 65
New York Giants (football) 2, 11, 13, 14, 15, 16, 24, 40, 71, 72, 89, 90, 91, 92, 98, 100, 102, 104, 183, 200
New York Herald Tribune 11, 91, 112, 122, 123, 124, 127, 130
New York Times 13, 30, 35, 59, 80, 94, 100, 104, 120, 121, 130, 144, 154, 174, 180
New York University 89
New York Yankees (baseball) 25, 35, 43, 65, 78, 91, 92, 93, 98, 122, 126
New York Yankees (football) 78, 90, 91, 92, 95, 97, 98, 99, 100, 101, 102, 103, 104, 105, 125, 161, 182, 183, 184
New Yorker 37
Newark, NJ 92, 135
Newark Bears (football) 96, 99
Newman, Paul 1, 201
Newton, Arthur 148, 151, 152, 156, 176, 181, 186
Nice, France 113
Niles, CA 54
Nilson, Gunnar 149
Normal, IL 164
Normand, Mabel 54
North Hollywood, CA 194
North Pole 146
Northern Lights 52
Northwestern University 29
Nurmi, Paavo 39, 110, 148, 149

Oakland, CA 51, 52, 132, 147
Oakland Hotel (Oakland, CA) 132
Oakland Tribune 51
O'Brien, William 130

O'Donnell, Bob 65
Ogden, UT 159
Ohio Stadium ("Big Horseshoe") 40
Ohio State University 12, 23, 24, 40, 45
Ohio Wesleyan University 44, 45, 46
Oklahoma City, OK 142, 155, 159, 161, 196
Oklahoma City Chamber of Commerce 142, 178
Oklahoma City Fairgrounds 159, 161, 178
Oklahoma Military Academy 184
Oklahoma State Supreme Court 196
Old Laguna Pueblo, NM 156
Oldfield, Barney 46, 47, 48, 101, 110
Olds, Fred 155
Olympic Games 39, 59, 60, 61, 110, 125, 126, 138, 149, 181, 189
One Minute to Play 78, 79, 80, 102
Only Yesterday 85
Oorang Indians 67
Oraibi, AZ 149
Orr, Bobby 202
Oshkosh, WI 56

Pacific Coast League 80
Paddock, Charlie 125, 126
Palace Hotel (San Francisco) 132
Palmer, A. Mitchell 85
Paris, France 50, 108, 112, 116, 119, 137, 139, 185
Park Theatre (Champaign, IL) 22, 63
Parker, F.W. 50
Parker, Col. Tom 8
Pasadena, CA 151
Passaic, NJ 149, 169, 170, 172, 173
Passaic (NJ) American Legion 171
Passaic (NJ) High School 170
Paterson, NJ 84
Pawhuska, OK 155
Payne, Andy 152, 153, 156, 158, 160, 161, 162, 163, 164, 168, 169, 170, 175, 177, 178, 180, 181, 184, 195, 196
Payne, "Doc" 152, 160
Pedersen, John 159
Pegler, Westbrook 7, 12, 18, 25, 36, 37, 68, 99, 113, 124, 146, 157, 181, 193, 196
Penn State University 57
Pennock, Herb 126
Pennsylvania Railroad 62
Persick, Nick 164
Peterson, Robert 2, 64
Petticoat Junction 201
Pheidippedes 138
Philadelphia, PA 12, 17, 66, 71, 92, 98, 100, 108, 126, 130, 149, 187
Philadelphia Eagles 201
Philadelphia Quakers 96, 98, 99, 100
Phillips, Owen 89
Phoenix, AZ 89, 188
Pickens, William H. "Bill" 79, 109, 110, 111, 112, 113, 114, 115, 116, 117, 118, 127, 133, 135, 146, 149, 155, 171, 172, 174, 194

Pickford, Mary 54, 75, 134
Pierce Arrow (automobile) 159
Pierce Brothers Funeral Home (California) 196
Pigskin: The Early Years of Pro Football 64
Pitts, ZaSu 101
Pittsburgh, PA 62, 69, 72, 126, 130
Pocatello, ID 53
Pollard, Fritz 62, 72
Pollard, Harry 54
Polo Grounds (New York City) 11, 13, 14, 15, 19, 35, 61, 68, 71, 80, 89, 90, 98, 100, 174, 183
Pomona College 79
Port Chester, NY 151
Portland, OR 48, 50, 77, 131
Pottstown, PA 92
Pourville, France 115
Powell, William 6
The Prince and the Pauper (film) 201
Prince of Wales 34, 112
Princeton University 57, 58, 61, 92, 93
Pro Football Hall of Fame 62, 195
Prohibition 99, 144
Promontory, UT 139
Providence, RI 135, 182
Providence Journal 72
Providence Steam Roller 62, 72, 182, 183
Pulitzer Prize 201
Purcell, James Mark 38
Pyle, Anna (Mrs. Verner Ronk) 44, 45, 51, 147, 196, 200
Pyle, Charles (C.C. Pyle's grandson) 196, 200
Pyle, Charles C. viii, 1, 2, 5, 6, 7, 8, 9, 10, 11, 13, 15, 16, 17, 18, 19, 22, 23, 24, 25, 26, 32, 34, 40, 41, 42, 43, 44, 45, 46, 47, 48, 49, 50, 51, 52, 53, 54, 55, 56, 61, 62, 63, 64, 66, 68, 69, 73, 74, 75, 76, 77, 78, 79, 80, 82, 83, 88, 89, 90, 91, 92, 94, 95, 96, 97, 99, 100, 101, 102, 103, 104, 105, 107, 109, 111, 112, 113, 114, 115, 116, 117, 118, 119, 120, 121, 122, 123, 124, 125, 126, 127, 128, 129, 130, 131, 132, 133, 134, 135, 136, 137, 138, 140, 143, 144, 145, 146, 147, 148, 149, 150, 151, 152, 153, 154, 155, 156, 157, 158, 159, 160, 164, 165, 166, 167, 168, 169, 170, 171, 172, 173, 174, 175, 176, 177, 178, 179, 180, 181, 182, 183, 184, 185, 186, 187, 188, 189, 190, 191, 192, 193, 194, 195, 196, 197, 199, 200, 201, 202
Pyle, Ira 44, 45, 51, 132, 147, 190, 196, 200
Pyle, Mary Margaret "Kathy" (Malan) 51, 52, 53, 147, 196, 200
Pyle, Noah 43
Pyle, Sidney McMillan (Mrs. William) 43, 44, 45, 46, 49, 50, 147, 200
Pyle, William 43, 44, 45, 200

Quamawahu, Nicholas 149, 151
Queen Mary (of England) 109
Queens, New York 83

Quist, Hugo 148, 149

Racine, WI 96
Racing Romeo 101, 102
Radio Transmission Company of America 196
Ralston, Jobyna 102
Ranch Boys 191
Rea, Harry 164
Red Cross 51, 67, 165
Red Grange Handicap (horse race) 75
Redwood Highway Marathon (CA) 152
Reid, Wallace 23
Rice, Grantland 11, 13, 34, 36, 38, 96, 108
Richards, Claire 123
Richards, Jeannette 188
Richards, Vince 122, 123, 124, 126, 128, 130, 135
Rickard, Tex 42, 174, 179, 180
Ringo, Jim 201
Ripley, Robert 192, 193, 196
Ritz Restaurant (Passaic, NJ) 170
Road to Singapore 200
Roberts, Oral 8
Robinson, Pat 188
Rock Island Independents 96, 98
Rockford, IL 29
Rockne, Knute 29, 30, 42, 57
Rockwell, Tod 31
Rocky Mount, NC 60
Rodale Press 202
Rogers, Albert 174
Rogers, Clem 152
Rogers, Will 152, 160, 169, 185
Rolla, MO 154, 164
Ronk, Verner 51
Roosevelt, Pres. Theodore 2, 58
Roosevelt, Theodore, Jr. 58
Rose Bowl 25, 61, 65, 96
Rothschild, Albert 150
Route 66 141, 142, 143, 146, 160, 165, 166, 184, 200, 202
Route 66 Association 141, 166
Runyon, Damon 1, 12, 19, 35, 36, 37, 38, 39, 72, 73, 75, 76, 77, 89, 106, 109, 110, 111
Ruppert, Col. Jacob 43, 86
Russell, Martha Lindsay (C.C. Pyle's second wife) 55
Russian River 51
Ruth, Claire 43
Ruth, George Herman "Babe" 1, 7, 13, 16, 19, 25, 32, 33, 34, 35, 36, 37, 39, 41, 43, 73, 80, 81, 87, 122, 126, 130, 146
Ruth, Helen 43

St. Louis, MO 12, 30, 36, 69, 92, 164, 184
St. Louis Cardinals (baseball) 92, 98, 126
St. Moritz, Switzerland 119
St. Paul, MN 17
Salm von-Hoogstraeten, Count Ludwig 195
Salo, Amelia 170, 195

Salo, John 149, 156, 157, 160, 162, 164, 166, 169, 170, 171, 175, 186, 189, 195
San Antonio, TX 134
San Bernardino, CA 151
San Diego, CA 77, 133, 194
Sandwich, Canada 159
San Francisco, CA 50, 51, 77, 101, 132, 133, 139, 152, 194, 196
San Francisco Bay, CA 110
San Francisco Bay Terminal 132
San Francisco Chronicle 132
Santa Fe Station (Los Angeles) 78
Santa Monica, CA 79, 110, 118, 141, 146, 149
Santa Rosa, CA 51, 52, 147, 193, 200
Santa Rosa Junior College 200
Satex Film Company 55
Saturday Afternoon Club (Santa Rosa, CA) 51
Saturday Evening Post 37
Schacht, Al 128
Schallenberger, W.E. 20, 78
Schuster, George, Sr. 139
Scotland 112
Scott, Lon 140, 141, 142, 143
Scott, Ralph 66, 97, 101, 161
Scranton, PA 194
Seattle, WA 77
Selig Polyscope Company 54
Seven Springs, NM 156
Shaddox, Vivian 153, 162, 184
The Shadow Box (play) 201
Shanghai, China 50
Shangreaux, Lily 196, 202
Sherlock Holmes 54
Shibe Park (Philadelphia) 12, 100
Silverton, OR 48, 49
Singletary, Alec 142
Smith, Andrew 57
Smith, Gov. Al 127
Smith, Harry 132, 167
Snodgrass, Harvey 122, 131, 135
Soldier Field (Chicago) 100
Sonoma County (CA) Federation of Women's Clubs 51
Souminen, Dr. Arne 152, 156, 159, 160
South Bend, IN 57, 167
Spalding Company Catalog 158
Spencer, Leon 188
Spokane, WA 139, 159
Spoor, George 54
Spring Valley Country Club (Elyria, OH) 168
Springfield, IL 164
Springfield, MO 143
Stagg, Amos Alonzo 29, 31, 56, 57
Staley, Augustus Eugene (A.E.) 65
Staley Starch Company 65
Stanfield, AZ 188
Stanford University 45, 58, 75, 96
Staten Island, NY 170
Staten Island Stapletons 62
Staunton, IL 164

Steinbeck, John 141
Sternaman, Ed "Dutch" 23, 24, 65, 69, 77, 96
Sternaman, Joey 16, 96, 100
Stevens, Stanley 172, 178
Stockholm, Sweden 59
Stoolman, Almon W. 62, 63
Stuhldreher, Harry 12, 95
Suffern, NY 170, 171
Suratt, Veleska 165
Sutherland, Jock 183
Swanson, Gloria 54
Sweden 159
Syracuse University 59

Tahlequah, OK 196
Tammany Hall (New York City) 14
Tampa, FL 75, 84
Tampa Cardinals 75
The Tennessee Partner 48
Terre Haute, IN 165
Theater Margarita (Eureka, CA) 50
Thompson, Charles 188
Thompson, Luke 12, 28
Thompson, Wildfire 175, 178
Thoreau, NM 156
Thorpe, Charles 58
Thorpe, Jim 27, 34, 39, 58, 59, 60, 61, 62, 63, 64, 66, 67, 75, 161, 184, 187, 189, 190
The Three Musketeers 52
Tilden, "Big" Bill 2, 106, 107, 108, 118, 120, 123, 127, 130
Tilley, Hope 55
Tilley, Paul 55
Time Magazine 13, 191
Times Square (New York City) 178
Tinee, Mae 80
Toledo, OH 168
Toledo Maroons 62
Tony Awards 1, 201
Toronto, Canada 126, 130
Trafton, George 103
Transcontinental Railroad 139
Trenton, NJ 187
Tryon, Eddie 38, 98, 99, 103
Tucumcari, NM 157, 158
Tulane University 75
Tulsa, OK 140, 142, 161, 162, 178
Tunney, Gene 14, 82
Turpin, Ben 54
Twain, Mark 49
Twentieth Century Limited 89
Twenty-third Regiment Armory (Brooklyn, NY) 135
Two Guns, AZ 156
Tyler Moore, Mary 201

Umek, Guisto 175, 189
Uncle Tom's Cabin 52, 54
Underwood, John 67
United News 144

U.S. Army 139
U.S. Lawn Tennis Association 106, 111, 112,
   119, 125, 128
U.S. Library of Congress 2
U.S. Marine Corps 28
U.S. Merchant Marine 169
U.S. Military Academy (West Point) 11, 58,
   59, 100
U.S. National Guard 115
U.S. National Tennis Championships 106
U.S. Naval Academy 29, 93, 100
U.S. Navy 65
U.S. Open (Tennis Championships) 107, 109,
   114, 121, 122
U.S. Women's Amateur (Golf) Championship
   119
University of Alabama 38, 61, 98
University of Chicago 29, 40, 56
University of Georgia 61
University of Illinois 7, 20, 22, 23, 24, 28,
   29, 30, 31, 34, 38, 39, 40, 45, 62, 65, 66,
   73, 77
University of Indiana 23
University of Iowa 98, 195
University of Kansas 45
University of Michigan 25, 29, 30, 31, 32,
   34, 37, 39, 45, 93, 103, 195
University of Minnesota 38
University of Missouri 42
University of Montana 102
University of Nebraska 26, 30, 38, 45
University of Notre Dame 11, 23, 29, 30, 42,
   57, 72, 96
University of Pennsylvania 23, 38, 39, 57,
   59, 99
University of Pittsburgh 59, 183
University of Southern California 102
University of Virginia 58
University of Washington 76, 92
University of Wisconsin 97
USA Today 201

Valentino, Rudolph 19
Vanderbilt, William K. 47
Vanderbilt Hotel (New York City) 5, 7, 8,
   175, 179
Vanity Fair 37
Vega, Texas 159
Ventura Fairgrounds (Ventura, CA) 102
Victorville, CA 151
Villa, Pancho 55
Virginia Theatre (Champaign, IL) 22, 63
Visa 51
Von Flue, Frank 181

Wabash College 40
Walker, Jimmy 127
Wallace, Frank 170, 172
Wallis, Michael 141
Walsh, Christy 43

Wantinnen, Olli 149, 166
Ward, Geoffrey 47, 81
Warner, Glenn "Pop" 29, 59, 63
Washington, D.C. 2, 16, 17, 19, 69, 110, 139,
   177
Washington Post 58
Washington Senators 33, 128
Waverly, NY 169
WEAF Radio 17
Webster, Levi T. ("Chief Tall Feather") 152
Weehawken, NJ 173, 174
Weissmuller, Johnny 34
Welco, Gilbert "Gibby" 183
Weldon, Charles "Dink" 28
Wellsville, NY 169
West Shore Terminal (Weehawken, NJ) 173
Westbrook, Walter 122
Western Union 47, 48
Weston, Edward Payson 139
Wheaton, IL 12, 27, 34, 40, 41, 73, 74, 80,
   182, 195
Wheaton College Archives & Special Collec-
   tions 2
Wheaton (IL) High School 28, 78
White Star Line 149
Wieslander, Hugo 60
Wightman Cup 106, 118
Wilkes-Barre, PA 27
Willard, Jess 81
Willen, Charles 115
Williams, Geoff 2, 50, 51, 55, 202
Williams, Joe 16
Williams, Richard 123
Williamsport, PA 27
Wills, Charles 118, 122
Wills, Helen 106, 117, 120, 122, 132, 133, 134,
   135
Wilmington, DE 187
Wilson, George "Wildcat" 76, 77, 92, 98,
   183
Wilson, Pres. Woodrow 34, 58, 85, 94
Wimbledon (Tennis Championships) 82,
   106, 108, 109, 116
Winston, Alexander 47
Winter Garden Ice Palace (Los Angeles) 101
Winter Garden Maroons 101
Wood, Natalie 139
Wood, Sam 78, 80, 101
Woolf, Bob 202
World Series 11, 95
World War I (a.k.a. "The Great War") 28,
   36, 62, 83, 84, 97, 115, 139, 165, 169
World War II 82, 196
Wrigley Field (Chicago) see "Cubs Park"
Wrigley Field (Los Angeles) 189

Yale Bowl 39, 61
Yale University 57, 58, 61
Yankee Stadium (New York City) 78, 90, 91,
   98, 99, 102, 104, 126, 169

Yost, Fielding "Hurry-Up" 25, 29, 31, 45
Young, Tom 158, 169

Zaharias, Babe 119

Zambrino, Frank 23
Zuppke, Bob 25, 28, 29, 38, 39, 40, 41, 42, 65, 66, 77